Get the eBook FREE!
(PDF, ePub, Kindle, and liveBook all included)

We believe that once you buy a book from us, you should be able to read it in any format we have available. To get electronic versions of this book at no additional cost to you, purchase and then register this book at the Manning website.

Go to https://www.manning.com/freebook and follow the instructions to complete your pBook registration.

That's it!
Thanks from Manning!

T0100172

Fast Python

HIGH PERFORMANCE TECHNIQUES FOR LARGE DATASETS

TIAGO RODRIGUES ANTÃO

MANNING

SHELTER ISLAND

Manning Publications Co.
20 Baldwin Road
PO Box 761
Shelter Island, NY 11964

Development editor:	Frances Lefkowitz
Technical development editor:	Al Krinker
Review editor:	Mihaela Batinić
Production editor:	Andy Marinkovich
Copy editor:	Alisa Larson
Proofreader:	Keri Hales
Technical proofreader:	Andy Miles
Typesetter:	Gordan Salinovic
Cover designer:	Marija Tudor

ISBN 9781617297939
Printed in the United States of America

contents

preface   ix
acknowledgments   xi
about this book   xii
about the author   xvii
about the cover illustration   xviii

PART 1 FOUNDATIONAL APPROACHES.....................................1

1 An urgent need for efficiency in data processing   3

1.1 How bad is the data deluge?   4

1.2 Modern computing architectures and high-performance computing   7

Changes inside the computer   8 ▪ *Changes in the network   10*
The cloud   11

1.3 Working with Python's limitations   12

The Global Interpreter Lock   13

1.4 A summary of the solutions   14

iii

2 *Extracting maximum performance from built-in features*   **17**

2.1   Profiling applications with both IO and computing workloads   18

*Downloading data and computing minimum temperatures   19
Python's built-in profiling module   21   ▪   Using local caches to
reduce network usage   22*

2.2   Profiling code to detect performance bottlenecks   23

*Visualizing profiling information   24   ▪   Line profiling   25
The takeaway: Profiling code   27*

2.3   Optimizing basic data structures for speed: Lists, sets,
and dictionaries   28

*Performance of list searches   28   ▪   Searching using sets   29
List, set, and dictionary complexity in Python   30*

2.4   Finding excessive memory allocation   32

*Navigating the minefield of Python memory estimation   32
The memory footprint of some alternative representations   35
Using arrays as a compact representation alternative to lists   37
Systematizing what we have learned: Estimating memory usage of
Python objects   38   ▪   The takeaway: Estimating memory usage
of Python objects   39*

2.5   Using laziness and gencrators for big-data pipelining   39
Using generators instead of standard functions   40

3 *Concurrency, parallelism, and asynchronous processing*   **43**

3.1   Writing the scaffold of an asynchronous server   46

*Implementing the scaffold for communicating with clients   48
Programming with coroutines   49   ▪   Sending complex data
from a simple synchronous client   50   ▪   Alternative approaches
to interprocess communication   52   ▪   The takeaway: Asynchronous
programming   52*

3.2   Implementing a basic MapReduce engine   52

*Understanding MapReduce frameworks   53   ▪   Developing a very
simple test scenario   54   ▪   A first attempt at implementing a
MapReduce framework   54*

3.3   Implementing a concurrent version of a
MapReduce engine   55

*Using concurrent.futures to implement a threaded server   55
Asynchronous execution with futures   57   ▪   The GIL and
multithreading   59*

3.4 Using multiprocessing to implement MapReduce 60

A solution based on concurrent.futures 60 ▪ A solution based on the multiprocessing module 62 ▪ Monitoring the progress of the multiprocessing solution 63 ▪ Transferring data in chunks 65

3.5 Tying it all together: An asynchronous multithreaded and multiprocessing MapReduce server 68

Architecting a complete high-performance solution 68 ▪ Creating a robust version of the server 72

4 **High-performance NumPy 75**

4.1 Understanding NumPy from a performance perspective 76

Copies vs. views of existing arrays 76 ▪ Understanding NumPy's view machinery 81 ▪ Making use of views for efficiency 86

4.2 Using array programming 88

The takeaway 89 ▪ Broadcasting in NumPy 90 ▪ Applying array programming 92 ▪ Developing a vectorized mentality 94

4.3 Tuning NumPy's internal architecture for performance 97

An overview of NumPy dependencies 97 ▪ How to tune NumPy in your Python distribution 99 ▪ Threads in NumPy 100

PART 2 HARDWARE 103

5 **Re-implementing critical code with Cython 105**

5.1 Overview of techniques for efficient code re-implementation 106

5.2 A whirlwind tour of Cython 107

A naive implementation in Cython 108 ▪ Using Cython annotations to increase performance 110 ▪ Why annotations are fundamental to performance 111 ▪ Adding typing to function returns 113

5.3 Profiling Cython code 114

Using Python's built-in profiling infrastructure 115 ▪ Using line_profiler 116

5.4 Optimizing array access with Cython memoryviews 119

The takeaway 121 ▪ Cleaning up all internal interactions with Python 121

5.5   Writing NumPy generalized universal functions
       in Cython   122
              The takeaway   124

5.6   Advanced array access in Cython   124
              *Bypassing the GIL's limitation on running multiple threads at a
              time   127 ▪ Basic performance analysis   130 ▪ A spacewar
              example using Quadlife   131*

5.7   Parallelism with Cython   132

6 *Memory hierarchy, storage, and networking*   135

6.1   How modern hardware architectures affect Python
       performance   137
              *The counterintuitive effect of modern architectures on
              performance   137 ▪ How CPU caching affects algorithm
              efficiency   138 ▪ Modern persistent storage   139*

6.2   Efficient data storage with Blosc   140
              *Compress data; save time   140 ▪ Read speeds (and memory
              buffers)   142 ▪ The effect of different compression algorithms on
              storage performance   143 ▪ Using insights about data
              representation to increase compression   144*

6.3   Accelerating NumPy with NumExpr   144
              *Fast expression processing   145 ▪ How hardware architecture
              affects our results   146 ▪ When NumExpr is not appropriate   147*

6.4   The performance implications of using the
       local network   147
              *The sources of inefficiency with REST calls   148 ▪ A naive client
              based on UDP and msgpack   148 ▪ A UDP-based server   150
              Dealing with basic recovery on the client side   151 ▪ Other
              suggestions for optimizing network computing   152*

PART 3   APPLICATIONS AND LIBRARIES FOR MODERN
         DATA PROCESSING 155

7 *High-performance pandas and Apache Arrow*   157

7.1   Optimizing memory and time when loading data   158
              *Compressed vs. uncompressed data   158 ▪ Type inference of
              columns   160 ▪ The effect of data type precision   162 ▪ Recoding
              and reducing data   164*

7.2   Techniques to increase data analysis speed   166

*Using indexing to accelerate access   166 ▪ Row iteration
strategies   167*

7.3   pandas on top of NumPy, Cython, and NumExpr   170

*Explicit use of NumPy   170 ▪ pandas on top of NumExpr   171
Cython and pandas   173*

7.4   Reading data into pandas with Arrow   174

*The relationship between pandas and Apache Arrow   175
Reading a CSV file   176 ▪ Analyzing with Arrow   178*

7.5   Using Arrow interop to delegate work to more efficient
languages and systems   179

*Implications of Arrow's language interop architecture   179
Zero-copy operations on data with Arrow's Plasma server   180*

8 **Storing big data   186**

8.1   A unified interface for file access: fsspec   187

*Using fsspec to search for files in a GitHub repo   187 ▪ Using fsspec to
inspect zip files   189 ▪ Accessing files using fsspec   189 ▪ Using URL
chaining to traverse different filesystems transparently   190 ▪ Replacing
filesystem backends   190 ▪ Interfacing with PyArrow   191*

8.2   Parquet: An efficient format to store columnar data   191

*Inspecting Parquet metadata   192 ▪ Column encoding with
Parquet   194 ▪ Partitioning with datasets   196*

8.3   Dealing with larger-than-memory datasets the
old-fashioned way   197

*Memory mapping files with NumPy   198 ▪ Chunk reading and
writing of data frames   199*

8.4   Zarr for large-array persistence   201

*Understanding Zarr's internal structure   202 ▪ Storage of arrays
in Zarr   204 ▪ Creating a new array   206 ▪ Parallel reading and
writing of Zarr arrays   208*

PART 4   ADVANCED TOPICS 211

9 **Data analysis using GPU computing   213**

9.1   Making sense of GPU computing power   215

*Understanding the advantages of GPUs   215 ▪ The relationship
between CPUs and GPUs   217 ▪ The internal architecture
of GPUs   218 ▪ Software architecture considerations   219*

9.2   Using Numba to generate GPU code   220

*Installation of GPU software for Python   220 ▪ The basics of GPU
programming with Numba   221 ▪ Revisiting the Mandelbrot
example using GPUs   224 ▪ A NumPy version of the Mandelbrot
code   227*

9.3   Performance analysis of GPU code: The case
of a CuPy application   228

*GPU-based data analysis libraries   228 ▪ Using CuPy: A GPU-based
version of NumPy   229 ▪ A basic interaction with CuPy   229 ▪ Writing
a Mandelbrot generator using Numba   230 ▪ Writing a Mandelbrot
generator using CUDA C   232 ▪ Profiling tools for GPU code   234*

10   *Analyzing big data with Dask   238*

10.1   Understanding Dask's execution model   240

*A pandas baseline for comparison   240 ▪ Developing a Dask-based
data frame solution   241*

10.2   The computational cost of Dask operations   243

*Partitioning data for processing   244 ▪ Persisting intermediate
computations   245 ▪ Algorithm implementations over distributed
data frames   246 ▪ Repartitioning the data   249 ▪ Persisting
distributed data frames   251*

10.3   Using Dask's distributed scheduler   252

*The dask.distributed architecture   253 ▪ Running code using
dask.distributed   257 ▪ Dealing with datasets larger than
memory   262*

appendix A   *Setting up the environment   265*
appendix B   *Using Numba to generate efficient low-level code   269*

index   275

preface

A few years ago, a Python-based pipeline that my team was working on suddenly ground to a halt. A process just kept using CPU and was not finalizing. This function was critical to the company and we needed to solve the problem sooner rather than later. We looked at the algorithm and it seemed OK—in fact, it was quite a simple implementation. After many hours with several engineers looking at the problem, we found that it all boiled down to searching on a list—a very big list. The problem was trivially solved after converting the list into a set. We ended up with a much smaller data structure with search times in milliseconds, not hours.

I had several epiphanies at that time:

- It was a trivial problem, but our development process was not concerned with performance issues. For example, if we had routinely used a profiler, we would have discovered the performance bug in minutes, not hours.
- This was a win-win situation: we ended up consuming less time and less memory. Yes, in many cases, there are tradeoffs to be made, but in others, there are some really effective results with no downsides.
- From a larger perspective, this situation was also a win-win. First, faster results are great for the company's bottom line. Second, a good algorithm uses less CPU time, which means less electricity, and the use of less electricity (i.e., resources) is better for the planet.
- While our single case doesn't do much to save energy, it dawned on me that many programmers are designing similar solutions.

I decided to write this book so other programmers could benefit from my epiphanies. My objective is to help seasoned Python programmers to design and implement solutions that are more efficient, along with with an understanding of the potential tradeoffs. I wanted to take a holistic approach to the subject by discussing pure Python and important Python libraries, taking an algorithmic perspective and considering modern hardware architectures and their implications, and discussing CPU and storage performance. I hope this book helps you to be more confident in approaching performance problems while developing in the Python ecosystem.

acknowledgments

I would like to thank development editor Frances Lefkowitz for her infinite patience. I would also like to thank my daughter and wife, who had to endure my absence the last few years while I was writing this book. Thanks also to the production team at Manning who helped create this book.

To all the reviewers: Abhilash Babu Jyotheendra Babu, Andrea Smith, Biswanath Chowdhury, Brian Griner, Brian S Cole, Dan Sheikh, Dana Robinson, Daniel Vasquez, David Paccoud, David Patschke, Grzegorz Mika, James Liu, Jens Christian B. Madsen, Jeremy Chen, Kalyan Reddy, Lorenzo De Leon, Manu Sareena, Nik Piepenbreier, Noah Flynn, Or Golan, Paulo Nuin, Pegah T. Afshar, Richard Vaughan, Ruud Gijsen, Shashank Kalanithi, Simeon Leyzerzon, Simone Sguazza, Sriram Macharla, Sruti Shivakumar, Steve Love, Walter Alexander Mata López, William Jamir Silva, and Xie Yikuan—your suggestions helped make this a better book.

about this book

The purpose of this book is to help you write more efficient applications in the Python ecosystem. By more efficient, I mean that your code will use fewer CPU cycles, less storage space, and less network communication.

The book takes a holistic approach to the problem of performance. We not only discuss code optimization techniques in pure Python, but we also consider the efficient use of widely used data libraries, like NumPy and pandas. Because Python is not sufficiently performant in some cases, we also consider Cython when we need more speed. In line with this holistic approach, we also discuss the impact of hardware on code design: we analyze the impact of modern computer architectures on algorithm performance. We also examine the effect of network architectures on efficiency, and we explore the usage of GPU computing for fast data analysis.

Who should read this book?

This book is intended for an intermediate to advanced audience. If you skim the table of contents, you should recognize most of the technologies, and you probably have used quite a few of them. Except for the sections on IO libraries and GPU computing, little introductory material is provided: you need to already know the basics. If you are currently writing code to be performant and facing real challenges in dealing with so much data efficiently, then this book is for you.

To gain the most benefit from this book, you should have at least a couple of years of Python experience and know Python control structures and what lists, sets, and dictionaries are. You should have experience with some of the Python standard libraries like os, sys, pickle, and multiprocessing. To take the best advantage of the techniques I present here, you should also have some level of exposure to standard data analysis libraries, like NumPy—with at least minimal exposure to arrays—and pandas—with some experience with data frames.

It would be helpful if you are aware of, even if you have no direct exposure to, ways to accelerate Python code through either foreign language interfaces to C or Rust or know of alternative approaches, like Cython or Numba. Experience dealing with IO in Python will also help you. Given that IO libraries are less explored in the literature, we will start from the very beginning with formats like Apache Parquet and libraries like Zarr.

You should know the basic shell commands of Linux terminals (or MacOS terminals). If you are on Windows, please have either a Unix-based shell installed or know your way around the command line or PowerShell. And, of course, you need Python software installed on your computer.

In some cases, I will provide tips for the cloud, but cloud access or knowledge is not a requirement for reading this book. If you are interested in cloud approaches, then you should know how to do basic operations like creating instances and accessing the storage of your cloud provider.

While you do not have to be academically trained in the field, a basic notion of complexity costs will be helpful—for example, the intuitive notion that algorithms that scale linearly with data are better than algorithms that scale exponentially. If you plan on using GPU optimizations, you are not expected to know anything at this stage.

How this book is organized: A road map

The chapters in this book are mostly independent, and you can jump to whichever chapter is important to you. That being said, the book is divided into four parts.

Part 1, *Foundational Approaches* (chapters 1–4), covers introductory material.

- Chapter 1 introduces the problem and explains why we must pay attention to efficiency in computing and storage. It also introduces the book's approach and offers suggestions for navigating it for your needs.
- Chapter 2 covers the optimization of native Python. We also discuss the optimization of Python data structures, code profiling, memory allocation, and lazy programming techniques.
- Chapter 3 discusses concurrency and parallelism in Python and how to make the best use of multiprocessing and multithreading (including the limitations of parallel processing when using threads). This chapter also covers asynchronous processing as an efficient way to deal with multiple concurrent requests with low workloads, typical of web services.
- Chapter 4 introduces NumPy, a library that allows you to process multidimensional arrays efficiently. NumPy is at the core of all modern data processing techniques, and as such, it is treated as a fundamental library. This chapter shares specific NumPy techniques to develop more efficient code, such as views, broadcasting, and array programming.

Part 2, *Hardware* (chapters 5 and 6), is mostly concerned with extracting the maximum efficiency of common hardware and networks.

- Chapter 5 covers Cython, a superset of Python that can generate very efficient code. Python is a high-level interpreted language and, as such, is not expected to be optimized for the hardware. There are several languages, such as C or Rust, that are designed to be as efficient as possible at the hardware level. Cython belongs to that domain of languages: while it is very close to Python, it compiles to C code. Generating the most efficient Cython code requires being mindful of how the code maps to an efficient implementation. In this chapter, we learn how to create efficient Cython code.
- Chapter 6 discusses the effect of modern hardware architectures on the design of efficient Python code. Given the way modern computers are designed, some counterintuitive programming approaches may be more efficient than expected. For example, in some cases, dealing with compressed data may be faster than dealing with uncompressed data, even if we need to pay the price of uncompressing the algorithm. This chapter also covers the effect of CPU, memory, storage, and network on Python algorithm design. We discuss NumExpr, a library that can make NumPy code more efficient by using the properties of modern hardware architecture.

Part 3, *Applications and Libraries for Modern Data Processing* (chapters 7 and 8), looks at the typical applications and libraries used in modern data processing.

- Chapter 7 concentrates on using pandas, the data frame library used in Python, as efficiently as possible. We'll look at pandas-related techniques to optimize code. Unlike most chapters in the book, this one builds from an earlier chapter. pandas works on top of NumPy, so we will draw from what we learn in chapter 4 and discover NumPy-related techniques to optimize pandas. We also look at how to optimize pandas with NumExpr and Cython. Finally, I introduce Arrow, a library that, among other functionalities, can be used to increase the performance of processing pandas data frames.
- Chapter 8 examines the optimization of data persistence. We discuss Parquet, a library to process columnar data efficiently, and Zarr, which can process very large on-disk arrays. We also start a discussion about how to deal with datasets that are larger than memory.

Part 4, *Advanced Topics* (chapters 9 and 10), deals with two final, and very different, approaches: working with GPUs and using the Dask library.

- Chapter 9 looks at the uses of graphical processing units (GPUs) to process large datasets. We will see that the GPU computing model—using many simple processing units—is quite adequate to deal with modern data science problems. We use two different approaches to take advantage of GPUs. First, we will discuss existing libraries that provide similar interfaces to libraries that you know, such as CuPy as a GPU version of NumPy. Second, we will cover how to generate code to run on GPUs from Python.

- Chapter 10 discusses Dask, a library that allows you to write parallel code that scales out to many machines—either on-premises or in the cloud—while providing familiar interfaces similar to NumPy and pandas.

The book also includes two appendixes.

- Appendix A walks you through the installation of software necessary to use the examples in this book.
- Appendix B discusses Numba, an alternative to Cython to generate efficient low-level code. Cython and Numba are the main avenues to generate low-level code. To solve real-world problems, I recommend Numba. Why, then, did I dedicate an entire chapter to Cython and put Numba at the back of the book? Because the main purpose of this book is to give you a solid foundation for writing efficient code in the Python ecosystem, and Cython, with its extra hurdles, allows us to dig deeper in terms of understanding what is going on.

About the code

This book contains many examples of source code both in numbered listings and in line with normal text. In both cases, source code is formatted in a `fixed-width font like this` to separate it from ordinary text. Sometimes code is also in **bold** to highlight code that has changed from previous steps in the chapter, such as when a new feature adds to an existing line of code.

In many cases, the original source code has been reformatted; we've added line breaks and reworked indentation to accommodate the available page space in the book. In rare cases, even this was not enough, and listings include line-continuation markers (➥). Additionally, comments in the source code have often been removed from the listings when the code is described in the text. Code annotations accompany many of the listings, highlighting important concepts.

You can get executable snippets of code from the liveBook (online) version of this book at https://livebook.manning.com/book/fast-python. The complete code for the examples in the book is available for download from GitHub at https://github.com/tiagoantao/python-performance, and from the Manning website at www.manning.com. I will update the repository when bugs are found or when major developments to Python and existing libraries require some revisions. As such, please expect some changes in the book repository. You will find a directory for each chapter in the repository.

Whatever code style you prefer, I have adapted the code herein to work well in a printed book. For example, I tend to be partial to long and descriptive variable names, but these do not work well with the limitations of book form. I try to use expressive names and follow standard Python conventions like PEP8, but book legibility takes precedence. The same is valid for type annotations: I would like to use them, but they get in the way of code readability. In some very rare cases, I use an algorithm to increase readability, even though it doesn't deal with all corner cases or add much to the explanation.

In most cases, the code in this book will work with the standard Python interpreter. In some limited scenarios, IPython will be required, especially for the expedient performance analysis. You can also use Jupyter Notebook.

Details about the installation can be found in appendix A. If any chapter or section requires special software, that will be noted in the appropriate place.

liveBook discussion forum

Purchase of *Fast Python* includes free access to liveBook, Manning's online reading platform. Using liveBook's exclusive discussion features, you can attach comments to the book globally or to specific sections or paragraphs. It's a snap to make notes for yourself, ask and answer technical questions, and receive help from the author and other users. To access the forum, go to https://livebook.manning.com/book/fast-python/discussion. You can also learn more about Manning's forums and the rules of conduct at https://livebook .manning.com/discussion.

Manning's commitment to our readers is to provide a venue where a meaningful dialogue between individual readers and between readers and the author can take place. It is not a commitment to any specific amount of participation on the part of the author, whose contribution to the forum remains voluntary (and unpaid). We suggest you try asking the author some challenging questions lest their interest stray! The forum and the archives of previous discussions will be accessible from the publisher's website for as long as the book is in print.

Hardware and software

You can use any operating system to run the code in this book. That being said, Linux is where most production code tends to be deployed, so that is the preferred system. MacOS X should also work without any adaptations. If you use Windows, I recommend that you install Windows Subsystem for Linux (WSL).

An alternative to all operating systems is Docker. You can use the Docker images provided in the repository. Docker will provide a containerized Linux environment to run the code.

I recommend you have at least 16 GB of memory and 150 GB of free disk space. Chapter 9, with GPU-related content, requires an NVIDIA GPU, at least based on the Pascal architecture; most GPUs released in the last five years should cover this requirement. More details about preparing your computer and software to get the most from this book can be found in appendix A.

about the author

TIAGO RODRIGUES ANTÃO has a BEng in Informatics and a PhD in bioinformatics. He currently works in the biotech field. Tiago uses Python with all its libraries to perform scientific computing and data engineering tasks. More often than not, he also uses low-level programming languages such as C and Rust to optimize critical parts of algorithms. He currently develops on an infrastructure based on Amazon AWS, but for most of his career, he used on-premises computing and scientific clusters.

In addition to working in the industry, his experience with the academic side of scientific computing includes two data analysis post-docs at Cambridge University and Oxford University. As a research scientist at the University of Montana, he created, from scratch, the entire scientific computing infrastructure for the analysis of biological data.

Tiago is one of the co-authors of *Biopython,* a major bioinformatics package written in Python, and is author of the book *Bioinformatics with Python Cookbook* (Packt, 2022), which is in its third edition. He has also authored and co-authored many important scientific articles in the field of bioinformatics.

about the cover illustration

The figure on the cover of *Fast Python* is captioned "Bourgeoise de Passeau," or "Bourgeoise of Passeau," taken from a collection by Jacques Grasset de Saint-Sauveur, published in 1797. Each illustration is finely drawn and colored by hand.

In those days, it was easy to identify where people lived and what their trade or station in life was just by their dress. Manning celebrates the inventiveness and initiative of the computer business with book covers based on the rich diversity of regional culture centuries ago, brought back to life by pictures from collections such as this one.

## Part 1

Foundational Approaches

In part 1 of this book, we will discuss foundational approaches regarding performance with Python. We will cover native Python libraries and fundamental data structures, and how Python can—without external libraries—make use of parallel processing techniques. An entire chapter on NumPy optimization is also included. While NumPy is an external library, it's so crucial to modern data processing that it's as foundational as pure Python approaches.

An urgent need for efficiency in data processing

An enormous amount of data is being collected all the time, at intense speeds, and from a broad scope of sources. It is collected whether or not there is currently a use for it. It is collected whether or not there is a way to process, store, access, or learn from it. Before data scientists can analyze it, before designers and developers and policymakers can use it to create products, services, and programs, software engineers must find ways to store and process it. Now more than ever those engineers need efficient ways to improve performance and optimize storage.

In this book, I share a collection of strategies for performance and storage optimization that I use in my own work. Simply throwing more machines at the problem is often neither possible nor helpful. So the solutions I introduce here rely more on understanding and exploiting what we all have at hand: coding approaches, hardware and system architectures, available software, and, of course, nuances of the Python language, libraries, and ecosystem.

Python has emerged as the language of choice to do, or at least glue, all the heavy lifting around this data *deluge*, as the cliches call it. Indeed, Python's popularity in data science and data engineering is one of the main drivers of the language's growth, helping to push it to one of the top three most popular languages, according to a majority of developer surveys. Python has its own unique set of advantages and limitations for dealing with big data, and its lack of speed certainly presents challenges. On the plus side, as you'll see, there are many different angles, approaches, and workarounds to making Python work more efficiently with large amounts of data.

Before we get to the solutions, we need to fully comprehend the problem(s), and that is what we'll do in much of this first chapter. We will spend a few moments looking more closely at the computing challenges presented by the deluge of data to orient ourselves to what exactly we are dealing with. Next, we'll examine the role of hardware, network, and cloud architectures to see why the old solutions, such as increasing CPU speed, are no longer adequate. Then we'll turn to the particular challenges that Python faces when dealing with big data, including Python's threading and CPython's Global Interpreter Lock (GIL). Once we've fully understood the need for new approaches to making Python perform better, I'll present an overview of the solutions that you'll learn in this book.

1.1 How bad is the data deluge?

You may be aware of two computing laws, Moore's and Edholm's, that together offer a dramatic picture of the exponential growth of data along with the lagging ability of computing systems to deal with that data. Edholm's Law states that data rates in telecommunications double every 18 months, while Moore's law predicts that the number of transistors that can fit on a microchip doubles every two years. We can take Edholm's data transfer rate as a proxy for the amount of data collected and Moore's transistor density as an indicator of speed and capacity in computing hardware. When we put them together we find a six-month lag between how fast and how much data we collect, and our ability to process and store it. Because exponential growth can be tricky to understand in words, I've plotted the two laws against each other in one graph, shown in figure 1.1

The situation described by this graph can be seen as a fight between what we need to analyze (Edholm's law) versus the power that we have to do that analysis (Moore's law). The graph actually paints a rosier picture than what we have in reality. We will

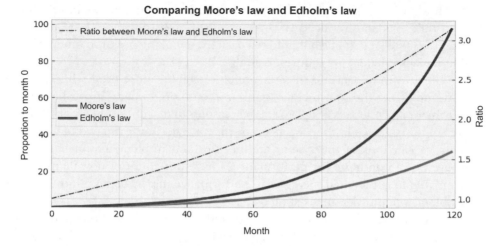

Figure 1.1 The ratio between Moore's law and Edholm's law suggests that hardware will always lag behind the amount of data being generated. Moreover, the gap will increase over time.

see why in chapter 6 when we discuss Moore's law in the context of modern CPU architectures. To focus here on data growth, let's look at one example, internet traffic, which is an indirect measure of data available. As you can see in figure 1.2, the growth of internet traffic over the years tracks Edholm's law quite well.

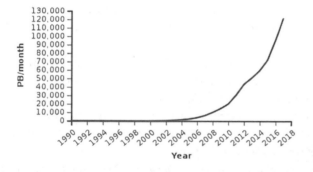

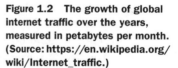

Figure 1.2 The growth of global internet traffic over the years, measured in petabytes per month. (Source: https://en.wikipedia.org/wiki/Internet_traffic.)

In addition, 90% of the data humankind has produced happened in the last two years (see "Big Data and What It Means," http://mng.bz/v1ya). Whether the quality of this new data is proportional to its size is another matter altogether. The point is that data produced will need to be processed and that processing will require resources.

It's not just the amount of available data that presents software engineers with obstacles. The way all this new data is represented is also changing in nature. Some project that by 2025, around 80% of data could be unstructured, ("Tapping the power of unstructured data," http://mng.bz/BlP0). We will get into the details later in the book, but simply put, unstructured data makes data processing more demanding from a computational perspective.

How do we deal with all this growth in data? It turns out that we mostly don't. More than 99% of data produced is never analyzed, according to *The Guardian* (http:// mng.bz/Q8M4). Part of what holds us back from making use of so much of our data is that we lack efficient procedures to analyze it.

The growth of data and the concomitant need for more processing has developed into one of the most pernicious mantras about computing: "If you have more data, just throw more servers at it." For many reasons, that is not often a viable or appropriate solution. Instead, when we need to increase the performance of an existing system, we can look at the system architecture and implementation and find places where we can optimize for performance. I have lost count of how many times I have been able to get ten-fold increases in performance just by being mindful of efficiency problems when reviewing existing code.

What is crucial to understand is that the relationship between the amount of increased data to analyze, and the complexity of the infrastructure needed to analyze it, is hardly linear. Solving these problems requires more time and ingenuity on the developer's part than in machines. This is true not only with cloud environments but also with in-house clusters and even with single-machine implementations. A few use cases will help to make this clear. For example:

- *Your solution requires only a single computer, but suddenly you need more machines.* Adding machines means you will have to manage the number of machines, distribute the workload across them, and make sure the data is partitioned correctly. You might also need a file system server to add to your list of machines. The cost of maintaining a server farm, or just a cloud, is *qualitatively* much more than maintaining a single computer.
- *Your solution works well in-memory but then the amount of data increases and no longer fits your memory.* To handle the new amount of data stored in disk will normally entail a major rewrite of your code. And, of course, the code itself will grow in complexity. For instance, if the main database is now on disk, you may need to create a cache policy. Or you may need to do concurrent reads from multiple processes, or, even worse, concurrent writes.
- *You use a SQL database and suddenly you reach the maximum throughput capacity of the server.* If it's only a read capacity problem, then you might survive by just creating a few read replicas. But if it is a write problem, what do you do? Maybe you set up sharding.[1] Or do you decide to completely change your database technology in favor of some supposedly better performant NoSQL variant?
- *If you are dependent on a system in the cloud based on vendor proprietary technologies, you might discover that the ability to scale indefinitely is more marketing talk than technological reality.* In many cases, if you hit performance limits, the only realistic solution is to change the technology that you are using, a change that requires enormous time, money, and human energy.

---

[1] *Sharding* is the partitioning of data so that parts of it reside in different servers.

I hope these examples make the case that growth is not just a question of "adding more machines," but instead entails substantial work on several fronts to deal with the increased complexity. Even something as "simple" as a parallel solution implemented on a single computer can bring with it all the problems of parallel processing (races, deadlocks, and more). These more efficient solutions can have a dramatic effect on complexity, reliability, and cost.

Finally, we could make the case that even if we *could* scale our infrastructure linearly (we can't, really), there would be ethical and ecological problems to consider: forecasts put energy consumption related to a "tsunami of data" at 20% of global electricity production ("Tsunami of Data," http://mng.bz/X5GE), and there is also a problem of landfill disposal as we update hardware.

The good news is that becoming computationally more efficient when handling big data helps us to reduce our computing bill, the complexity of the architecture for our solution, our storage needs, our time to market, and our energy footprint. And sometimes, more efficient solutions might even come with minimal implementation costs. For example, the judicious use of data structures might reduce computing time at no substantial development cost.

On the other hand, many of the solutions we'll look at will have a development cost and will add an amount of complexity themselves. When you look at *your* data and forecasts for its growth, you will have to make a judgment call on where to optimize, as there are no clear-cut recipes or one-size-fits-all solutions. That being said, there might be just one rule that can be applied across the board: if the solution is good for Netflix, Google, Amazon, Apple, or Facebook, then probably it is *not* good for you, unless, of course, you work for one of these companies.

The amount of data that most of us will see will be substantially lower than the biggest technological companies use. It will still be enormous, and it will still be hard, but it will probably be a few orders of magnitude lower. The somewhat prevailing wisdom that what works for those companies is also a good fit for the rest of us is, in my opinion, just wrong. Generally, less complex solutions will be more appropriate for most of us.

As you can see, this new world with extreme growth, both in quantity and complexity, of both data and algorithms requires more sophisticated techniques to perform computation and storage in an efficient and cost-conscious way. Don't get me wrong: sometimes you *will* need to scale up your infrastructure. But when you architect and implement your solution, you can still use the same mindset of focusing on efficiency. It's just that the techniques will be different.

1.2 Modern computing architectures and high-performance computing

Creating more efficient solutions does not happen in an abstract void. First, we have our domain problem to consider—that is, what real problem you are trying to solve. Equally important is the computing architecture where our solution will be run. Computing architectures play a major role in determining the best optimization techniques, so we have to take them into consideration when we devise our software solutions. In this section, we will take a look at the main architectural problems that affect the design and implementation of our solutions.

1.2.1 Changes inside the computer

Radical changes are happening *inside* the computer. First, we have CPUs that are increasing processing power mostly in the number of parallel units, not raw speed, as they did in the past. Computers can also be equipped with graphics processing units (GPUs), which were originally developed for graphics processing only but now can be used for general computing as well. Indeed, many efficient implementations of AI algorithms are done for GPUs. Unfortunately, at least from our perspective, GPUs have a completely different architecture than CPUs: they are composed of thousands of computing units that are expected to do the same "simple" computation across all units. The memory model is also completely different. These differences mean that programming GPUs require a radically different approach from programming CPUs.

To understand how we can use GPUs for data processing, we need to understand their original purpose and architectural implications. GPUs, as the name indicates, were developed to help with graphics processing. Some of the most computationally demanding applications are actually games. Games, and graphic applications in general, are constantly updating millions of pixels on the screen. The hardware architecture devised to solve this problem has many small processing cores. Its quite easy for a GPU to have thousands of cores, while a CPU typically has less than 10. GPU cores are substantially simpler and mostly run the same code on each core. They are thus very good for running a massive number of similar tasks, like updating pixels.

Given the sheer amount of processing power in GPUs, there was an attempt to try to use that power for other tasks with the appearance of general-purpose computing on graphics processing units (GPGPU). Because of the way GPU architectures are organized, they are mostly applicable to tasks that are massively parallel in nature. It turns out that many modern AI algorithms, like ones based on neural networks, tend to be massively parallel. So there was a natural fit between the two.

Unfortunately, the difference between CPUs and GPUs is not only in the number of cores and their complexity. GPU memory, especially on the most computationally powerful, is separated from the main memory. Thus, there is also the problem of transferring data between the main memory and GPU memory. So we have two massive problems to consider when targeting GPUs.

For reasons that will become clear in chapter 9, programming GPUs with Python is substantially more difficult and less practical than targeting CPUs. Nonetheless, there is still more than enough scope to make use of GPUs from Python.

While less fashionable than the advances in GPUs, monumental changes have also come to how CPUs can be programmed. And, unlike GPUs, we can easily use most of these CPU changes in Python. CPU performance increases are being delivered differently by manufacturers than in the past. Their solution, driven by the laws of physics, is to build in more parallel processing, not more speed. Moore's law is sometimes stated as the doubling of speed every 24 months, but that is actually not the correct definition: it relates instead to the transistor density doubling every two years. The linear relationship between increased speed and transistor density broke more than a decade ago, and speed has mostly plateaued since then. Given that data has continued to grow along with algorithm complexity, we are in a pernicious situation. The first line of solutions coming from CPU manufacturers is allowing more parallelism: more CPUs per computer, more cores per CPU, and simultaneous multithreading. Processors are not really accelerating sequential computations anymore but allowing for more concurrent execution. This concurrent execution requires a paradigm shift in how we program computers. Before, the speed of a program would "magically" increase when you changed CPUs. Now, increasing speed depends on the programmer being aware of the shift in the underlying architecture to the parallel programming paradigm.

There are many changes in the way we program modern CPUs, and as you will see in chapter 6, some of them are so counterintuitive they are worth keeping an eye on from the onset. For example, while CPU speeds have leveled in recent years, CPUs are still orders of magnitude faster than RAM. If CPU caches did not exist, then CPUs would be mostly idle, as they would spend most of the time waiting for RAM. This means that sometimes it is *faster* to work with compressed data, including the cost of decompression, than with raw data. Why? If you can put a compressed block on the CPU cache, then those cycles that otherwise would be idle waiting for RAM access could be used to decompress the data with CPU cycles to spare that could be used for computation! A similar argument could work for compressed file systems: they sometimes can be faster than raw file systems. There are direct applications of this in the Python world; for example, by changing a simple Boolean flag regarding the choice of the internal representation of NumPy arrays, you take advantage of cache locality problems and speed up your NumPy processing considerably. We have some access times and sizes for different kinds of memory in table 1.1, including CPU cache, RAM, local disk, and remote storage. The key point here is not the precise numbers but the orders of magnitude in difference in both size and access time.

Table 1.1 Memory hierarchy with sizes and access times for a hypothetical, but realistic modern desktop

Type	Size	Access time
CPU		
L1 cache	256 KB	2 ns
L2 cache	1 MB	5 ns
L3 cache	6 MB	30 ns
RAM		
DIMM	8 GB	100 ns

Table 1.1   Memory hierarchy with sizes and access times for a hypothetical, but realistic modern desktop *(continued)*

Type	Size	Access time
Secondary storage		
SSD	256 GB	50 μs
HDD	2 TB	5 ms
Tertiary storage		
NAS - Network Access Server	100 TB	Network dependent
Cloud proprietary	1 PB	Provider dependent

Table 1.1 includes tertiary storage, which happens *outside* the computer. There have also been changes there, which we will address in the next section.

1.2.2   Changes in the network

In high-performance computing settings, we use the network as both a way to add more storage and, especially, to increase computing power. While we would like to solve our problems using a single computer, sometimes relying on a compute cluster is inevitable. Optimizing for the architectures with multiple computers—be it in the cloud or on-premises—will be a part of our journey to high performance.

Using many computers and external storage brings a whole new class of problems related to distributed computing: network topologies, sharing data across machines, and managing processes running across the network. There are many examples. For instance, what is the price of using REST APIs on services that require high performance and low latency? How can we deal with the penalties of having remote filesystems; can we mitigate those?

We will be trying to optimize our usage of the network stack and for that, we will have to be aware of it at all levels shown in figure 1.3. Outside the network, we have our code and Python libraries, which make choices about the layers below. At the top of the network stack, a typical choice for data transport is HTTPS with a payload based on JSON.

While this is a perfectly reasonable choice for many applications, there are more performant alternatives for cases where network speed and lag matter. For example, a binary payload might be more efficient than JSON. Also, HTTP might be replaced by a direct TCP socket. But there are more radical alternatives like replacing the TCP transport layer: most internet application protocols use TCP, although there are a few exceptions like DNS and DHCP, which are both UDP based. The TCP protocol is highly reliable, but there is a performance penalty to be paid for that reliability. There will be times when the smaller overhead of UDP will be a more efficient alternative and the extra reliability is not needed.

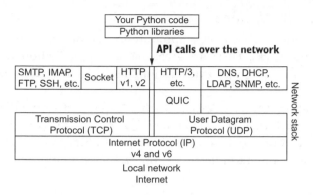

Figure 1.3   **API calls via the network stack. Understanding the alternatives available for network communication can dramatically increase the speed of internet-based applications.**

Below transport protocols, we have the internet protocol (IP) and the physical infrastructure. The physical infrastructure can be important when we design our solutions. For example, if we have a very reliable local network, then UDP, which can lose data, will be more of an alternative than it would be in an unreliable network.

1.2.3   *The cloud*

In the past, most data processing implementations were made to function on a single computer or on an on-premises cluster maintained by the same organization that runs the workload. Currently, cloud-based infrastructure where all servers are "virtual" and maintained by an external entity, is becoming increasingly common. Sometimes, as with so-called serverless computing, we do not even deal with servers directly.

The cloud is not just about adding more computers or network storage. It's also about a set of proprietary extensions on how to deal with storage and compute resources, and those extensions have consequences in terms of performance. Furthermore, virtual computers can throw a wrench in some CPU optimizations. For example, in a bare metal machine, you can devise a solution that is considerate of cache locality problems, but in a virtual machine, you have no way of knowing whether your cache is being preempted by another virtual machine being executed concurrently. How do we keep our algorithms efficient in such an environment? Also, the cost model of cloud computing is completely different—time is literally money—and, as such, efficient solutions become even more important.

Many of the compute and storage solutions in the cloud are also proprietary and have very specific APIs and behaviors. Using such proprietary solutions also has consequences on performance that should be considered. As such, and while most problems pertaining to traditional clusters are also applicable to the cloud, sometimes there will be specific problems that will need to be dealt with separately. Now that we have a view of the architectural possibilities and limitations that will shape our applications, let's turn to the advantages and disadvantages of Python for high-performance computing.

1.3   *Working with Python's limitations*

Python is widely used in modern data process applications. As with any language, it has its advantages and its drawbacks. There are great reasons to use Python, but here we are more concerned with dealing with Python's limitations for high-performance data processing.

Let's not sugarcoat reality: Python is spectacularly ill-equipped to handle high-performance computing. If performance and parallelism were the only consideration, nobody would use Python. Python has an amazing ecology of libraries for doing data analysis, great documentation, and a wonderfully supportive community. That is why we use it, not computational performance.

There is a saying that goes something like this "There are no slow languages, only slow language implementations." I hope you allow me to disagree. It is not fair to ask the implementors of a dynamic, high-level language like Python (or, say, JavaScript for that matter) to compete in terms of speed with lower-level languages like C, C++, Rust, or Go.

Features like dynamic typing and garbage collection will pay a price in terms of performance. And that is fine: there are many cases where programmer time is more valuable than compute time. But let's not bury our heads in the sand: more declarative and dynamic languages will pay a price in computation and memory. It's a balance.

That being said, this is no excuse for poorly performant language implementations. In this regard, how does CPython, the flagship Python implementation that you are probably using, fare? A complete analysis would not be easy, but you can do a simple exercise: write a matrix multiplication function and time it. Then, for example, run it with another Python implementation like PyPy. Then convert your code to JavaScript (a fair comparison as the language is also dynamic; an unfair comparison would be would C) and time it again.

Spoiler alert: CPython will not fare well. We have a language that is naturally slow and a flagship implementation that does not seem to have speed as its main consideration. Now, the good news is that most of these problems can be overcome. Many people have produced applications and libraries that will mitigate most performance problems. You can still write code in Python that will perform very well with a small memory footprint. You just have to write code while attending to Python's warts.

> **NOTE** In most of the book, when we talk about Python, we are referring to the CPython implementation. All exceptions to this rule will be explicitly called out.

Given Python's limitations regarding performance, optimizing our Python code sometimes will not be enough. In those cases, we will end up rewriting that part in a lower-level language or, at the very least, annotating our code so that it gets rewritten in a lower-level language by some code conversion tool. The part of the code that we will need to rewrite is normally very small, so we are decidedly *not* ditching Python. When we do this last stage of optimization, probably more than 90% of the code will still be Python. This is what many core scientific libraries like NumPy, scikit-learn, and SciPy actually do: their most computationally demanding parts are usually implemented in C or Fortran.

1.3.1 *The Global Interpreter Lock*

In discussions about Python's performance, its GIL, or Global Interpreter Lock, inevitably comes up. What exactly is the GIL? While Python has the concept of threads, CPython has a GIL, which only allows a single thread to execute at a point in time. Even on a multicore processor, you only get a single thread executing at a single point in time.

Other implementations of Python, like Jython and IronPython, do not have a GIL and can use all cores in modern multiprocessors. But CPython is still the reference implementation for which all the main libraries are developed. In addition, Jython and IronPython are, respectively, JVM and .NET dependent. As such, CPython, given its massive library base, ends up being the default Python implementation. We will briefly discuss other implementations in the book, most notably PyPy, but in practice, CPython is queen.

To understand how to work around the GIL, it is useful to remember the difference between *concurrency* and *parallelism*. Concurrency, you may recall, is when a certain number of tasks can *overlap* in time, though they may not be *running* at the same time. They can, for example, interleave. Parallelism is when tasks are executed at the same time. So, in Python, concurrency is possible, but parallelism is not . . . or is it?

Concurrency without parallelism is still quite useful. The best example of this comes from the JavaScript world and Node.JS, which is overwhelmingly used to implement the backend of web servers. In many server-side web tasks, most of the time is actually spent waiting for IO; that is a great time for a thread to *voluntarily* relinquish control so that other threads can continue with computation. Modern Python has similar asynchronous facilities, and we will be discussing them.

But back to the main problem: does the GIL impose a serious performance penalty? In most cases, the answer is a surprising no. There are two main reasons for this:

- Most of the high-performance code, those tight inner loops, will probably have to be written in a lower-level language as we've discussed.
- Python provides mechanisms for lower-level languages to release the GIL.

This means that when you enter a part of the code rewritten in a lower-level language, you can instruct Python to continue with other Python threads in parallel with your low-level implementation. You should only release the GIL if that is safe—for example, if you do not write to objects that may be in use by other threads.

Also, *multiprocessing* (i.e., running multiple processes simultaneously) is not affected by the GIL, which only affects threads, so there is still plenty of space to deploy parallel solutions even in pure Python.

So, in theory, the GIL is a concern with regard to performance, but in practice, it rarely is the source of problems that cannot be overcome. We will dive deep into this subject in chapter 3.

1.4   *A summary of the solutions*

This book is about getting high performance from Python, but code does not run in a vacuum. You can only devise efficient code if you take into consideration the broader perspective of data and algorithm demands as well as computing architectures. While it's impossible to go into every architectural and algorithmic detail in one book, my aim with these is to help you understand the implications of CPU design, GPUs, storage alternatives, network protocols and cloud architectures, and other system considerations (figure 1.4) so you can make sound decisions for improving the performance of your Python code. This book should equip you to assess the advantages and drawbacks of your computing architecture, whether it is a single computer, a GPU-enabled computer, a cluster, or a cloud environment, and implement the necessary changes to take full advantage of it.

Hardware ecology

On-premises/cloud/hybrid		
Computing	Storage	Network
Metal	CPU cache	Topology
VM	RAM	Protocols
Cloud instance	File system	Speed
Serverless	SQL	Latency
	NoSQL	
	Cloud proprietary	
	Network attached storage	

Figure 1.4   **Underlying hardware architectures must be taken into account when choosing high-performance coding solutions.**

The goal of this book is to introduce you to a range of solutions and show you how and where each one is best applied, so you can select and implement the most efficient solution for your particular set of resources, goals, and problems. We will spend considerable time working through examples so you can see for yourself the effects, both positive and negative, of these approaches. There is no mandate to apply all the approaches, nor is there a prescribed order in which to apply them. Each approach has its greater or lesser gains in performance and efficiency, along with its tradeoffs. If you understand what you have at your disposal in your system and in available strategies for improving aspects of that system, you can pick and choose where to spend your time and resources. To help you make sense of the approaches, table 1.2 presents a summary of the techniques presented in the book and the component or domain of the system development process that they target.

Table 1.2   **Purpose of each chapter in the book**

Domain	Application	Chapter
Getting the most of your Python interpreter	Python interpreter	2 Extracting maximum performance from built-in features
Understanding Python's internal functionality to extract the most computing power from your computer	Python interpreter	3 Concurrency, parallelism, and asynchronous processing

Extracting maximum performance from built-in features

This chapter covers

- Profiling code to find speed and memory bottlenecks
- Making more efficient use of existing Python data structures
- Understanding Python's memory cost of allocating typical data structures
- Using lazy programming techniques to process large amounts of data

There arc many tools and libraries to help us write more efficient Python. But before we dive into all the external options to improve performance, let's first take a closer look at how we can write pure Python code that is more efficient, in both computing and IO performance. Indeed many, although ccrtainly not all, Python performance problems can be solved by being more mindful of Python's limits and capabilities.

To demonstrate Python's own tools for improving performance, let's use them on a hypothetical, although realistic problem. Let's say you are a data engineer tasked with preparing the analysis of climate data around the world. The data will be based on the Integrated Surface Database from the US National Oceanic and Atmospheric Administration (NOAA; http://mng.bz/ydge). You are on a tight deadline, and you will only be able to use mostly standard Python. Furthermore, buying more processing power is out of the question due to budgetary constraints. The data will start to arrive in one month, and you plan on using the time before it arrives to increase code performance. Your task, then, is to find the places in need of optimization and to increase their performance.

The first thing that you want to do is to profile the existing code that will ingest the data. You know that the code that you already have is slow, but before you try to optimize it, you need to find empirical evidence of the bottlenecks. Profiling is important because it allows you to search, in a rigorous and systematic way, for bottlenecks in your code. The most common alternative, guesstimating, is particularly ineffective here because many slowdown points can be quite unintuitive.

Optimizing pure Python code is the low-hanging fruit, but it is also where most problems tend to reside, so optimizing can often be quite advantageous. In this chapter, we will see what pure Python offers out of the box to help us develop more performant code. We will start by profiling the code, using several profiling tools, to detect problem areas. Then we will focus on Python's basic data structures: lists, sets, and dictionaries. Our goal here will be to improve the efficiency of these data structures and to allocate memory to them in the best way for optimal performance. Finally, we will see how modern Python lazy programming techniques can help us to improve the performance of our data pipeline.

This chapter will only discuss optimizing Python without external libraries, but we will still use some external tools to help us optimize performance and access data. We will be using Snakeviz to visualize the output of Python profiling, as well as line_profiler to profile code line by line. Finally, we will use the requests library to download data from the internet.

If you use Docker, the default image has all you need. If you follow the instructions for Anaconda Python from appendix A, you are all set. Let's now start our profiling process by downloading data from weather stations and studying the temperature at each station.

2.1   *Profiling applications with both IO and computing workloads*

Our first objective will be to download data from a weather station and get the minimum temperature for a certain year on that station. Data on NOAA's site has CSV files, one per year and then per station. For example, the file https://www.ncei.noaa .gov/data/global-hourly/access/2021/01494099999.csv has all the entries for station

01494099999 for the year 2021. This includes, among other entries, temperature and pressure, recorded potentially several times a day.

Let's develop a script to download the data for a set of stations on an interval of years. After downloading the data of interest, we will get the minimum temperature for each station.

2.1.1 Downloading data and computing minimum temperatures

Our script will have a simple command-line interface, where we pass a list of stations and an interval of years of interest. Here is the code to parse the input (the code can be found in 02-python/sec1-io-cpu/load.py):

```
import collections
import csv
import datetime
import sys

import requests

stations = sys.argv[1].split(",")
years = [int(year) for year in sys.argv[2].split("-")]
start_year = years[0]
end_year = years[1]
```

To ease the coding part, we will be using the requests library to get the file. Here is the code to download the data from the server:

```
TEMPLATE_URL = "https://www.ncei.noaa.gov/data/global-hourly/access/{year}/
➥ {station}.csv"
TEMPLATE_FILE = "station_{station}_{year}.csv"

def download_data(station, year):
    my_url = TEMPLATE_URL.format(station=station, year=year)
    req = requests.get(my_url)        ←────┐
    if req.status_code != 200:              │ Requests makes it easy to access web content.
        return  # not found
    w = open(TEMPLATE_FILE.format(station=station, year=year), "wt")
    w.write(req.text)
    w.close()


def download_all_data(stations, start_year, end_year):
    for station in stations:
        for year in range(start_year, end_year + 1):
            download_data(station, year)
```

This code will write each downloaded file to disk for all the requested stations across all years. Now, let's get all the temperatures in a single file:

```
def get_file_temperatures(file_name):
  with open(file_name, "rt") as f:
    reader = csv.reader(f)
```

```
                     header = next(reader)
                     for row in reader:
    We ignore            station = row[header.index("STATION")]
  entries for            # date = datetime.datetime.fromisoformat(row[header.index('DATE')])
  which the            tmp = row[header.index("TMP")]
  data is not          temperature, status = tmp.split(",")
  available.    ┌─┐   if status != "1":
                └─▷       continue
                         temperature = int(temperature) / 10
                         yield temperature
```

The format for the temperature field includes a subfield with the status quality of the data.

Let's now get all temperatures and the minimum temperature per station:

```
def get_all_temperatures(stations, start_year, end_year):
    temperatures = collections.defaultdict(list)
    for station in stations:
        for year in range(start_year, end_year + 1):
            for temperature in get_file_temperatures(
➡   TEMPLATE_FILE.format(station=station, year=year)):
                    temperatures[station].append(temperature)
    return temperatures


def get_min_temperatures(all_temperatures):
    return {station: min(temperatures) for station, temperatures in
➡   all_temperatures.items()}
```

Now we can tie everything together: download the data, get all temperatures, compute the minimum per station, and print the results:

```
download_all_data(stations, start_year, end_year)
all_temperatures = get_all_temperatures(stations, start_year, end_year)
min_temperatures = get_min_temperatures(all_temperatures)
print(min_temperatures)
```

For example, to load the data for stations 01044099999 and 02293099999 for the year 2021, we do

```
python load.py 01044099999,02293099999 2021-2021
```

with the output being

```
{'01044099999': -10.0, '02293099999': -27.6}
```

Now, the real fun starts. Our goal is to continue to download lots of data from lots of stations over many years. To handle this quantity of data, we want to make the code as efficient as possible. The first step in making the code more efficient is to profile it in an organized and thorough way to find the bottlenecks slowing it down. For this, we will use Python's built-in profiling machinery.

2.1.2 Python's built-in profiling module

As we want to make sure our code is as efficient as possible, the first thing we need to do is to find existing bottlenecks in that code. Our first port of call will be profiling the code to check each function's time consumption. For this, we run the code via Python's cProfile module. This module is built into Python and allows us to obtain profiling information from our code. Make sure you do not use the profile module, as it is orders of magnitude slower; it's only useful if you are developing profiling tools yourself.

We can run the profiler with:

```
python -m cProfile -s cumulative load.py 01044099999,02293099999 2021-
    2021 > profile.txt
```

Remember that running Python with the -m flag will execute the module, so we are running the cProfile module. This is Python's recommended module to gather profiling information. We are asking for profile statistics ordered by cumulative time. The easiest way to use the module is by passing our script to the profiler in a module call like this:

```
375402 function calls (370670 primitive calls) in 3.061 seconds        ⟵

        Ordered by: cumulative time            Basic summary information can be found on the first
                                               line: the number of function calls and total run time.

   ncalls  tottime  percall  cumtime  percall filename:lineno(function)
    158/1    0.000    0.000    3.061    3.061 {built-in method builtins.exec}
        1    0.000    0.000    3.061    3.061 load.py:1(<module>)
        1    0.001    0.001    2.768    2.768 load.py:27(download_all_data)
        2    0.001    0.000    2.766    1.383 load.py:17(download_data)
        2    0.000    0.000    2.714    1.357 api.py:64(get)
        2    0.000    0.000    2.714    1.357 api.py:16(request)
        2    0.000    0.000    2.710    1.355 sessions.py:470(request)
        2    0.000    0.000    2.704    1.352 sessions.py:626(send)
     3015    0.017    0.000    1.857    0.001 socket.py:690(readinto)
     3015    0.017    0.000    1.829    0.001 ssl.py:1230(recv_into)
   [...]
        1    0.000    0.000    0.000    0.000 load.py:58(get_min_temperatures)
```

The computing costs of our code (computing is done in **get_min_temperatures**) are neglegible.

The output is ordered by cumulative time, which is all the time spent inside a certain function. Another output is the number of calls per function. For example, there is only a single call to download_all_data (which takes care of downloading all data), but its cumulative time is almost equal to the total time of the script. You will notice two columns called percall. The first one states the time spent on the function *excluding* the time spent on all the subcalls. The second one includes the time spent on subcalls. In the case of download_all_data, it is clear that most time is consumed by some of the subfunctions.

In many cases, when you have some intensive form of I/O like here, there is a strong possibility that I/O dominates in terms of time needed. In our case, we have both network I/O (getting the data from NOAA) and disk I/O (writing it to disk). Network costs can vary widely, even between runs, as they are dependent on many connection points along the way. As network costs are normally the biggest time sink, let's try to mitigate those.

2.1.3 *Using local caches to reduce network usage*

To reduce network communication, let's save a copy for future use when we download a file for the first time. We will build a local cache of data. We will use the same code as the previous, save for the function download_all_data (the code can be found in 02-python/sec1-io-cpu/load_cache.py):

```
import os
def download_all_data(stations, start_year, end_year):
  for station in stations:
    for year in range(start_year, end_year + 1):
      if not os.path.exists(TEMPLATE_FILE.format(
        station=station, year=year)):          ◁——
        download_data(station, year)
```

> **We check whether the file already exists and only download it if not.**

The first run of the code will take the same time as the previous solution, but a second run will not require any network access. For example, given the same run as the previous, it goes from 2.8 s to 0.26 s—more than an order of magnitude increase. Remember that due to high variability in network access, the time to download files can vary substantially in your case. This is yet another reason to consider caching network data: having a more predictable execution time:

```
python -m cProfile -s cumulative load_cache.py 01044099999,02293099999
  2021-2021 > profile_cache.txt
```

Now, the result is different in where time is consumed:

```
299938 function calls (295246 primitive calls) in 0.260 seconds

   Ordered by: cumulative time

ncalls  tottime  percall  cumtime  percall filename:lineno(function)
156/1    0.000    0.000    0.260    0.260 {built-in method builtins.exec}
    1    0.000    0.000    0.260    0.260 load_cache.py:1(<module>)
    1    0.008    0.008    0.166    0.166 load_cache.py:51(
  get_all_temperatures)
33650    0.137    0.000    0.156    0.000 load_cache.py:36(
  get_file_temperatures)
[...]
    1    0.000    0.000    0.001    0.001 load_cache.py:60(
    get_min_temperatures)
```

While the time to run decreased one order of magnitude, IO is still top. Now, it's not the network but disk access. This is mostly caused by the computation being acually low.

> **WARNING** Caches, as this example shows, can speed up code by orders of magnitude. However, cache management can be problematic and is a common source of bugs. In our example, the files never change over time, but there are many use cases for caches where the source might be changing. In that case, the cache management code needs to recognize that problem. We will revisit caches in other parts of the book.

We are now going to consider a case where CPU is the limiting factor.

2.2 Profiling code to detect performance bottlenecks

Here we look at code where CPU is the resource costing the most time in a process. We'll take all stations in the NOAA database and compute the distance between them, a problem of complexity n2.

In the repository, you will find a file (02-python/sec2-cpu/locations.csv) with all the geographical coordinates of the stations (the code can be found in 02-python/sec2-cpu/distance_cache.py):

```python
import csv
import math


def get_locations():
    with open("locations.csv", "rt") as f:
        reader = csv.reader(f)
        header = next(reader)
        for row in reader:
            station = row[header.index("STATION")]
            lat = float(row[header.index("LATITUDE")])
            lon = float(row[header.index("LONGITUDE")])
            yield station, (lat, lon)


def get_distance(p1, p2):          ◁──┐  This is the code to compute the
    lat1, lon1 = p1                   │  distance between two stations.
    lat2, lon2 = p2

    lat_dist = math.radians(lat2 - lat1)
    lon_dist = math.radians(lon2 - lon1)
    a = (
        math.sin(lat_dist / 2) * math.sin(lat_dist / 2) +
        math.cos(math.radians(lat1)) * math.cos(math.radians(lat2)) *
        math.sin(lon_dist / 2) * math.sin(lon_dist / 2)
    )
    c = 2 * math.atan2(math.sqrt(a), math.sqrt(1 - a))
    earth_radius = 6371
    dist = earth_radius * c

    return dist


def get_distances(stations, locations):
```

```
    distances = {}
    for first_i in range(len(stations) - 1):
        first_station = stations[first_i]
        first_location = locations[first_station]
        for second_i in range(first_i, len(stations)):
            second_station = stations[second_i]
            second_location = locations[second_station]
            distances[(first_station, second_station)] = get_distance(
                first_location, second_location)
    return distances
```

> As we are comparing all the stations between each other, the complexity is of the order n^2.

```
locations = {station: (lat, lon) for station, (lat, lon) in get_locations()}
stations = sorted(locations.keys())
distances = get_distances(stations, locations)
```

The previous code will take a long time to run. It also takes a lot of memory. If you have memory problems, limit the number of stations that you are processing. Let's now use Python's profiling infrastructure to see where most time is spent.

2.2.1   *Visualizing profiling information*

Again, we use Python's profiling infrastructure to find pieces of code that are delaying execution. But to better inspect the trace, we'll use an external visualization tool, SnakeViz (https://jiffyclub.github.io/snakeviz/).

We start by saving a profile trace:

```
python -m cProfile -o distance_cache.prof distance_cache.py
```

The -o parameter specifies the file where the profiling information will be stored. After that, we have the call to our code as usual.

> **NOTE** Python provides the pstats module to analyze traces written to disk. You can do python -m pstats distance_cache.prof, which will start a command-line interface to analyze the cost of our script. You can find more information about this module in the Python documentation or in the profiling section of chapter 5.

To analyze this information, we will use the web-based visualization tool, SnakeViz. You just need to do snakeviz distance_cache.prof. This will start an interactive browser window (figure 2.1 shows a screenshot).

> **Familiarizing yourself with the SnakeViz interface**
>
> This would be a good time to play with the SnakeViz interface a bit. For example, you can change the style from Icicle to Sunburst (arguably cuter but with less information as the file name disappears). Reorder the table at the bottom. Check the Depth and Cutoff entries. Do not forget to click some of the colored blocks, and, finally, return to the main view by clicking Call Stack and choosing the 0 entry.

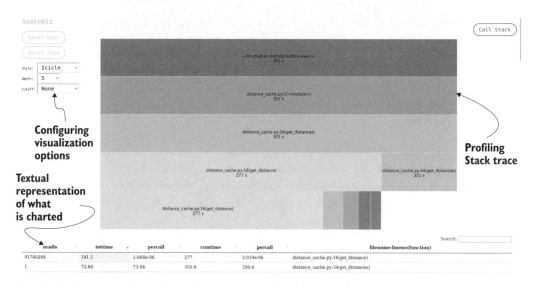

Figure 2.1 Using SnakeViz to inspect profiling information of our script

Most of the time is spent inside the function `get_distance`, but exactly where? We can see the cost of some of the math functions, but Python's profiling doesn't allow us to have a fine-grained view of what happens inside each function. We only get aggregate views for each trigonometric function. Yes, there is some time spent in `math.sin`, but given that we use it in several lines, where exactly are we paying a steep price? For that, we need to recruit the help of the line profiling module.

2.2.2 *Line profiling*

Built-in profiling, like we used previously, allowed us to find the piece of code that was causing a massive delay. But there are limits to what we can do with it. We'll discuss those limits here and introduce line profiling as a way to find further performance bottlenecks in our code.

 To understand the cost of each line of `get_distance`, we will use the `line_profiler` package, which is available at https://github.com/pyutils/line_profiler. Using the line profiler is quite easy: you just need to add an annotation to `get_distance`:

```
@profile
def get_distance(p1, p2):
```

You might have noticed that we have not imported the `profile` annotation from anywhere. This is because we will be using the convenience script `kernprof` from the `line_profiler` package that will take care of this. Let's then run the line profiler in our code:

```
kernprof -l lprofile_distance_cache.py
```

Be prepared for the instrumentation required by the line profiler to slow the code substantially, by several orders of magnitude. Let it run for a minute or so and, after that, interrupt it (`kernprof` would probably run for many hours if you let it complete). If you interrupt it, you will still have a trace. After the profiler ends, you can have a look at the results with the command:

```
python -m line_profiler lprofile_distance_cache.py.lprof
```

If you look at the output shown in listing 2.1, you can see that it has many calls that take a long time. So we will probably want to optimize that code. At this stage, as we are discussing only profiling, we will stop here, but afterward, we would need to optimize those lines (we will do so later in this chapter). If you are interested in optimizing this piece of code, have a look at chapter 6 about Cython or appendix B on Numba as they provide the most straightforward avenues to increase the speed.

Listing 2.1   The output of the `line_profiler` package for our code

```
Timer unit: 1e-06 s
```
The total running time for our code

```
Total time: 619.401 s
File: lprofile_distance_cache.py
Function: get_distance at line 16
```

The information that we are getting for each line that is being profiled. For each line, we get the number of times the line is called, the sum of the time spent on the line, the time per call, and the percentage of time on the line.

```
Line #      Hits         Time    Per Hit   % Time  Line Contents
==============================================================
    16                                             @profile
    17                                             def get_distance(p1, p2):
    18  84753141   36675975.0      0.4      5.9        lat1, lon1 = p1
    19  84753141   35140326.0      0.4      5.7        lat2, lon2 = p2
    20
    21  84753141   39451843.0      0.5      6.4        lat_dist = math.
➥ radians(lat2 -lat1)
    22  84753141   38480853.0      0.5      6.2        lon_dist = math.
➥ adians(lon2 - lon1)
    23  84753141   28281163.0      0.3      4.6        a = (
    24 169506282   84658529.0      0.5     13.7          math.sin(lat_dist / 2)
➥ * math.sin(
➥ lat_dist / 2) +
    25 254259423  118542280.0      0.5     19.1          math.cos(math.radians(
➥ lat1)) * math.cos(
➥ math.radians(
➥ lat2)) *
    26 169506282   81240276.0      0.5     13.1          math.sin(lon_dist / 2)
➥ * math.sin(
➥ lon_dist / 2)
    27                                                 )
    28  84753141   65457056.0      0.8     10.6        c = 2 * math.atan2(
➥ math.sqrt(a),
➥ math.sqrt(1 - a))
    29  84753141   29816074.0      0.4      4.8        earth_radius = 6371
```

```
30   84753141    33769542.0       0.4        5.5        dist = earth_radius * c
31
32   84753141    27886650.0       0.3        4.5        return dist
```

Hopefully, you will find line_profiler's output substantially more intuitive than the output from the built-in profiler.

2.2.3   The takeaway: Profiling code

As we've seen, overall built-in profiling is a big help as a first approach; it is also substantially faster than line profiling. But line profiling is significantly more informative, mostly because built-in Python profiling doesn't provide a breakdown inside the function. Instead, Python's profiling only provides cumulative values per function, as well as showing how much time is spent on subcalls. In specific cases, it is possible to know if a subcall belongs to another function, but, in general, that is not possible. An overall strategy for profiling needs to take all this into account.

The strategy we used here is a generally sensible approach: first, try the built-in Python profiling module cProfile because it is fast and does provide some high-level information. If that is not enough, use line profiling, which is more informative but also slower. Remember, here we are mostly concerned with locating bottlenecks; later chapters will provide ways to optimize the code. Sometimes just changing parts of an existing solution is not enough and a general re-architecturing will be necessary; we will also discuss that in due time.

Other profiling tools

Many other utilities can be useful if you are profiling code, but a profiling section would not be complete without a reference to one of these, the timeit module. This is probably the most common approach that newcomers take to profile code and you can find endless examples using the timeit module on the Internet. The easiest way to use the timeit module is by using IPython or Jupyter Notebook, as these systems make timeit very streamlined. Just add the %timeit magic to what you want to profile, for example, inside iPython:

```
In [1]: %timeit list(range(1000000))
27.4 ms ± 72.5 µs per loop (mean ± std. dev. of 7 runs, 10 loops each)

In [2]: %timeit range(1000000)
180 ns ± 33.6 ns per loop (mean ± std. dev. of 7 runs, 10000000 loops
⇒ each)
```

This gives you the run time of several runs of the function that you are profiling. The magic will decide how many times to run and report basic statistical information. In the previous snippet, you have the difference between a range(1000000) and a list(range(1000000)). In this specific case, timeit shows that the lazy version of range is two orders of magnitude faster than the eager one.

(continued)

You will be able to find more details in the documentation of the `timeit` module, but for most use cases, the `%timeit` magic of IPython will be enough to access its functionality. You are encouraged to use IPython and its magic, but in most of the rest of the book, we will use the standard interpreter. You can read more about the `%timeit` magic here: https://ipython.readthedocs.io/en/stable/interactive/magics.html.

Now that you are familiar with both a toolset and an approach to profiling, let's direct our attention to a different subject: optimizing the usage of Python data structures.

2.3 Optimizing basic data structures for speed: Lists, sets, and dictionaries

Next, we will try to find inefficient uses of Python basic data structures and rewrite pieces of code more efficiently. To demonstrate this process, we will continue to use the temperature data from NOAA. But here our challenge is to determine whether certain temperatures occurred in a station during a specified time interval.

We will reuse the code from the first section of the chapter to read the data (the code can be found in `02-python/sec3-basic-ds/exists_temperature.py`). What we are interested in, for the sake of this example, is the data from station 01044099999 for the years 2005 to 2021:

```
stations = ['01044099999']
start_year = 2005
end_year = 2021
download_all_data(stations, start_year, end_year)
all_temperatures = get_all_temperatures(stations, start_year, end_year)
first_all_temperatures = all_temperatures[stations[0]]
```

`first_all_temperatures` has a list of temperatures for the station. We can get some basic stats with `print(len(first_all_temperatures), max(first_all_temperatures), min(first_all_temperatures)))`. We have 141,082 entries with a maximum of 27.0 C and a minimum of -16.0 C.

2.3.1 Performance of list searches

Checking whether a temperature is in the list is a matter of `temperature in first_all_temperatures`. Let's get a rough estimate of how much time it takes to check whether -10.7 is in the list:

```
%timeit (-10.7 in first_all_temperatures)
```

The output on my computer is:

```
313 µs ± 6.39 µs per loop (mean ± std. dev. of 7 runs, 1,000 loops each)
```

Let's now try this query with a value that we know is not on the list:

```
%timeit (-100 in first_all_temperatures))
```

The result is:

```
2.87 ms ± 20.3 µs per loop (mean ± std. dev. of 7 runs, 100 loops each)
```

This is roughly one order of magnitude slower than our search for -10.7.

Why such low performance in the second search? Because to complete this search, the in operator does a sequential scan starting from the beginning of the list. This approach means, in a worst-case scenario, that the entire list will be searched, which is exactly the case when the element that we are looking for (-100) is *not* on the list. For small lists, it adds a trivial amount of time to start the search at the top and go straight through. But as the list grows, as well as the number of searches that you might have to do on those ever-growing lists, the time adds up significantly.

At this stage, we have no numbers to compare against, but it's safe to assume that ranges between a millisecond and even a microsecond are not very encouraging. This should be doable in orders-of-magnitude less time.

2.3.2   Searching using sets

Let's see whether we can do better by switching our data structure from lists to sets. Let's convert our ordered list into a set and try to do a search

```
set_first_all_temperatures = set(first_all_temperatures)

%timeit (-10.7 in set_first_all_temperatures)
%timeit (-100 in set_first_all_temperatures)
```

with the time costs being

```
62.1 ns ± 3.27 ns per loop (mean ± std. dev. of 7 runs,
➡ 10,000,000 loops each)
26.6 ns ± 0.115 ns per loop (mean ± std. dev. of 7 runs,
➡ 10,000,000 loops each)
```

This is several orders of magnitude faster than the solutions in the previous section! But why such an improvement? There are two main reasons: one is related to set size and another is related to complexity. The complexity part will be discussed in the next subsection. Here we'll look at the role of set size.

With regards to the size, remember that the original list had 141,082 elements. But with a set, all repeated values are collapsed into a single value—and there are plenty of repeated elements on the original list. The set size is reduced to print(len(set_first_all_temperatures)), which is 400 elements (350 times fewer). No wonder searching is so much faster as the size of the structure is much smaller.

The takeaway is that we should be aware of possible repeated elements in a list and know that there are potential advantages of using sets so the search can happen on much smaller data structures. But there is also a more profound difference between the implementation of lists and sets in Python.

2.3.3   *List, set, and dictionary complexity in Python*

The improved performance from the previous example was mostly due to the de facto reduction in the size of the data structure when we switched from a list to a set. This begs the question: what would happen if there was no repetition, so both the list and the set were the same size? Let's find out. We can simulate this with a range, which will specify that all elements will be different:

```
a_list_range = list(range(100000))
a_set_range = set(a_list_range)

%timeit 50000 in a_list_range
%timeit 50000 in a_set_range
%timeit 500000 in a_list_range
%timeit 500000 in a_set_range
```

So now we have a range of 0 to 99,999 that is implemented as both a list and a set. We search both data structures for 50,000 and 500,000. Here are the timings:

```
455 µs ± 2.68 µs per loop (mean ± std. dev. of 7 runs, 1,000 loops each)
40.1 ns ± 0.115 ns per loop (mean ± std. dev. of 7 runs,
➡ 10,000,000 loops each)
936 µs ± 9.37 µs per loop (mean ± std. dev. of 7 runs, 1,000 loops each)
28.1 ns ± 0.107 ns per loop (mean ± std. dev. of 7 runs,
➡ 10,000,000 loops each)
```

The set implementation still has much better performance. That is because in Python (to be more precise, CPython) a set is implemented with a hash. Finding an element thus has the cost of searching a hash. Hash functions come in many flavors and have to deal with many design problems. But when comparing lists and sets, we can generally assume that set lookup is mostly constant and will perform as well with a collection of size 10 or 10 million. This is not actually correct, but it is reasonable for understanding, in an intuitive way, why set lookups compare favorably against list lookups.

Remember also that a set is usually implemented like a dictionary, without values, which means that when you search on a dictionary key, you get the same performance as searching on a set. However, sets and dictionaries are not the silver bullets that they might seem here. For example, if you want to search an interval, an ordered list is substantially more efficient. In an ordered list, you can find the lowest element and then traverse from that point up until you find the first element above the interval and then stop. In a set or dictionary, you would have to do a lookup for each element in the interval. So if you know the value you are searching for, then a dictionary can be extremely fast. But if you are looking in an interval, then it suddenly stops being a reasonable option; an ordered list with a bisection algorithm would perform much better.

Given that lists are so pervasive and easy to use in Python, there are many cases where more appropriate data structures exist. But it is worth stressing that lists are a fundamental data structure that has many good use cases. The point is to be mindful of your options, not to banish lists.

TIP Be careful when using in to search inside large lists. If you browse through Python code, the pattern of using in to find elements in a list (the method index of list objects is, in practice, the same thing) is quite common. This is not a problem for small lists as the time penalty is quite small and perfectly reasonable, but it can be serious with large lists.

From a very down-to-earth software engineering perspective, the use of in with lists can go from an unnoticed problem in development to a massive problem in production. The common pattern is a developer testing with small data examples, because feeding big data is normally not practical with most unit testing. The real data might be very large, however, and once it's introduced, it could bring a production system to a halt.

A more systematic solution would be to test the code—maybe not always but at least from time to time—with very large data sets. This can occur in different stages of testing, from unit to end-to-end testing. This should not be construed as an argument against using in with lists. Just be mindful of the discrepancies between performance during development and production due to data size.

By the way, for most searching operations, there is a substantially better family of data structures than lists, sets, or dictionaries: trees. But in this chapter, we are evaluating Python's built-in data structures, which do not include trees.

The whole topic of choosing appropriate algorithms and data structures is the subject of many books and often makes up some of the most difficult courses for a computer science degree. The point is not to have an exhaustive discussion of the topic but to make you aware of the most common alternatives in Python. If you believe existing Python data structures are not enough for your needs, you may want to consider other types of data structures. This book's focus is on Python, but other resources will cover data structures outside of Python; for example, *Data Structures and Algorithms in Python*, by Michael T. Goodrich, Roberto Tamassia, and Michael H. Goldwasser (Wiley 2013), provides a good introduction.

Another helpful resource is Python's own data on TimeComplexity (https://wiki.python.org/moin/TimeComplexity). Here you can look up the time complexity of a wide range of operations over many Python data structures.

So far in this chapter we have focused on time performance. But that is not the only factor when dealing with performance problems with large data sets. Let's turn to another important factor: conserving memory.

2.4   *Finding excessive memory allocation*

Memory consumption can be crucial for performance, and it's not just that you might run out of memory. Effective memory allocation can allow for more processes to be run in parallel on the same machine. Even more significantly, judicious memory use might allow for in-memory algorithms.

Let's return to our familiar scenario, the NOAA database, to see how we can reduce the disk consumption of our data. To do this, we will start with a study of the content of the data files. Our objective here is to load a few of those files and do some statistics on character distributions.

```python
def download_all_data(stations, start_year, end_year):
    for station in stations:
        for year in range(start_year, end_year + 1):
            if not os.path.exists(TEMPLATE_FILE.format(
                ➥ station=station, year=year)):
                download_data(station, year)


def get_all_files(stations, start_year, end_year):
    all_files = collections.defaultdict(list)
    for station in stations:
        for year in range(start_year, end_year + 1):
            f = open(TEMPLATE_FILE.format(station=station, year=year), 'rb')
            content = list(f.read())
            all_files[station].append(content)
            f.close()
    return all_files


stations = ['01044099999']
start_year = 2005
end_year = 2021
download_all_data(stations, start_year, end_year)
all_files = get_all_files(stations, start_year, end_year)
```

`all_files` now has a dictionary where each item contains the contents for all the files related to a station. Let's study the memory usage of this.

2.4.1   *Navigating the minefield of Python memory estimation*

Python provides a function in the sys module, `getsizeof`, that supposedly returns the memory occupied by an object. We can get an understanding of the memory occupied by our dictionary using the following code:

```python
print(sys.getsizeof(all_files))
print(sys.getsizeof(all_files.values()))
print(sys.getsizeof(list(all_files.values())))
```

The result is:

```
240
40
64
```

getsizeof might not return what you expect. The files on the disk are in the mega-byte range, so estimates below 1 KB sound quite suspicious. getsizeof is actually returning the size of the containers (the first is a dictionary, the second is an iterator, and the third is a list) *without* accounting for the content. So, we have to account for two things occupying memory: the content of the container and the container itself.

> **NOTE**   Note that there is no problem with the getsizeof implementation in the language; it is just that the expectation of an unsuspecting user is typically of something different—namely, that it would return the memory footprint of everything referred in the object. If you read the official documentation, you will even find instructions for a recursive implementation that solves most problems. For us, the intricacies of getsizeof are mostly a starting point to discuss CPython memory allocation in depth.

Let's get some basic information about our station data:

```
station_content = all_files[stations[0]]
print(len(station_content))
print(sys.getsizeof(station_content))
```

The output is:

```
17
248
```

Our dictionary has only one entry, corresponding to a single station. It contains a list with 17 entries. The list itself takes 248 bytes, but remember, that doesn't include the content. Now let's inspect the size of the first entry:

```
print(len(station_content[0]))
print(sys.getsizeof(station_content[0]))
print(type(station_content[0]))
```

The length is 1,303,981, corresponding to the size of the file. We have a getsizeof of 10,431,904. This is around eight times the size of the underlying file. Why eight times? Because each entry is a pointer to a character, and a pointer is 8 bytes in size. At this stage, this looks quite bad, as we have a large data structure, and we haven't yet accounted for the data proper. Let's have a look at a single character:

```
print(sys.getsizeof(station_content[0]))
print(type(station_content[0]))
```

This is colossal in size. The output is 28 with a type of int. So every character, which should take only one 1 byte, is represented by 28 bytes. Hence, we have 10,431,904 for the size of the list plus 28 * 1,303,981 (36,511,468) for a grand total of 46,943,372. This is 36 times bigger than the original file! Fortunately, the situation is not as bad as it seems, but we can do much better. We will start by seeing that Python (or rather, CPython) is quite smart with memory allocation.

CPython can allocate objects in a more sophisticated way, and it turns out that our approach to computing memory allocation is quite naive. Let's compute the size of only the inner content, but instead of going through all the integers in our matrix, we will make sure that we are not double-counting. In Python, if an object is used many times, it gets the same id. So if we see the same id many times, we should only count a single memory allocation:

```
single_file_data = station_content[0]
all_ids = set()
for entry in single_file_data:        The id function allows us to get
    all_ids.add(id(entry))    ◁────  the unique ID of an object.
print(len(all_ids))
```

The previous code gets the unique identifier for all of our numbers. In CPython, that happens to be memory location. CPython is smart enough to see that the same string content is being used over and over again—remember that each ASCII character is represented by an integer between 0 and 127—and, as such, the output of the previous code is 46.

So, dumb allocation of memory would be dreadful, but Python (or, to be more precise, CPython) is much smarter. The memory cost of this solution is just the list infrastructure (10,431,904). Note that in our case, we only have 46 distinct characters; with such a small subset, Python is quite good at smart memory allocation. Do not expect this best-case scenario to occur at all times because it will depend on your data pattern.

Object caching and reuse in Python

Python tries to be as smart as possible with object reuse, but we need to be careful with expectations. The first reason is that this is *implementation-dependent*. CPython is different from other Python implementations in terms of this behavior.

Another reason is that even CPython makes no promises about most of its allocation policies from version to version. What works for your specific version might change in a different version.

Finally, even if you have a fixed version, how things work might not be completely obvious. Consider this code in Python 3.7.3 (this might vary on other versions):

```
s1 = 'a' * 2         Here we are getting the string
s2 = 'a' * 2    ◁──  aa by multiplying a times 2.
s = 2
s3 = 'a' * s    ◁──
s4 = 'a' * s         Here we are getting the string aa by
print(id(s1))        multiplying a times s which is 2.
print(id(s2))
print(id(s3))
print(id(s4))        All these strings are equal
print(s1 == s4) ◁──  in terms of content.
```

The result will be:

```
140002256425568
140002256425568
140002256425904
140002256425960
True
```

With the size of the string as a variable, the allocator is not able to determine that the content is the same, even if the size is the same. If this simple example works like this, what about more complicated cases? Of course, you can still use knowledge of how the allocator works, and for code, you have control over the Python version, this makes special sense. But adjust your expectations accordingly.

We are using a file representation based on a list of numbers. What if we considered alternative representations?

2.4.2 The memory footprint of some alternative representations

We are now going to consider some simple alternatives to representing a file. Some will be better; some will be worse. The main point here is to understand the underlying cost of each alternative. Instead of using integers to represent each character, we could use strings of length 1—something like this:

```
single_file_str_list = [chr(i) for i in single_file_data]
```

This approach would even be worse than the one that we used before. Just look at the size of each string with a single character:

```
print(sys.getsizeof(single_file_str_list[0]))
```

This returns 50, whereas the representation for our previous integer representation was only 28. This is a step backward, so we won't be doing it.

Python object overheads are quite bad with lots of small objects. Why do small numbers require 28 bytes and single character strings, 50 bytes? It turns out that every Python object requires at least 24 bytes of overhead, and to that overhead, you have to add the overhead of the object type, which will vary from type to type. As we have seen, it's bigger for strings than byte arrays (figure 2.2).

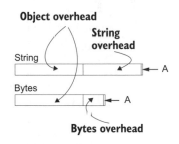

Figure 2.2 Object overhead for strings and bytes

The internal representation of strings and numbers

Python has an efficient internal representation for strings, which can vary and thus confuse expectations about memory allocation:

```
from sys import getsizeof
getsizeof('')
getsizeof('c')
getsizeof('c' * 10000)
getsizeof('ç' * 10000)
getsizeof('ç')
getsizeof('☺')
getsizeof('☺' * 10000)
```

The output would be:

```
49
50
10049
10073
74
80
40076
```

The empty string takes 49 bytes; the c string takes 50; 10,000 c's take 10049 bytes. So far so good. But a c with a cedilla takes 74 and 10,000 ç's take 10,073. If you are a bit confused now, know that a single confused smiley takes 80 bytes and 10,000 of those take 40,076 bytes.

Python 3 strings represent Unicode characters, but there is a nuance: the internal representation is optimized as a function of the string being represented. For details, you can see PEP 393–*Flexible String Representation*. For Latin-1 characters (a super-set of ASCII), Python uses 1 byte (the c with a cedilla is part of that set), but for other types of characters it can take up to 4 bytes (in the case of our confused emoji). But from our perspective, string sizes are difficult to calculate.

Integers have also an optimized implementation. The precision is arbitrary, but for signed integers fitting 30 bits, we get the smaller representation possibility of 28 bytes (the number 0 is an exception; it is represented by 24 bytes only, which you might recall is the smallest object size possible due to CPython's object overhead).

There is a more obvious representation for a file: instead of using a list of one-character strings, we can use *a string with the whole file*:

```
single_file_str = ''.join(single_file_str_list)
print(sys.getsizeof(single_file_str))
```

This will be a size of 1,304,030—the size of our file plus the string object overhead. While this is an obvious and simple solution, we will continue with the approach of containers of sequences of bytes because, as it turns out, those approaches can still be improved.

2.4.3 *Using arrays as a compact representation alternative to lists*

Here we will look at how an alternative container to elements might be substantially more efficient in terms of memory: arrays. Let's revisit the implementation of our `get_all_files` function:

```
def get_all_files_clean(stations, start_year, end_year):
    all_files = collections.defaultdict(list)
    for station in stations:
        for year in range(start_year, end_year + 1):
            f = open(TEMPLATE_FILE.format(station=station, year=year), 'rb')
            content = f.read()              ⟵————————
            all_files[station].append(content)    The original implementation
            f.close()                             had content = list(f.read()).
    return all_files
```

The line `content = list(f.read())` was converting the output of the `read` function into a list. Now, we implemented it without the list call, returning a byte array. Let's check the object size:

```
print(type(single_file_data))
print(sys.getsizeof(single_file_data))
```

The type is `bytes`, and the size including data is 1,304,014.

Arrays are of fixed size and can only contain objects of the same type. Hence, their representation can be made much more compact: it can be stored with the object overhead. Recall that for our integers, there was a 28-byte size for a storage of, really, a single byte of data.

> **Memory occupation in lists**
>
> When you allocate a list, Python creates an extra space for potential future additions, so the list will normally have more space than you expect. This makes insertions substantially cheaper because there is no need to allocate memory every time a new element is added—just when the extra space allocated is exhausted. The cost, of course, is the memory overhead. As a rule, such overhead is not serious unless you have lots of tiny lists; that is, the "lots of tiny objects" argument is especially true for lists. While knowing this is interesting, the overhead is normally OK with all other cases.

Much of the code related to array management is available in the `array` module. Except for this chapter, however, we won't be using the `array` module anymore; instead, we will use NumPy, which supersedes it in many ways. But the point here has less to do with the module and more with understanding and getting rid of the object overhead.

At this stage, you should have an insight into the costs and pitfalls of object memory allocation in Python. Finally, we'll now try to understand how to compute the memory usage of Python objects.

2.4.4 Systematizing what we have learned: Estimating memory usage of Python objects

At this stage, you have the basis to understand how memory allocation works. Now that you have a grasp of the underlying principles, we will try to devise some code to allow us to gather all the knowledge of the previous section into a utility function that gives a good approximation of the memory footprint.

We'll now distill all the tidbits that we learned in the rest of the section. In the following discussion, we'll write a function that will return the estimated memory size of an object. It will return both the size of all the objects along with the expenditure on containers. If you look at the following code, you should be able to find ID tracking, container counting (including mapper objects like dictionaries where we need to track both the key and the value), and string and array management.

Computing the size of general objects is a veritable minefield (it is actually not possible in general for external objects using Python only approaches). Our code in listing 2.2 tries to be smart by not double-counting repeated objects and containers/iterators that report the full size of the container and the content (like strings or arrays; the code can be found in `02-python/sec4-memory/compute_allocation.py`).

Listing 2.2   Computing the size of general Python objects

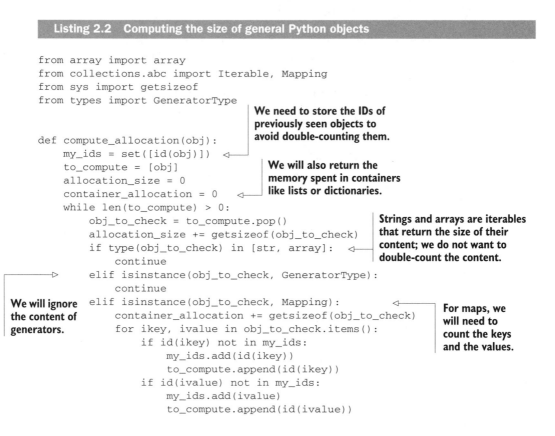

```python
from array import array
from collections.abc import Iterable, Mapping
from sys import getsizeof
from types import GeneratorType


def compute_allocation(obj):
    my_ids = set([id(obj)])          ◁   We need to store the IDs of
    to_compute = [obj]                    previously seen objects to
    allocation_size = 0                   avoid double-counting them.
    container_allocation = 0         ◁   We will also return the
    while len(to_compute) > 0:             memory spent in containers
        obj_to_check = to_compute.pop()    like lists or dictionaries.
        allocation_size += getsizeof(obj_to_check)
        if type(obj_to_check) in [str, array]:   ◁   Strings and arrays are iterables
            continue                                 that return the size of their
        elif isinstance(obj_to_check, GeneratorType):   content; we do not want to
            continue                                     double-count the content.
        elif isinstance(obj_to_check, Mapping):   ◁
            container_allocation += getsizeof(obj_to_check)
            for ikey, ivalue in obj_to_check.items():
                if id(ikey) not in my_ids:
                    my_ids.add(id(ikey))
                    to_compute.append(id(ikey))
                if id(ivalue) not in my_ids:
                    my_ids.add(ivalue)
                    to_compute.append(id(ivalue))
```

We will ignore the content of generators.

For maps, we will need to count the keys and the values.

```
    elif isinstance(obj_to_check, Iterable):          ◄──────┐   Finally, for other
        container_allocation += getsizeof(obj_to_check)      │   iterators, we will
        for inner in obj_to_check:                           │   need to check
            if id(inner) not in my_ids:                      │   the size.
                my_ids.add(id(inner))
                to_compute.append(inner)
    return allocation_size, allocation_size - container_allocation
```

Here we are using an iterative approach to compute memory allocation. This is a type of algorithm that would have lent itself to a recursive implementation, but due to Python's lack of proper support for good tail call optimization and recursive implementations in general, we will use an iterative approach.

Computing the size of objects from external libraries that are implemented in a system programming language like C or Rust will mostly depend on the implementation making that information available in some form. For those libraries, consult the documentation for details.

> **WARNING** There are memory profiler libraries for Python that you could try to use instead. I have a mixed experience with the reliability of estimates from some of the tools available, which is not shocking due to the minefield that is memory estimation in Python. If you use them, be careful.

There are more lower-level ways to check the memory allocation of Python, but we will discuss those when we use NumPy. In this chapter, we restrict ourselves to Python without external libraries.

2.4.5 *The takeaway: Estimating memory usage of Python objects*

To summarize, estimating the size of memory objects is not as easy as one might expect. sys.getsizeof doesn't report all the object sizes, and as such, extra effort is needed to accurately compute object sizes. In the general case, the problem is not even solvable: libraries written in low-level languages might not report the size of the allocations that they do.

Lean memory allocation has several side advantages. One is allowing the run of more parallel processes in cases where memory is the limiting factor, as it sometimes is. Another advantage is that it may create room for using in-memory algorithms, which are faster than algorithms, which need disk space and are much slower due to disk access.

2.5 *Using laziness and generators for big-data pipelining*

We now shift our attention to a feature that was extensively introduced with Python 3: lazy semantics. Lazy semantics delays any computation until the data is required and not before. This is extremely helpful to process large amounts of data, as sometimes computation (and related memory allocation) doesn't need to be done or can be spread over time. If you use generators, you are using lazy semantics already. Python 3 is way lazier than Python 2 as functions like range, map, and zip became lazy. A lazy approach will allow you to process more data, typically with substantially less memory, and permit the creation of data pipelines inside the code in a much easier way.

2.5.1 *Using generators instead of standard functions*

Let's revisit the original code of the first section of this chapter:

```
def get_file_temperatures(file_name):
    with open(file_name, "rt") as f:
        reader = csv.reader(f)
        header = next(reader)
        for row in reader:
            station = row[header.index("STATION")]
            # date = datetime.datetime.fromisoformat(
            ➥ row[header.index('DATE')])
            tmp = row[header.index("TMP")]
            temperature, status = tmp.split(",")
            if status != "1":
                continue
            temperature = int(temperature) / 10
            yield temperature
```

A yield in a definition indicates a generator.

get_file_temperatures is a generator (notice the yield). Let's run the generator:

```
temperatures = get_file_temperatures(TEMPLATE_FILE.format(
➥ station="01044099999", year=2021))

print(type(temperatures))
print(sys.getsizeof(temperatures))
```

The type reported will be generator, and the size of the structure will be 112. In reality, not much was done as generators are lazy. Only when you start iterating through it will the code execute as needed:

```
for temperature in temperatures:
    print(temperature)
```

Every time the for loop is repeated, the generator code will be called to provide a new value.

There are several advantages of this approach. The first, and biggest, one is that you will not need to have memory allocated for all temperatures as each one will be processed in turn. Contrast this with a list where you need memory to maintain all the temperatures at the same time. This can be quite important when a function returns very large data structures with many elements—the difference between having enough memory to execute the code or not.

Second, sometimes we do not need to get all the results, and as such, being eager just spends time in useless computation. Imagine, for example, that you wanted to write a function to see whether there is at least one temperature below zero. You don't need to get all results: computation can stop as soon as a single value is below zero.

It's quite trivial to make an eager version of a generator, as simple as:

```
temperatures = list(temperatures)
```

In this case, you lose the advantage of generators, but there are situations where that might be useful. For example, when the compute time is not long and the memory used by the list representation is tolerable, then in circumstances where you need to visit the results many times, an eager version makes more sense.

NOTE One of the biggest differences between Python 2 and Python 3 is that many built-ins that were eager became lazy. For example, in our case, `zip`, `map`, and `filter` would behave in very different ways in Python 2

Generators can be used to reduce the memory footprint and, in some cases, compute time. So when you are writing code that returns sequences, ask yourself whether it makes sense to convert it to a generator.

Summary

- Detection of performance bottlenecks is not easy to do in an intuitive, nonempirical way. Profiling is the necessary first step to be able to find exactly where performance lacks. "Gut feelings" tend to be wrong when finding performance problems, and empirical approaches almost always win.
- Python's internal profiling system is very useful, but it is sometimes difficult to interpret. Visualization tools like SnakeViz can help us make sense of profiling information.
- Python's internal profiling system has substantial limitations in helping us find the exact spot where a bottleneck occurs. Tools like line_profiler can be substantially more precise at the expense of running very slowly to collect information.
- While CPU performance is typically our first port of call for performance optimization, memory usage is equally important and can have major indirect benefits. For example, a solution that has poor memory optimization and requires an out-of-memory algorithm may sometimes be replaced with a fully in-memory approach, producing enormous time gains.
- Python provides basic data structures that can be used and misused to affect performance. For example, searching for elements in unordered lists can become quite expensive. We have to be mindful of the complexity cost of many operations over Python's basic data structures. These data structures appear in all Python programs and are typically low-hanging fruit that can have a massive effect on performance.
- Having a basic understanding of the computational complexity—Big-O notation—of Python's data structures is crucial for writing efficient code. Be sure to check these from time to time as Python versions change, and sometimes the underlying implementation is replaced, thus changing the performance of the algorithm.

- Lazy programming techniques allow us to develop programs that tend to have smaller memory footprints. They sometimes also make it possible to outright avoid large parts of a computation.
- All the content of this chapter is of wide applicability—both profiling and pure Python optimizations—and it can be used before any techniques discussed in the rest of the book.

Concurrency, parallelism, and asynchronous processing

This chapter covers
- Using asynchronous processing to design applications with reduced wait times
- Threading in Python and its limitations on writing parallel applications
- Making multiprocessing applications to take full advantage of multicore computers

Modern CPU architectures allow for more than one sequential program to be executed at the same time, permitting impressive gains in processing speeds. In fact, speeds can increase right up to the number of parallel processing units (e.g., CPU cores) that are available. The bad news is that to take advantage of all this parallel processing speed for our programs, we need to make our code parallel-aware, and Python is ill-suited for writing parallel solutions. Most Python code is sequential, so it is not able to use all the available CPU resources. Furthermore, the implementation of the Python interpreter is, as we will see, not tuned for parallel processing. In other words, our usual Python code cannot make use of modern hardware's capabilities, and it will always run at a much lower speed than the hardware allows. So we need to devise techniques to help Python make use of all the available CPU power.

In this chapter, we will learn how to do just that, starting with some approaches you may be familiar with in general but that have some unique Python twists. We will discuss concurrency, multithreading, and parallelism the Python way, including some strong limitations around multithreaded programming.

We will also learn about asynchronous programming methods, which allow us to efficiently serve many concurrent requests without any need for parallel solutions. Asynchronous programming has been around for quite some time, and it is popular in the JavaScript/Node.JS world, but only recently has it become standardized in Python with the addition of new modules to facilitate asynchronous programming.

For this chapter, let's assume that you are a developer working for a big software company. You are tasked with developing a MapReduce framework that is expected to be extremely fast. All the data will be in-memory, and everything will have to be done on a single computer. Furthermore, your service will have to be able to handle requests from several clients, most of whom are automated AI bots, at the same time. To tackle this project, you will use concurrent and parallel programming techniques, including multithreading and multiprocessing, to speed up the processing of MapReduce requests. In addition, you'll use asynchronous programming to efficiently process many simultaneous queries from users.

We will divide the problem into two parts. In the first section of the chapter, we will build a server that is able to handle multiple requests simultaneously. Then we need to create the MapReduce framework itself, and this will take up most of the chapter after section 3.1. We will consider three different ways to build the framework: sequential, multithreaded, and multiprocess. This will allow you to see several approaches at work, along with their benefits, tradeoffs, and limitations. In the final section, we'll put the two parts together and connect the server with the MapReduce framework, allowing us to understand how to architect a solution that integrates all the parts in an efficient way.

To make the chapter topics and organization clearer, figure 3.1 provides a visual roadmap of the chapter. It shows the approaches that we will investigate as well as how they are connected to each other and/or used together. In the upper left corner of each box, you'll find the section number where you'll learn about each technique.

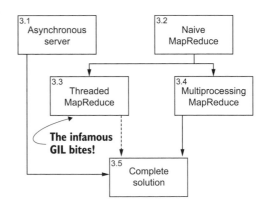

Figure 3.1 Chapter roadmap

Sequential processing, concurrency, and parallelism

Before we start, let's briefly review the meaning of sequential processing, concurrency, and parallelism. Although these are basic concepts, many experienced developers still get them confused, so here's a quick refresher to make sure we're all using the terms in the same way.

Parallelism is the easiest concept to explain: tasks run in parallel when they are running at the same time. Concurrent tasks *may* run in any order: they may be run in parallel or in sequence, depending on the language and OS. So all parallel tasks are concurrent but not the other way around.

The term *sequential* can be used in two different ways. First, it can mean that a certain set of tasks need to be run in a strict order. For example, to write in your computer, you have to first turn it on: the ordering, or sequence, *is imposed by the tasks themselves*. The second task can only happen after the execution of the first one.

Sometimes, however, sequential is used to mean a limitation that the *system* imposes on the order of the execution of tasks. For example, only one person at a time is allowed to go through a metal detector in an airport, even if two would be able to fit through it simultaneously.

Finally, there is the concept of preemption: this happens when a task is interrupted (involuntarily) for another one to run. This is related to scheduling policies among tasks and requires a piece of software or hardware to do it, called a *scheduler*.

The alternative to preemptive multitasking is cooperative multitasking: your code is responsible to tell the system when it can be interrupted to be swapped by another task. The following figure tries to make some of these concepts clearer.

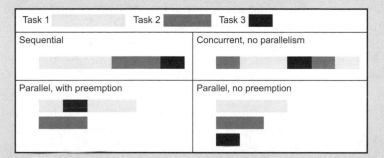

Understanding sequential, concurrent, and parallel models. Sequential execution occurs when all tasks are executed in sequence and never interrupted. Concurrent execution with no parallelism adds the possibility of a task being interrupted by another and later resumed. Parallelism occurs when several tasks are run at the same time. Even with parallelism, it is quite common for preemption to still occur as the number of processors/cores may not be enough for all tasks. A dream scenario is when there are more processors than tasks: this allows parallel execution of all tasks without the need for any preemption.

NOTE We will not go over the basic features of Python multithreading and multiprocessing. Many introductory guides can fill the gap for you if you need a refresher, including *Python Concurrency with Asyncio,* by Matthew Fowler (Manning, 2022; https://www.manning.com/books/python-concurrency-with-asyncio).

3.1   *Writing the scaffold of an asynchronous server*

While our main job is to use a MapReduce framework to process requests, we will start by building the part of the server that receives the requests (i.e., provides an interface to clients). Processing the requests properly will be a matter for the rest of the chapter. In this section, we will write a server that will accept connections from all clients and receive MapReduce requests (both data and code). In doing this, we will see how asynchronous programming can help create efficient servers, even without the use of parallelism.

> **The rise of asynchronous programming**
>
> Asynchronous programming was made popular in the JavaScript world, especially on the server with NodeJS. It is a particularly good model when we have a lot of slow IO streams that need monitoring. The most obvious example is a web server where most use-case data exchange is limited in size and the amount of processing is fast, typically in the order of milliseconds. But the asynchronous model can also help us to write clean concurrent and parallel programs. Furthermore, as we will see in the rest of the chapter, the asynchronous approach is also useful for more orthodox data analysis scenarios.
>
> To clarify, being asynchronous is orthogonal to being single-threaded, multithreaded, or multiprocess. You can have asynchronous systems on top of any of these.

First, let's look at one of the major problems that synchronous processing creates, so we can compare the synchronous solutions to the asynchronous solutions. Synchronous programming is the more common approach in the Python world and would probably be the first port of call for most Python programmers. But a synchronous (and single-process) version of a server will block while waiting for the user input. Since the user can take 1 ms or 1 h to actually write a request after opening the connection, in a synchronous world that would mean that all other clients would be on hold during this time. There are three potential solutions here (figure 3.2):

1   We just block (label 1 in figure 3.2). This means that while that connection is being processed, everything else (e.g., attending to other users) is nonresponsive. This blocking of all connections is unacceptable.

2   We have a multithreaded or multiprocessing solution where a single thread or process is started to take care of a request (label 2 in figure 3.2). This means that the main process is released to take care of other incoming requests. A single-threaded solution is possible and lighter for cases where we have lots of IO channels producing little information.

3   Finally, when a blocking call occurs, the alternative is for the code to somehow release execution control so that other pieces of code can be executed while the data is arriving (label 3 in figure 3.2). This is the solution that we will be exploring here: asynchronous processing with a single thread.

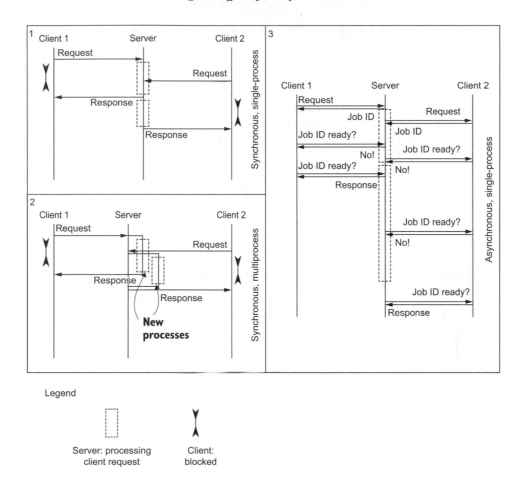

Figure 3.2   Several architectures covering synchronous single-process/thread, synchronous multiprocess, and asynchronous single-process implementations for a server

There are plenty of alternatives to these three options. For example, the solution at the end of the chapter will actually be a mix of solutions 2 and 3. Another very common alternative in solution 2 is to have a pool of prelaunched processes to speed up the response. For solution 3, we are assuming that the computing tasks can be interrupted (an assumption we will relax later in the chapter). Finally, with Python, as you might know, multithreaded code is normally (although not always) nonparallel; we will get into this later. As we address our MapReduce project, we will discuss all of these solutions as well as their problems. We will follow the process depicted in figure 3.1. First, we'll attempt a naive solution with no parallelism at all.[1] Then, we try a thread-based solution, which falls short of our needs. After that, we will develop a multiprocessing

---

[1] While the first solution that we will implement with asynchronous communication is naive for our use case, it is very good in other situations. For example, it is perfectly reasonable for most web servers as NodeJS demonstrates. As always, what is naive or what is best depends on your specific problem.

solution that will finally increase performance. In the final section, when we tie the network interface developed in this section with the multiprocess solution, we will find a place where threaded code still can be of use, although not for parallelism.

> **TIP**   The solution presented here is *a* solution. There are plenty of alternative approaches. Even if this was the best solution possible (it is not), concessions were made for the sake of explanation: what is defined as *best* varies with your criteria. Also, different problems will require completely different approaches.

> What you should take from here is not a set of clear-cut rules but, instead, a set of techniques and insights that will help you devise the best solution for your own problem and your specific criteria.

For now, let's get back to our asynchronous, single-threaded, and single-process server.

3.1.1   *Implementing the scaffold for communicating with clients*

Our server will be based on the TCP protocol and answer on port 1936. It is available in the repository in `03-concurrency/sec1-async/server.py`. Here is the top level of the scaffold that processes client requests:

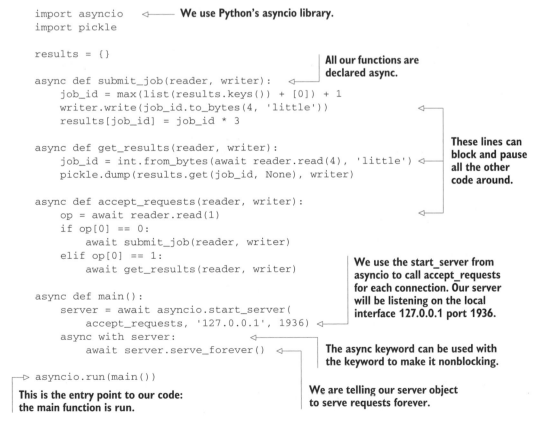

```
import asyncio     <——— We use Python's asyncio library.
import pickle

results = {}
                                              All our functions are
                                              declared async.
async def submit_job(reader, writer):     <—┘
    job_id = max(list(results.keys()) + [0]) + 1
    writer.write(job_id.to_bytes(4, 'little'))              <—┐
    results[job_id] = job_id * 3

async def get_results(reader, writer):                        These lines can
    job_id = int.from_bytes(await reader.read(4), 'little')  <—  block and pause
    pickle.dump(results.get(job_id, None), writer)            │ all the other
                                                              │ code around.
async def accept_requests(reader, writer):
    op = await reader.read(1)                               <—┘
    if op[0] == 0:
        await submit_job(reader, writer)
    elif op[0] == 1:
        await get_results(reader, writer)         We use the start_server from
                                                  asyncio to call accept_requests
async def main():                                 for each connection. Our server
    server = await asyncio.start_server(          will be listening on the local
        accept_requests, '127.0.0.1', 1936)  <—┐ interface 127.0.0.1 port 1936.
    async with server:              <—┐
        await server.serve_forever()   <—┐
                                        │   The async keyword can be used with
                                        │   the keyword to make it nonblocking.
  ┌─> asyncio.run(main())
  │                                     We are telling our server object
  │ This is the entry point to our code: to serve requests forever.
  └ the main function is run.
```

This code is just a scaffold for now; we will complete the code in the last section of the chapter when we tie everything together. Still, there is a lot to unpack here. The fundamental question is why do it this way at all? Why not just do a "typical" synchronous version?

The main reason is that the functions related to annotation 3—in our case, reads and writes from the network—can take an undetermined amount of time. Furthermore, network speeds are orders of magnitude slower than CPU speeds. Were we to block there, we would be working substantially below potential and also making other users wait needlessly.

All the Python infrastructure that you've just seen—`async`, `await`, and the `asyncio` module—exists to prevent blocking calls to stop other parts of the code that are independent of it in a single-threaded application.

3.1.2 *Programming with coroutines*

The `asynchronous` functions like the ones in the previous section (i.e., the ones created with `async def`) are called *coroutines*. Coroutines are functions that voluntarily release control of execution. There is another part of the system, an executor, that manages all coroutines and runs them according to some policy.

When you call a coroutine from inside another coroutine using `await`, you are actually telling Python that control can be diverted elsewhere at this stage. This is called *cooperative scheduling*, as releasing control is voluntary and needs to be explicitly done by the coroutine code.

Compare a coroutine system with the threading systems of most operating systems: there, threads are forcefully preempted and have no control over when they are run. That is called *preemptive scheduling*. Typical threaded code does not need to explicitly mark where it can be interrupted because it will be interrupted by force. Python threads, in this sense, work like OS system threads. It's just for `async` code that voluntary preemption applies.

A typical example could be a program that is waiting for some network data and writing to a disk (typically an IO task). It could work like this—note that this is sequential, so there's no need for threads:

1 The main program schedules with the asynchronous executor two coroutines: one to wait for a network connection, and the other to write to a disk.
2 The executor selects—maybe randomly—the network coroutine to start.
3 The network coroutine sets up network listening. It then waits for connections. There are no connections at the moment so it *voluntarily* tells the executor to do something else.
4 The executor starts the disk coroutine.
5 The disk coroutine starts writing to the disk. Writing is going slowly compared to CPU speeds, so the coroutine tells the executor to do something else.
6 The executor continues the network coroutine.

7   There are still no connection requests; the network coroutine yields.
8   The executor schedules the disk coroutine.
9   The disk coroutine finalizes writing and terminates its work.
10 The executor lets the network coroutine run forever as there is nothing more to do. If the network coroutine yields, the executor just goes back to it.
11 The network coroutine eventually answers a connection or maybe times out.
12 The executor concludes and passes control back to the main program.

This section, along with the final one, provides examples of coroutines—remember that all `async def` are coroutines. But let's do a small (a scaffold) test with the following subset of the previous code:

```
import asyncio

async def accept_requests(reader, writer):
    op = await reader.read(1)
    # ...

result = accept_requests(None, None)
print(type(result))
```

Let's see what `async` offers us here. If the code above doesn't have the `async` keyword, we would expect it to throw an exception (on `reader.read()`) as `reader` would be `None`. However, calling `accept_requests` like this doesn't execute a function but instead returns a coroutine, which is what `async def` actually creates.

The `await` call in our code tells Python that `accept_requests` can be suspended at that point and that something else might be run instead. Therefore, while we are waiting for the `reader` to send data, Python can do other stuff until the data arrives. If coroutines feel a bit like generators (as discussed in chapter 2) in the sense that execution is delayed and can be suspended, then you are on the right track.

3.1.3   *Sending complex data from a simple synchronous client*

To interact with our server, we will write a simple synchronous client. This serves as an example of a more synchronous type of code, which is more common in the Python world and is quite enough for our client needs. But, more important, we also take the opportunity to show how to do the communication of data and code between processes. While the server will be further developed later, this is actually the final version of the client.

Our client will submit both our code (the code can be found in `03-concurrency/sec1-async/client.py`) and data and will then probe the server until an answer is returned:

```
import marshal
import pickle
import socket
from time import sleep
```

marshal is used to submit code.

pickle is used to submit most high-level Python data structures.

```
def my_funs():          ◁─────┐  Our functions are defined
    def mapper(v):             │  in a single function that
        return v, 1            │  returns functions.

    def reducer(my_args):
        v, obs = my_args
        return v, sum(obs)
    return mapper, reducer


def do_request(my_funs, data):                                      We create a network
    conn = socket.create_connection(('127.0.0.1', 1936))   ◁──┘   connection here.
    conn.send(b'\x00')
    my_code = marshal.dumps(my_funs.__code__)      ◁───┐
    conn.send(len(my_code).to_bytes(4, 'little'))       │  We create a byte
    conn.send(my_code)                                  │  representation of
    my_data = pickle.dumps(data)                        │  our code.
    conn.send(len(my_data).to_bytes(4, 'little'))
    conn.send(my_data)
    job_id = int.from_bytes(conn.recv(4), 'little')   ◁───┐
    conn.close()                                           │  We receive the job_id
                                                           │  and take care of the
    print(f'Getting data from job_id {job_id}')            │  encoding ourselves.
    result = None
    while result is None:
        conn = socket.create_connection(('127.0.0.1', 1936))
        conn.send(b'\x01')
        conn.send(job_id.to_bytes(4, 'little'))
        result_size = int.from_bytes(conn.recv(4), 'little')
        result = pickle.loads(conn.recv(result_size))
        conn.close()
    sleep(1)
    print(f'Result is {result}')


if __name__ == '__main__':
    do_request(my_funs, 'Python rocks. Python is great'.split(' '))
```

We will keep connecting until the result is ready.

There is a lot to unpack here as well. Let's start with the network code: we create a TCP connection with Python's socket interface, and we use that API to send and receive data. All calls are potentially blocking, which is OK for this client.

Probably the most important part of this code to retain is the various alternatives to transfer data. In Python, the pickle module is the most common way to serialize data, which can then be transferred across processes. But it's not an all encompassing solution, for example, it cannot be used to transfer code. For code, we use the marshal module. We also use the to_bytes function of the int object to serve as a reminder that we can take care of the encoding ourselves in more corner-case situations. The most common of these is when we need a solution that is both compact and fast—two things that pickle is not. Of course, in that scenario, we will have the burden of encoding/decoding ourselves. We will revisit this when we deal with IO.

We transfer our code inside a function, `my_funs`, that returns functions. An alternative dialect would be to use objects. To use this code, open a terminal and start the server with:

```
python server.py
```

Then run the client with:

```
python client.py
```

The output will be:

```
Getting data from job_id 1
Result is [Number between 1 and 4]
```

3.1.4   *Alternative approaches to interprocess communication*

A more common approach for client/server communication would be to use a REST interface over HTTPS, but REST is not really helpful when we are trying to understand underlying concepts. We will revisit the performance effect of alternative network communication strategies in chapter 6. In any case, a realistic implementation would surely require at least some form of encryption.

3.1.5   *The takeaway: Asynchronous programming*

Asynchronous programming can be effective in processing lots of simultaneous user requests. Two conditions must be present for `async` to improve the response time. First, communication with external processes must be limited. Second, the amount of CPU processing per request also should be small. Since both of these conditions tend to be at work with web servers, `async` programming can generally be helpful with most web applications.

Furthermore, although we concentrated on the fundamentals of `async` programming in this section, there is much more to be said about core asynchronous functionality with Python. I encourage you to read up on language functionalities like asynchronous iterators (`async for`) and context managers (`async with`). There is also a burgeoning field of asynchronous libraries like aiohttp for HTTP communication as alternatives to the well-known synchronous requests libraries.

3.2   *Implementing a basic MapReduce engine*

Now let's get on with our main objective in the chapter, which is to *implement* a MapReduce framework. In the first section, we took care of the communication architecture *around* the framework. In this section, we will start implementing the core of the solution. This section will set up the basic solution from which we will derive more computationally efficient versions later in the chapter.

3.2.1   *Understanding MapReduce frameworks*

Let's start with deconstructing a MapReduce framework to see what components go into it. From a theoretical perspective, MapReduce computations are separated into at least two halves: a map and a reduce part. Let's see this in action with a typical example of a MapReduce application: word counting. In this case, we'll use two lines from Shakespeare's *The Tempest*: "I am a fool. To weep at what I am glad of." You can see this input in a MapReduce in figure 3.3. Other than map and reduce, in practice, other components need to exist. For example, the results from a map need to be shuffled before being sent to reduce processes: if the two instances of the word am were sent to distinct reduce processes, the count would not be correct.

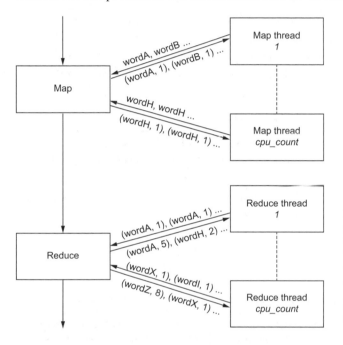

Figure 3.3   **The basics of a map_reduce framework using word counting as an example. Traditional MapReduce frameworks have several processes or threads implementing the map and result steps. In many cases, these can be distributed across several computers.**

Word counting could be implemented with a map function that would emit an entry for every word found with a count of 1, and a reduce function would sum all the map entries for the same word. So map would emit:

```
I, 1
am, 1
a, 1
fool, 1
To, 1
weep, 1
at, 1
what, 1
I, 1
am, 1
glad, 1
of, 1
```

And reduce would then generate:

```
I, 2
a, 1
fool, 1
To, 1
weep, 1
at, 1
what, 1
am, 2
glad, 1
of, 1
```

Somewhere in the middle, we need to shuffle the results so that a unique word would be seen only by a single reduce function. For example, if am was seen by two different reduce functions, then we would end up with two counts of 1 when we want to see one count of 2. In our server, the shuffle function is built-in; the user doesn't need to provide it.

3.2.2 *Developing a very simple test scenario*

Remember that we are *implementing* a MapReduce framework ourselves. While we won't be *users*, we will need to test our MapReduce framework. To do that, we will return to the most common exercise with MapReduce: counting words in a text. Our framework will then be used with many other problems, but for basic testing of the framework, counting words will suffice.

The *user code* to implement this would be as simple as the following. Remember this is not what we were commissioned to do; it's just the example that we will use for testing:

> We will be using functional notation on purpose as MapReduce has functional origins. If you use PEP 8, your syntax checker will complain as PEP 8 says, "Always use a def statement instead of an assignment statement that binds a lambda expression directly to an identifier." The way this is reported will depend on your linter. It's up to you whether you prefer to use this notation or the PEP 8 one, which would be of the form def emitter(word). We will be using this code to test the framework that we will build across the chapter.

```
emitter = lambda word: (word, 1)                    ◁─────────
counter = lambda (word, emissions): (work, sum(emissions))
```

3.2.3 *A first attempt at implementing a MapReduce framework*

Remember, the previous code is what your *user* will write. We will now implement a MapReduce engine, which is our real goal, that will count words and do much more. We will start with something that works but not much more, and we will develop an efficient engine through the rest of the chapter using threading, parallelism, and asynchronous interfaces (the first version is available in `03-concurrency/sec2-naive/naive_server.py`):

```
from collections import defaultdict

def map_reduce_ultra_naive(my_input, mapper, reducer):
    map_results = map(mapper, my_input)

    shuffler = defaultdict(list)
    for key, value in map_results:
        shuffler[key].append(value)

    return map(reducer, shuffler.items())
```

You can now use this with:

```
words = 'Python is great Python rocks'.split(' ')
list(map_reduce_ultra_naive(words, emiter, counter))
```

`list` forces the lazy map call to actually execute (see chapter 2 if you have doubts about lazy semantics), and so you will get the output:

```
[('Python', 2), ('is', 1), ('great', 1), ('rocks', 1)]
```

While the previous implementation is quite clean from a conceptual point of view, from an operational perspective, it fails to grasp the most important operational expectation for a MapReduce framework—that its functions are run in parallel. In the next sections, we will make sure we create an efficient parallel implementation in Python.

3.3   *Implementing a concurrent version of a MapReduce engine*

Let's try a second time and do a concurrent framework, this time by using multithreading. We will use the threaded executor from the `concurrent.futures` module to manage our MapReduce jobs. We are doing this to have a solution that is not only concurrent but also parallel (i.e., allowing us to use all the compute power available)—at least that is what we hope.

3.3.1   *Using concurrent.futures to implement a threaded server*

We start with `concurrent.futures` because it is more declarative and higher level than the most commonly used `threading` and `multiprocessing` modules. These are foundational modules in the field, and we will use `multiprocessing` in the next section, as its lower-level interface will allow us to allocate CPU resources more precisely.

Here is the new version (the code is available in `03-concurrency/sec3-thread/threaded_mapreduce_sync.py`):

```
from collections import defaultdict
from concurrent.futures import ThreadPoolExecutor as Executor   ◁─── 
```
> **We use the threaded executor from the concurrent.futures module.**

```
def map_reduce_still_naive(my_input, mapper, reducer):
    with Executor() as executor:   ◁─── 
```
> **The executor can work as a context manager.**

```
map_results = executor.map(mapper, my_input)

distributor = defaultdict(list)
for key, value in map_results:
    distributor[key].append(value)

results = executor.map(reducer, distributor.items())
return results
```

We use a very simple shuffler function.

Executors have a map function with blocking behavior.

Our function again takes some input along with `mapper` and `reducer` functions. The executor from `concurrent.futures` is responsible for thread management, although we can specify the number of threads we want. If not, the default is related to `os.cpu_count`; the actual number of threads varies across Python versions. This is summarized in figure 3.4.

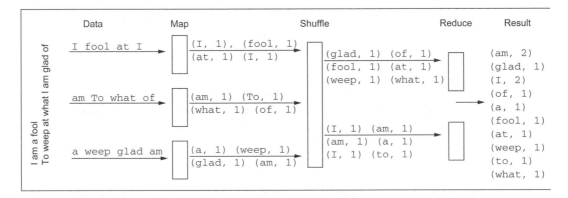

Figure 3.4   Threaded execution of our MapReduce framework

Remember that we need to make sure that the results for the same object (a word in our example) are sent to the correct reduce function. In our case, we implement a very simple version in the `distributor` default dictionary that creates an entry per word.

The previous code can have a fairly big memory footprint, especially because the shuffler will hold all results in memory, although in a compact fashion. But for the sake of simplicity, we will leave it as it is.

Exactly how the number of workers is managed is more or less a black box with `concurrent.futures`. As such, we do not know for what it has been optimized. Consequently, if we want to make sure we are extracting the maximum performance, we must be in full control of how the execution is done. If you want to fine-tune worker management, you will need to use the `threading` module directly.[2] We will see how to do this in the next section.

---

[2] Another alternative is to implement a `concurrent.futures` executor yourself, but in that case, you would need an understanding of the underlying modules like `threading` and `multiprocessing` anyway.

You can try this solution with

```
words = 'Python is great Python rocks'.split(' ')
print(list(map_reduce_still_naive(words, emiter, counter)))
```

and the output will be the same as in the previous section.

However, the previous solution has a problem: it doesn't allow any kind of interaction with the ongoing outside program. That is, when you do `executor.map`, you will have to wait until the complete solution is computed. This is irrelevant with an example with five words, but you might want to have some feedback with very large texts. For example, you want to be able to report the percentage of progress done while the code runs. This requires a somewhat different solution.

3.3.2 *Asynchronous execution with futures*

First, let's just code the map part to understand what is going on (the code is available in `03-concurrency/sec3-thread/threaded_mapreduce.py`):

```
from collections import defaultdict
from concurrent.futures import ThreadPoolExecutor as Executor

def async_map(executor, mapper, data):
    futures = []
    for datum in data:
        futures.append(executor.submit(mapper, datum))   ◄──  We use submit instead
    return futures                                             of map when calling the
                                                              executor.
def map_less_naive(executor, my_input, mapper):
    map_results = async_map(executor, mapper, my_input)
    return map_results
```

While the map function of the executor waits for results, `submit` doesn't. We will see what that means when we run this soon.

We will change our emitter to be able to track what is going on:

```
from time import sleep

def emitter(word):
    sleep(10)
    return word, 1
```

The sleep call is there to slow down the code, allowing us to track what is going on even with a simple example. Let's use our map function as it is:

```
with Executor(max_workers=4) as executor:
    maps = map_less_naive(executor, words, emitter)
    print(maps[-1])
```

If you print the last item from the list, you might get something unexpected:

```
<Future at 0x7fca334e0e50 state=pending>
```

You do not get (`'rocks'`, 1), but instead you get a *future*. A future represents a potential result that can be subject to `await` and checked for its state. We can now allow the user to track progress like this:

> We put only four executors to let us track progress as we have five tasks.

```
with Executor(max_workers=4) as executor:
    maps = map_less_naive(executor, words, emitter)
    not_done = 1
    while not_done > 0:
        not_done = 0
        for fut in maps:
            not_done += 1 if not fut.done() else 0
            sleep(1)
        print(f'Still not finalized: {not_done}')
```

Checks whether the future is done

> We print status while there are still tasks to be done.

> Sleeps for a bit as we do not want a barrage of text

If you run the previous code, you will get a few lines with `Still not finalized…`. Typically for the first 10 s, you will see five and then just one. As there are four workers, it takes 10 s to do the first four, and then the final one can start. Given that this is concurrent code, this can change a bit from run to run, so the way threads are preempted can vary every time you run this code: it is nondeterministic.

There is one final piece of the puzzle left to do, which will be in the last version of the threaded executor: we need a way for the caller to be able to be informed of the progress. The caller will have to pass a callback function, which will be called when an important event occurs. In our case, that important event will be tracking the completion of all map and reduce jobs. This is implemented in the following code:

```
def report_progress(futures, tag, callback):
    done = 0
    num_jobs = len(map_returns)
    while num_jobs > done:
        done = 0
        for fut in futures:
            if fut.done():
                done +=1
        sleep(0.5)
        if callback:
            callback(tag, done, num_jobs - done)
```

> report_progress will require a callback function that will be called every half second with statistical information about jobs done.

```
def map_reduce_less_naive(my_input, mapper, reducer, callback=None):
    with Executor(max_workers=2) as executor:
        futures = async_map(executor, mapper, my_input)
        report_progress(futures, 'map', callback)
        map_results = map(lambda f: f.result(), futures)
        distributor = defaultdict(list)
        for key, value in map_results:
            distributor[key].append(value)
```

We report the progress for all map tasks.

> Because the results are actually futures, we need to get those from the future objects.

```
        futures = async_map(executor, reducer, distributor.items())
        report_progress(futures, 'reduce', callback)
        results = map(lambda f: f.result(), futures)
    return results
```

We report the progress for all reduce tasks.

Because the results are actually futures, we need to get those from the future objects.

So, every 0.5 s while the map and reduce are running, the user-supplied callback function will be executed. A callback can be as simple or as complicated as you want, although it should be fast as everything else will be waiting for it. For the word count example that we use for testing, we have a very simple one:

```
def reporter(tag, done, not_done):
    print(f'Operation {tag}: {done}/{done+not_done}')
```

Note that the callback function signature is not arbitrary: it has to follow the protocol imposed by `report_progres`, which requires as arguments the tag and the number of done and not done tasks.

If you run

```
words = 'Python is great Python rocks'.split(' ')
results = map_reduce_less_naive(words, emitter, counter, reporter)
```

you will have a few lines printing the ongoing status of the operation, followed by the result:

```
Operation map: 3/5
Operation reduce: 0/4
('is', 1)
('great', 1)
('rocks', 1)
('Python', 2)
```

It would not be too difficult, for example, to use the return value as an indicator to the MapReduce framework to cancel the execution. This would allow us to change the semantics of the callback function to interrupt the process.

Unfortunately, this solution is concurrent but not parallel. This is because Python (or rather, CPython) only executes one thread at a time, courtesy of the infamous CPython GIL, the Global Interpreter Lock. Let's look closer at the GIL and how it handles this role in the next section.

3.3.3 The GIL and multithreading

While CPython makes use of OS threads so they are preemptive threads, the GIL imposes a restriction so that only one thread can run at a time. So, you might have a multithreaded program running on a multicore computer, but you will end up with no parallelism. It's actually a bit worse than that: the performance of thread swapping can be quite bad in multicore computers due to the friction between the GIL, which doesn't allow more than one thread to run at a time, and the CPU and OS, which are actually optimized to do the opposite.

This book includes a section on multithreading because any book related to performance would be incomplete without it. But truth be told, if you want performance, Python threads are rarely the best solution.

GIL problems are overrated. The fact is that if you need to do high-performance code at the thread level, Python is probably too slow anyway. At least the CPython implementation, but probably also Python's dynamic features, impose a cost. You will want to implement any extremely efficient code in a lower-level language like C or Rust or by using a system like Cython or Numba, which we will study later on.

The GIL provides a few escape routes for lower-level code implemented in other languages: when you enter your lower-level solution you can actually release the GIL and use parallelism to your heart's content. This is what libraries like NumPy, SciPy, and scikit-learn do. They have multithreaded code written in C or Fortran that releases the GIL and is actually parallel. So your code case can still be parallel in a threaded world. It's just that the parallel part will not be written in Python.

But you can still write efficient parallel code in pure Python and do that at a level of computing granularity that makes sense in Python. You do this not with multithreading but with *multiprocessing*.

PyPy

While CPython is the standard implementation for Python, others exist like IronPython and Jython for .NET and the JVM, respectively. Another implementation worth mentioning is PyPy, which is not an interpreter but a just-in-time compiler. PyPy is not a drop-in replacement for CPython as many CPython libraries do not work directly with it. But it might be a faster implementation if the libraries supported are the ones you need. While PyPy is in many cases faster than CPython, it still does have a GIL, so it won't solve that problem. In this book, we will stick with CPython, but for a reasonable subset of efficiency cases, PyPy might be a potential alternative.

A final word: if you confuse *PyPy*, the Python implementation, with *PyPI*, the package repository, know that you are not alone.

3.4   *Using multiprocessing to implement MapReduce*

Due to the GIL, our multithreaded code is not really parallel. We can turn to two directions to solve this: we can re-implement our Python code in a lower-level language like C or Rust, or as our solution in this section, we can turn to multiprocessing to have parallelism and make usage of all CPU power available. Lower-level solutions will be addressed in later chapters.

3.4.1   *A solution based on concurrent.futures*

In theory, a solution based on concurrent.futures is quite simple. It is a design goal of the module to make it easy to change one of the imports from ThreadPoolExecutor to

ProcessPoolExecutor (this code is available in 03-concurrency/sec4-multiprocess/
futures_mapreduce.py):

```
from concurrent.futures import ProcessPoolExecutor as Executor
```

If you replace this line on the asynchronous version of the previous section, you will
notice that something is wrong as the code seems to freeze in the reduce part. We
need to dig down; as such, we will build a more informative report_progress function from the last section:

```
def report_progress(futures, tag, callback):
    done = 0
    while num_jobs > done:
        done = 0
        for fut in futures:
            if fut.done():
                done +=1
                print(fut)
                print(fut.exception())
        sleep(0.5)
        if callback:
            callback(tag, done, not_done)
```

We just added two prints. If we run the code again, we get:

```
<Future at 0x7f1ffff104c0 state=finished raised PicklingError>
Can't pickle <function <lambda> at 0x7f2000131ca0>: attribute lookup
  <lambda> on __main__ failed
```

It turns out that lambdas (remember that our counter function was written as a
lambda) cannot be pickled. Yet multiprocessing communication is done via the
pickle module. Therefore, our counter function cannot be transferred to the sub-
process as is. We can just rewrite it as a def function:

```
def counter(emitted):
    return emitted[0], sum(emitted[1])
```

This solves our specific test example, but the larger point is that you cannot simply do
a drop-in replacement from the threaded executor to the process-based one. What
other features might be different? Turn to the next section to find out.

> **Problems with data and code sharing using the Python multiprocessing
> module**
> We have now seen that transmitting lambdas across processes is not possible with
> a default pickle configuration. Or, if you want to do that, you have to implement your
> own protocol.

(continued)

Generally, if `pickle` cannot handle it, then you have to take care of that out-off-band as multiprocessing relies on `pickle` for communication. This might include objects from foreign libraries, especially if they have non-Python implementations.

File pointers, database connections, and sockets are either impossible to transfer or require extra care. With threads, all these object types can be shared, although we need to check whether they are thread-safe. Another problem with `pickle` is that it is quite slow. In cases where there is a lot of data to transfer, that might defeat the purpose of using multiprocessing altogether.

Using Python's communication primitives is perfectly fine for coarse-grained processing with low communication. But there should be some care in scenarios with a lot of communication overhead as the speed gained with multiprocessing might be lost in communication time.

3.4.2 A solution based on the multiprocessing module

`concurrent.futures` gives us a very simple interface to do concurrent processing. For more obvious problems, it can be quite efficient in terms of both programmer productivity and computing performance. But programming simplicity comes at a cost: we lose control of how code is executed. What is the order of execution of futures? While we define the maximum number of workers, how many are really available at a certain point in time? Are processes recycled or recreated from scratch for every task? With `concurrent.futures`, this is defined by the executor, and we have no control over it.

In our case, we actually would like to enforce some policies to achieve high performance. For example, we want to create all processes before work arrives or keep processes alive even when there are no tasks. This is because creating and destroying processes when requests arrive has an overhead that we prefer to pay when we are not dealing with processing those requests. We will begin by creating a process pool ourselves.

We will start with a simple solution that doesn't allow us to track progress in real-time (the code is available in `03-concurrency/sec4-multiprocess/mp_mapreduce_0.py`):

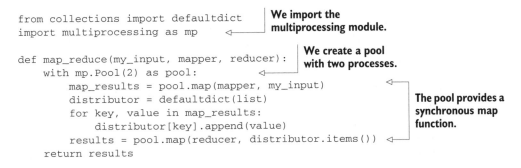

```
from collections import defaultdict          We import the
import multiprocessing as mp                 multiprocessing module.

def map_reduce(my_input, mapper, reducer):   We create a pool
    with mp.Pool(2) as pool:                  with two processes.
        map_results = pool.map(mapper, my_input)
        distributor = defaultdict(list)                  The pool provides a
        for key, value in map_results:                   synchronous map
            distributor[key].append(value)               function.
        results = pool.map(reducer, distributor.items())
    return results
```

This code is as simple as it gets. The only new line is the creation of a `Pool`. The pool is created every time a MapReduce operation is requested, so it's not persistent over multiple invocations: we are paying the price of pool creation for every execution.

`CPU_count` vs. `sched_getaffinity` to determine the pool size

The previous code specifies two processes to be created in our pool. In most cases, you will want this number to be a function of your computing power. The default for the pool is `os.cpu_count`, which is actually a misnomer: it normally reports the number of hyperthreads, not CPUs.

A slightly more rigorous alternative would be to use `len(os.sched_getaffinity())` as it reports all the cores that are accessible to you. Your computer might have more, but the OS, container, or virtual machine may have limited your access to part of them.

WARNING   The semantics of the `Pool.map` function is eager, whereas the built-in map function is lazy. As such this code is not semantically equivalent:

```
map(fun, data)
Pool.map(fun, data)
```

The first returns immediately and did not execute fun. `list(map(fun, data))` would be the eager equivalent. A typical development pattern is to replace `Pool.map` with map, as debugging code is easier if done in the same process. However, this is not entirely correct. On the `multiprocessing` side, you also have `imap`, which is a lazier version, and an asynchronous version in `map_async`.

3.4.3   *Monitoring the progress of the multiprocessing solution*

As it stands, `map_async` does not support progress tracking. Note that it has callback support, but it only calls the `callback` function when all the results become ready. We would like something more granular: the ability to have a call every time an element of the iterator is ready. That's what we need for progress tracking.

We will change the code to support it. While there is a `Pool.map_async` function that can be useful on many occasions, its callback system only reports the very end of the execution, and that is not enough. We need a slightly lower-level solution (this code is available in `03-concurrency/sec4-multiprocess/mp_mapreduce.py`):

```
def async_map(pool, mapper, data):
    async_returns = []
    for datum in data:
        async_returns.append(pool.apply_async(
            mapper, (datum, )))
    return async_returns

def map_reduce(pool, my_input, mapper, reducer, callback=None):
```

We use Pool.apply_async
to start individual jobs.

Note that the parameter to
the function is specified as
a tuple.

```
map_returns = async_map(pool, mapper, my_input)
report_progress(map_returns, 'map', callback)
map_results = [ret.get() for ret in map_returns]    ⊲─┐
distributor = defaultdict(list)                          Getting results from
for key, value in map_results:                           the async objects using
    distributor[key].append(value)                       its get method
returns = async_map(pool, reducer, distributor.items())
results = [ret.get() for ret in returns]
return results
```

The code is not much different from the `concurrent.futures` solution—to the point that we might ask whether the lack of flexibility from `concurrent.futures` is worthwhile for the extra simplicity.

Our `map_reduce` function now uses a pool provided by the user, allowing for pool recycling. This will generally be more efficient than starting new processes every time a new operation is done. In our example, there is almost no overhead, but in more complex examples, initialization of each process might be time- and resource-consuming.

To call this code, we now have to create the pool beforehand. This is simple:

We close the pool.

```
pool = mp.Pool()
results = map_reduce(pool, words, emitter, counter, reporter)
pool.close()
pool.join()    ⊲──── We wait for all the processes to terminate.
```

We could use a pool from a context manager here, but this allows us to see that cleaning up a pool is not just closing all the processes; it is also waiting for them to exit—the `join` call. A more forceful alternative to `close` would be to `terminate`, which would force existing processes to terminate even without finalizing any ongoing work.

Overcommitting or undercommitting CPU resources

When we create our pool, we are using the default size, `os.cpu_count()`, but there are many situations in which you will want to undercommit resources. There are even situations when overcommitting will be fine.

The most common reason for undercommitting is when the processes are IO bound: too much IO can easily trash the machine as a lot of processes can cause more IO load than the machine can handle. This is especially true for disk IO.

If the processes take a lot of memory, then you also need to scale down as you might have reduced performance due to memory cache usage. In the worst case, the OS might start killing processes if the computer runs out of memory.

A typical case for overcommitting is when you are waiting for the network. This means that processes might sit idle for a good part of the time, and so the CPU resource is available.

Paradoxically, overcommitting of CPU can be useful for some CPU-bound processes—for example, when CPU usage per process is not continuous but occurs in bursts or when there is a large setup time before the computation actually begins.

The `report_progress` function is almost the same: it calls the callback when a job has finished. The call to `Future.done` is replaced by `AsyncReturn.ready`:

```
def report_progress(map_returns, tag, callback):
    done = 0
    num_jobs = len(map_returns)
    while num_jobs > done:
        done = 0
        for ret in map_returns:
            if ret.ready():
                done += 1
        sleep(0.5)
        if callback:
            callback(tag, done, num_jobs - done)
```

You can now run the code, and it all works. But is the solution fast enough?

3.4.4 Transferring data in chunks

To answer the question of whether the solution is fast enough, we need to compare it to something else. As we have seen in the previous chapter and will revisit in a later one, chunking for disk writing can dramatically speed up disk write operations. Is that technique also good for CPU costs and interprocess communication?

To answer this question, we will make a minor change to our MapReduce architecture. We will add a splitting phase at the beginning that will send the data not as single elements but as chunks. Figure 3.5 introduces a new step to figure 3.3, which is responsible for splitting.

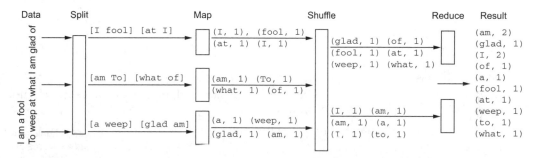

Figure 3.5   A `map_reduce` framework with splitting (really chunking in our case)

Our split is actually quite simple, but advanced MapReduce frameworks can do substantially more advanced optimizations here. We will start by looking at the code that submits chunked jobs and dechunks them on the pool processes (this code is in `03-concurrency/sec4-multiprocess/chunk_mp_mapreduce.py`):

```
def chunk(my_iter, chunk_size):
    chunk_list = []
    for elem in my_iter:
        chunk_list.append(elem)
```

> We now have the chunk generator that will split an iterator in lists of chunk_size.

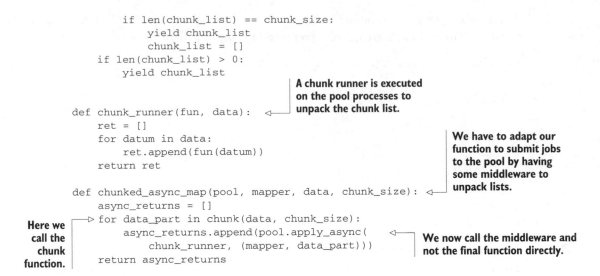

```
            if len(chunk_list) == chunk_size:
                yield chunk_list
                chunk_list = []
        if len(chunk_list) > 0:
            yield chunk_list
```

A chunk runner is executed on the pool processes to unpack the chunk list.

```
def chunk_runner(fun, data):
    ret = []
    for datum in data:
        ret.append(fun(datum))
    return ret
```

We have to adapt our function to submit jobs to the pool by having some middleware to unpack lists.

```
def chunked_async_map(pool, mapper, data, chunk_size):
    async_returns = []
    for data_part in chunk(data, chunk_size):
        async_returns.append(pool.apply_async(
            chunk_runner, (mapper, data_part)))
    return async_returns
```

Here we call the chunk function.

We now call the middleware and not the final function directly.

chunked_async_map is the code that will distribute the work across the pools. It calls the chunk generator to split the input into chunks of chunk_size. Note that it doesn't call the desired function directly anymore: the first thing that runs on the pool processes is chunk_runner, which will iterate each element of the chunk and call the real work function, fun.

You might think that there is a simpler implementation of the chunk generator, like this:

```
def chunk0(my_list, chunk_size):
    for i in range(0, len(my_list), chunk_size):
        yield my_list[i:i + chunk_size]
```

The problem with the implementation is that it requires a len(my_list), thus restricting our input to being a list. An iterator can be lazy and, hence, occupies less memory and probably requires less CPU to process.

We now need to change our top MapReduce function:

We add chunk_size as a parameter.

```
def map_reduce(
        pool, my_input, mapper, reducer, chunk_size, callback=None):
    map_returns = chunked_async_map(pool, mapper, my_input, chunk_size)
    report_progress(map_returns, 'map', callback)
    map_results = []
    for ret in map_returns:
        map_results.extend(ret.get())
    distributor = defaultdict(list)
    for key, value in map_results:
        distributor[key].append(value)
    returns = chunked_async_map(
      pool, reducer, distributor.items(), chunk_size)
    report_progress(returns, 'reduce', callback)
    results = []
```

We use extend instead of append.

We add chunk_size as a parameter.

```
    for ret in returns:
        results.extend(ret.get())
    return results
```

The only caveat is that the result of each execution is not a single element anymore, but a list of elements. So we have to extend the list and not append to it.

To have a better speed test, we will use Tolstoy's *Anna Karenina*, available at Project Gutenberg (http://gutenberg.org/files/1399/1399-0.txt). Here is the calling code:

```
words = [word                                              ◁       This reads all the
         for word in map(lambda x: x.strip().rstrip(),             text into a list.
             ' '.join(open(
                 'text.txt', 'rt', encoding='utf-8').readlines()).split(' '))
         if word != '' ]
chunk_size = int(sys.argv[1])     ◁——— The chunk size is a command line parameter.
pool = mp.Pool()
counts = map_reduce(pool, words, emitter, counter, chunk_size, reporter)
pool.close()
pool.join()
                                                          We print all the word
for count in sorted(counts, key=lambda x: x[1]):    ◁——  counts in increasing order.
    print(count)
```

I have run the previous code with a chunk size of 1, 10, 100, 1,000, and 10,000. The time for each case is depicted in table 3.1.

Table 3.1 Running times for different chunk sizes

Chunk size	Time (s)
1	114.2
10	12.3
100	4.3
1,000	3.1
10,000	3.1

The numbers in table 3.1 speak for themselves: chunking can massively increase the performance of our framework. Chunking is such an important concept that we will be revisiting it in other chapters.

> **TIP** If you use map from the Pool object, chunking is implemented for you for free. You just have to add the chunksize parameter. The same is true for map_async and imap. More generally, when you use a parallel library, be sure to check whether the chunking functionality is present. In many cases, you will not need to implement it yourself.

> **Shared memory**
>
> An alternative to the (implicit) message-passing solution presented here would be to use shared memory services. Naive shared memory models such as the ones available in Python's built-in libraries are notoriously very bug-prone to use, and as such, we will not address them here. If you need memory sharing, you are probably in a situation in which you will have to implement your code in a lower-level solution anyway. We will discuss shared memory in later contexts where we use lower-level approaches connected to our Python code to do processing.

3.5   *Tying it all together: An asynchronous multithreaded and multiprocessing MapReduce server*

We have spent the chapter testing out various approaches and combinations of approaches using parallelism, concurrency, threading, and synchronous and asynchronous programming. We will now choose the most effective of these strategies and put them together as we return to our example problem of developing an extremely fast MapReduce framework. Let's recall all the parameters of our problem: all data is in-memory, all the work will happen on a single computer, and our system will be handling requests from several clients, including automated AI bots. In this final section, we will finally develop a complete solution, ending up with a multiprocessing MapReduce implementation behind an asynchronous TCP server that will answer queries from multiple clients.

We have already built two of the pieces: the chunked MapReduce implementation from the previous section and the client we made way back in section 3.1. We can use these two pieces as-is. For everything else in this solution, read on.

3.5.1   *Architecting a complete high-performance solution*

We will design the architecture according to figure 3.6. The frontend interfacing with all the clients will be asynchronous. Work will be sent to another thread via a queue. That thread will be responsible for managing a pool of processes that will do the MapReduce work.

Our frontend TCP server will be implemented inside an asynchronous loop. There will be a second thread that is only responsible for managing the MapReduce multiprocessing pool.

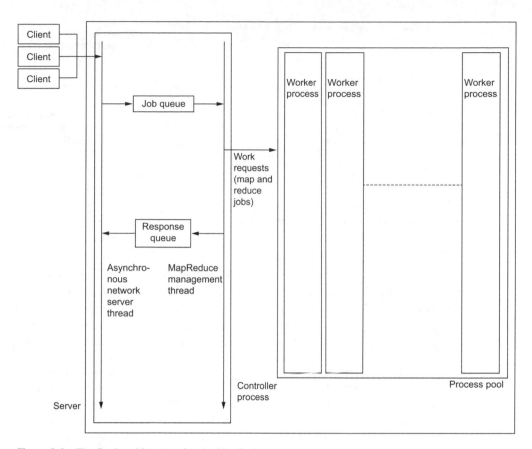

Figure 3.6 **The final architecture for the MapReduce server**

The communication between the two threads will use a `Queue` from the `queue` module. The entry code will set up the asynchronous server and the thread that manages the MapReduce pool (the code is in `03-concurrency/sec5-all/server.py`):

```
import asyncio
from queue import Queue, Empty
import multiprocessing as mp
import types

work_queue = Queue()                    This function is called
results_queue = Queue()                 on the new thread.
results = {}

def worker():                           The pool is created inside
    pool = mp.Pool()                    the worker thread.
    while True:                                      The worker thread waits
        job_id, code, data = work_queue.get()       for some work to do.
        func = types.FunctionType(code, globals(), 'mapper_and_reducer')
        mapper, reducer = func()
        counts = mr.map_reduce(pool, data, mapper, reducer, 100, mr.reporter)
```

```
        results_queue.put((job_id, counts))
    pool.close()
    pool.join()
```
**Results are put on
the response queue.**

```
async def main():
    server = await asyncio.start_server(accept_requests, '127.0.0.1', 1936)
    worker_thread = threading.Thread(target=worker)
    worker_thread.start()
    async with server:
        await server.serve_forever()
```
The thread is started.

**A thread is prepared,
pointing at worker
as the starting point.**

```
asyncio.run(main())
```

Our main entry point, `main`, prepares the asynchronous infrastructure as before and also creates and starts the thread that will manage the MapReduce pool, which is implemented in the function `worker`. `worker` creates the multiprocessing pool and deals with requests from the asynchronous server. Communication is done via FIFO (first-in, first-out) queues. The `queue` module makes sure that the queues are synchronized (i.e., that locking mechanisms are in place to assure threading doesn't cause inconsistent states). There is a `queue` to receive work and another to return the results. All the functions in `worker` are blocking because nothing is there to be processed on initialization: the clients are being dispatched by the asynchronous part.

> **NOTE** Queues are also a great way to communicate when you are using multiprocessing instead of threading. The `multiprocessing` module has a specific `Queue` class for this as managing interprocess communication is harder than multithreading versions. Some of the burden is passed to the user. Only objects that can be pickled can go through the queue. Because of `pickle` usage and interprocess communication, speed might become a concern, so be aware of that.

Let's start with job submission. The asynchronous part is now coded like this:

```
async def submit_job(job_id, reader, writer):
    writer.write(job_id.to_bytes(4, 'little'))
    writer.close()
    code_size = int.from_bytes(await reader.read(4), 'little')
    my_code = marshal.loads(await reader.read(code_size))
    data_size = int.from_bytes(await reader.read(4), 'little')
    data = pickle.loads(await reader.read(data_size))
    work_queue.put_nowait((job_id, my_code, data))
```
**We write
the data to
work_queue,
nonblocking.**

Our `submit_job` function now finally does something useful: it submits the job into the `work_queue`, which will be picked up by the thread running the `worker` function. We use `put_nowait` to avoid blocking when putting the result. In our case, this should not happen as the queue was initialized without constraints regarding size. However, we account here for the possibility of a queue with size limits, which you will need to consider and implement on the queue creation call in cases where there can be many messages on the queue.

The rest of the asynchronous code is as follows:

```
def get_results_queue():
    while results_queue.qsize() > 0:
        try:
            job_id, data = results_queue.get_nowait()
            results[job_id] = data
        except Empty:
            return
```

We get the size of the queue to see whether something has arrived.

We read the response from results_queue, nonblocking.

We provision for an empty queue.

```
async def get_results(reader, writer):
    get_results_queue()
    job_id = int.from_bytes(await reader.read(4), 'little')
    data = pickle.dumps(None)
    if job_id in results:
        data = pickle.dumps(results[job_id])
        del results[job_id]
    writer.write(len(data).to_bytes(4, 'little'))
    writer.write(data)


async def accept_requests(reader, writer, job_id=[0]):
    op = await reader.read(1)
    if op[0] == 0:
        await submit_job(job_id[0], reader, writer)
        job_id[0] += 1
    elif op[0] == 1:
        await get_results(reader, writer)
```

`accept_requests` is exactly the same as in the first section and shown here only for completion.

`get_results` has only a new line at the beginning: calling `get_results_queue`, which is responsible for checking whether the MapReduce concluded, and the results are transferred to the `results` dictionary. It is worth noting that the queue size determination via `qsize` is only approximate, so we have to consider an empty queue and avoid blocking until we wait for a message to arrive.

Locking and low-level synchronization with threading and multiprocessing

Run away from most lower-level primitives for locking! There is a plethora of standard synchronization primitives that both `threading` and `multiprocessing` support, including locks and semaphores, along with a few others. However, our perspective here is that if you need to use these low-level constructs, you probably need to implement the code in a lower-level language anyway. So, we will deal with such mechanisms later in the book when we address performance by re-implementing parts of the codes outside of standard Python.

While not directly related to performance, a multiprocess-related communication primitive commonly used is `Pipe`, as it allows communication with external applications using the standard input and output channels.

3.5.2 *Creating a robust version of the server*

Up to now, we have had little concern for errors and unexpected input. At this stage, we will make our code a little bit more robust. This will substantially increase the size of our implementation. We will make sure that when the server is shut down, the asynchronous server is stopped gracefully: the worker thread terminates, and the pool is properly closed.

Our main function will have to bulk up a little:

- We will need to trap the user request for interruption (typically Control-C) and cleanup at that stage.
- Because our asynchronous server can now be canceled, we have to catch that also.
- We will have to have a way to signal the working thread that it has to clean up.

Here is the implementation (the code is in `03-concurrency/sec5-all/server_robust.py`):

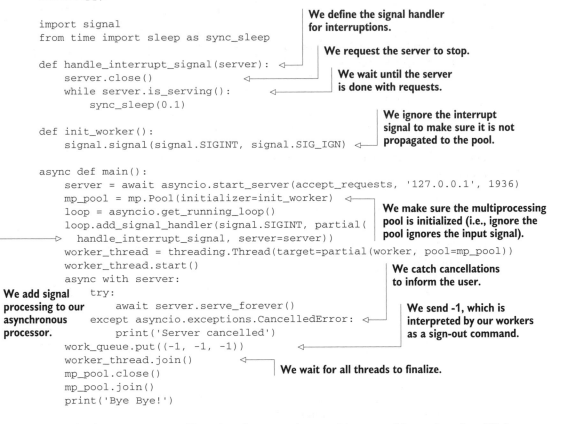

```python
import signal
from time import sleep as sync_sleep


def handle_interrupt_signal(server):
    server.close()
    while server.is_serving():
        sync_sleep(0.1)


def init_worker():
    signal.signal(signal.SIGINT, signal.SIG_IGN)


async def main():
    server = await asyncio.start_server(accept_requests, '127.0.0.1', 1936)
    mp_pool = mp.Pool(initializer=init_worker)
    loop = asyncio.get_running_loop()
    loop.add_signal_handler(signal.SIGINT, partial(
        handle_interrupt_signal, server=server))
    worker_thread = threading.Thread(target=partial(worker, pool=mp_pool))
    worker_thread.start()
    async with server:
        try:
            await server.serve_forever()
        except asyncio.exceptions.CancelledError:
            print('Server cancelled')
    work_queue.put((-1, -1, -1))
    worker_thread.join()
    mp_pool.close()
    mp_pool.join()
    print('Bye Bye!')
```

We define the signal handler for interruptions.

We request the server to stop.

We wait until the server is done with requests.

We ignore the interrupt signal to make sure it is not propagated to the pool.

We make sure the multiprocessing pool is initialized (i.e., ignore the pool ignores the input signal).

We add signal processing to our asynchronous processor.

We catch cancellations to inform the user.

We send -1, which is interpreted by our workers as a sign-out command.

We wait for all threads to finalize.

If you look at main, you will notice that now the pool is created here, just for efficiency, and now each process has an initializer function called init_worker. This is because when we press Control-C, we do not want the pool to interrupt as the signal is propagated to all of the pool. As such, we use the `signal` library and instruct each pool process (`signal.SIG_IGN`) to ignore the interrupt signal (`signal.SIGINT`).

We want our main thread to capture the interrupt signal and process it properly. Because we want to be able to control the asynchronous code from the signal, we need to use a different way to trap it: we call `add_signal_handler` to the loop. We need to pass the server object, and we do that with a partial function application. The handler `handle_interrupt_signal` cancels the server and waits until it's not serving any longer, as the cancellation might not be immediate.

When we run the asynchronous server, we now need to be aware of cancellations, so we catch that exception. Finally, we need to ask the monitor thread to clean up. Because the signal is passed only to the main thread, we need to do this with some communication mechanism: we just send `work` with a `job_id` of -1.

Managing errors and exceptions in multithreaded and multiprocessing code

Debugging multithreaded and multiprocessing code can be extremely frustrating even when using simple models of interprocess communication. We barely scratched the surface and somewhat unrealistically assumed that the architecture is well-behaved. If you are doing concurrent processing in your code, you should consider having good logging in place to help you catch problems. Whenever possible, you should try to make sure the problem is not related to concurrency (e.g., by trying to run any problematic code not in a pool or separate thread but on a single thread of a single process). For example, you can temporarily substitute a `multiprocessing.Pool.map` with a `list(map)`.

As the worker thread needs to explicitly clean up, we will need to implement that

```
def worker(pool):
    while True:
        job_id, code, data = work_queue.get()
        if job_id == -1:
            break                                    We break out of the
                                                     loop if job_id is -1.
        func = types.FunctionType(code, globals(), 'mapper_and_reducer')
        mapper, reducer = func()
        counts = mr.map_reduce(pool, data, mapper, reducer, 100, mr.reporter)
        results_queue.put((job_id, counts))
    print('Worker thread terminating')
```

Summary

- Asynchronous programming can be an effective approach to efficiently process many simultaneous requests when communication needs and the amount of processing required are small; this is the most common pattern with web servers.
- Python is a slow language in the sense that it has a slow flagship implementation. This makes the ability to run parallel code even more important.

- Python threading is not great for performance improvement. The Global Interpreter Lock (GIL) requires that only one thread can run at a time. That being said, some other implementations of Python (e.g., IronPython) don't have a GIL, and threaded code can be parallel.

- Threading can still be quite useful for architecture design purposes. While it is not the best avenue to approach performance, don't discard it outright. There are other perspectives beyond the scope of the book where it can still be relevant.

- With Python multiprocessing, it is possible to make use of all CPU cores in a computer even with just pure Python code.

- It is generally best to keep computing granularity coarse, and too much communication will probably slow down your solution. When you communicate across processes, be sure that the overhead of communication is not a substantial source of performance bottlenecks.

- Run away from shared memory and low-level locks when developing parallel code. If you think you need them, then implement a sequential solution in a lower-level language. Debugging parallel solutions with complex communication patterns is extremely difficult, as communication in parallel systems is mostly nondeterministic.

High-performance NumPy 4

This chapter covers

- Rediscovering NumPy from a performance perspective
- Leveraging NumPy views for computing efficiency and memory conservation
- Introducing array programming as a paradigm
- Configuring NumPy internals for efficiency

It is difficult to overstate the importance of NumPy for doing data analytics with Python. This book might as well be called *High-Performance Python with NumPy*. NumPy will be found somewhere in your stack: Do you use pandas? NumPy. Do you use scikit-learn? NumPy. Dask? NumPy. SciPy? NumPy. Matplotlib? NumPy. TensorFlow? NumPy. If you are doing data analytics in Python, almost surely your answer includes NumPy.

NumPy is a Python library that provides N-dimensional or multidimensional array objects such as matrices, which are two-dimensional, along with the functionality to manipulate them. The implementation is extremely efficient with its core written in Fortran and C. Many data analysis problems can be modeled at their core by N-dimensional arrays; this is why NumPy is pervasive in this field.

Given the importance and wide usage of NumPy in Python's data analysis, some topics related to it will be discussed in other chapters, notably:

- Vectorization of functions using Cython in chapter 5
- Internal memory organization of arrays in chapter 6
- Using NumExpr for fast numerical expression evaluation in chapter 6
- Using arrays larger than memory in chapters 8 and 10
- Efficient storage of arrays in chapters 8 and 10
- Making use of GPU computing for array processing in chapter 9

In this chapter, we will start with a refresher on NumPy. While this book assumes that you have had some exposure to NumPy, it is not uncommon that, even if you are using the library, it might be in an indirect manner. For example, you might be using pandas or Matplotlib and do very little direct NumPy programming yourself. This refresher focuses on NumPy concepts *from a performance perspective.* If you feel that you need a more thorough introduction, there are countless free examples on the web. The official one is really good: https://numpy.org/devdocs/user/quickstart.html. The NumPy site also provides a curated list of learning resources at https://numpy.org/learn/.

After the primer, we will examine array programming as a *programming model* where an operation is applied to more than one atomic value at a time. This approach is valuable both from a performance perspective and also as an elegant approach to writing code. In the final part of the chapter, we will discuss the effect of NumPy's internal architecture and dependencies on its performance—and we will learn how to fine-tune it.

4.1 Understanding NumPy from a performance perspective

In this section, and throughout this chapter, we will learn the key concepts and techniques through the use of a practical example: the development of simple image manipulation routines. Images are, on first approach, two-dimensional arrays (i.e., matrices) and thus lend themselves quite easily to NumPy manipulation. So we will assume we are developing a new image-processing software. Again, while this section is a kind of NumPy primer, it emphasizes how NumPy affects performance. So even if you know NumPy basics, you may learn something new about it here.

4.1.1 Copies vs. views of existing arrays

Our first task is to read an image from a file and perform several rotation operations on it. We will use NumPy directly to rotate the image, not the functions provided by the Pillow image library that we use to read the image. We will learn to do this with both NumPy memory copying and with view creation so we can compare their efficiency. Views are based on arrays that share the same memory but interpret it differently, so they are generally more efficient, although they cannot always be used, as we will see.

Let's start by loading a familiar image, the logo from Manning Publications, and then getting a NumPy array from it. Note that some operations like rotating an image can be conceived as nothing more than interpreting an array in a different way:

columns become rows and rows become columns. This is exactly what a NumPy view is: a different interpretation of the same raw data. We will divide this process into very small steps, as we need to carefully consider and understand each line (the code can be found in `04-numpy/sec1-basics/image_processing.py`):

```
import sys
import numpy as np
from PIL import Image

image = Image.open("../manning-logo.png").convert("L")
print("Image size:", image.size)
width, height = image.size
image_arr = np.array(image)
print("Array shape, array type:", image_arr.shape, image_arr.dtype)
print("Array size * item size: ", image_arr.nbytes)
print("Array nbytes:", image_arr.nbytes)
print("sys.getsizeof:", sys.getsizeof(image_arr))
```

> The convert("L") operation reduces the image to grayscale.

We use the Pillow library to load the Manning logo (figure 4.1), converting the image to grayscale. Every pixel will be represented by an unsigned byte. The size of the image is 182×45. The output is:

```
Image size: (182, 45)
Array shape, array type: (45, 182) uint8
Array size * item size:  8190
Array nbytes: 8190
sys.getsizeof: 8302
```

We then get an array representing the image data by using the function `np.array`. The reason this works with a Pillow image is not because NumPy knows what an image is, but because the image object implements `__array_interface__` which NumPy uses to construct an array representation.

We then print the array `shape`, which is 45×182. Notice that the *convention* for images—width followed by height—is the reverse of the convention followed by NumPy, which comes from mathematics—the number of rows followed by the number of columns. This nuance is substantially more important than it seems, and we will start to see this when we discuss different views of data in the next subsection. But the magnitude of the problem will become especially clear when we discuss memory representation in chapter 6.

We then print the data type of the array, which comes as `uint8` (i.e., unsigned integer of 8 bits, or a byte). A `uint8` is sufficient to keep enough information for grayscale images. Following that, we print the memory occupied by the array in two different ways: (1) by multiplying the number of items in the array (45 * 182 = 8190) times the size of each element (1 byte in our case), or (2) we can use the `nbytes` field directly.

Finally, we use the `getsizeof` function introduced in chapter 2 to get the size of the array *object*. This includes the raw array (8190) plus the Python and NumPy overhead and metadata (for a total of 8302).

We have seen a few ways to establish the size of our array—with and without object overhead. Now we will flip the image upside down. Image flipping can be done by copying the array or simply by changing our interpretation of the raw data, so it's a good example for introducing views. After we get the two flips, we will black out half of the original image:

```
flipped_from_view = np.flipud(image_arr)
flipped_from_copy = np.flipud(image_arr).copy()
image_arr[:, :width//2] = 0
removed = Image.fromarray(image_arr, "L")
image.save("image.png")
removed.save("removed.png")

flipped_from_view_image = Image.fromarray(flipped_from_view, "L")
flipped_from_view_image.save("flipped_view.png")
flipped_from_copy_image = Image.fromarray(flipped_from_copy, "L")
flipped_from_copy_image.save("flipped_copy.png")
```

Flips the image in the vertical axis. This is done using a view.

Takes a flipped image and creates a copy of it

Figure 4.1 shows the four images combined. `flipped_from_view` is created from a view of `image_arr`. This means that when you change `image_arr` with `image_arr[:, :width//2] = 0`, `flipped_from_view` will also be altered because the raw array is shared.

Views share the underlying raw array; copies don't. Therefore, the image of `flipped_from_copy` is not affected by the change on `image_arr`. As a side note, `Image.fromarray` creates a copy of the original array. That is why image.png and removed.png are different. If it had provided a view, then the images would be equal.

The underlying data structures supporting the images are shown in figure 4.2. Note that the original image was destroyed, and `image_arr` contains the blacked-out array.

image.png   removed.png

flipped_copy.png   flipped_view.png

Figure 4.1   The four images: the original Manning logo (image.png), the left part blacked out (removed.png), a vertical flip from a copy (flipped_copy.png), and a flip from a view (flipped_view.png)

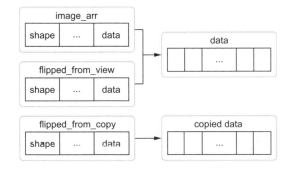

Figure 4.2   Many NumPy operations can generate new objects, or views, which share the raw data with the original objects. Sometimes that is not possible or desirable, and data is copied.

Sometimes it is not desirable to do view sharing. For example, you might not want to black out the original image. In that case, you need to make a copy so that the original object is preserved intact. There are also times when it is not possible to get the data as a view; we will see a case of this later in the section.

It is possible to see whether an array is based on another array:

```
print(flipped_from_copy.base, flipped_from_view.base)
print(flipped_from_view.base is image_arr)
print(flipped_from_view.base == image_arr)
```

Checks whether it is the same object

Checks whether all values of both arrays are equal

The output is:

```
None [[ 0 .... <long array>]]
True
[[ True  True  True ...  True  True  True]
```

`flipped_from_copy.base` will be `None` as it is its own fresh copy. `flipped_from_view.base` will have a value—a matrix. We can check whether it is the same object as `image_arr` by using `is`. Be careful: if you use `==`, you are getting a value-by-value comparison of all elements of the array. For `is`, you will get `True`; for `==` you will get an array of `True`.

> **TIP** The base of any view is not the object from which the view is derived but the very first object in the chain. So, for example, if you have `v2 = v1[:-1]` and `v1 = arr[::-1]`, `v2.base is arr` and `v1.base is arr` are both `True`, but `v2.base is v1` is not.

As we have seen, Numpy objects have a set of metadata like `shape` or `dtype`. The raw array data is in a field called `data`, which points to a Python built-in type, a `memoryview`. The `memoryview` class provides a lot of basic functionality from the Python side to deal with blocks of allocated memory with homogeneous types. For example, it implements indexing, slicing, and memory sharing.

It is possible to inquire whether NumPy arrays share memory, which is more general than being a view because `memoryviews` can be belong simultaneously to other objects and, potentially, other arrays without using a view to create them:

```
print(np.shares_memory(image_arr, flipped_from_copy),
      np.shares_memory(image_arr, flipped_from_view))
```

`np.shares_memory` will be `False` for `image_arr` and `flipped_from_copy` because we are dealing with a copy. It will be `True` for both `image_arr` and `flipped_from_view`. Generally, if `base` is shared, then memory is shared, but the reverse doesn't have to be true: memory can be shared without having the same base.

> **TIP** Determining whether two arrays share memory is not a trivial problem. In complex scenarios, it may take a lot of time, making it impractical. In those cases, there is a faster function, `may_share_memory`, to provide a guess whether two arrays share memory.

THE TAKEAWAY

The take-home point here is that *views tend to be substantially more efficient than copies.*
There are two main reasons for this. First, when you copy an array, you pay the computing price of copying the raw data whereas with views, only the view information is
remade. Probably more important, when you copy an array, you double the memory
that you need, which might not be feasible when you are dealing with large in-memory
arrays. In any case, don't forget that if you change any view, all objects that share the
same memory will be affected.

Let's run a short example to grasp the consequence of this difference in efficiency.
We will create an array with variable sizes and measure how long it takes to create both
a view and a copy (table 4.1):

```
import sys                  If you use iPython, remember that
import timeit   ⊲────┘      the %timeit magic is available.

import numpy as np

for size in [
  1, 10, 100, 1000, 10000, 100000, 200000, 400000, 800000, 1000000]:
    print(size)
    my_array = np.arange(size, dtype=np.uint16)
    print(sys.getsizeof(my_array))
    print(my_array.data.nbytes)
    view_time = timeit.timeit(
        "my_array.view()",
        f"import numpy; my_array = numpy.arange({size})")
    print(view_time)
    copy_time = timeit.timeit(
        "my_array.copy()",
        f"import numpy; my_array = numpy.arange({size})")
    print(copy_time)
    copy_gc_time = timeit.timeit(
        "my_array.copy()",
        f"import numpy;
          import gc; gc.enable(); my_array = numpy.arange({size})")
    print(copy_gc_time)

    print()
```

Table 4.1   Comparing the time and memory allocations between copies and views

Array size	Array memory (b)	View time	Copy time
1	2	0.171	0.281
10	20	0.137	0.259
100	200	0.139	0.286
1000	2000	0.162	0.502
10000	20000	0.142	2.275

Table 4.1 Comparing the time and memory allocations between copies and views *(continued)*

Array size	Array memory (b)	View time	Copy time
100000	200000	0.138	31.257
200000	400000	0.152	67.005
400000	800000	0.144	354.287
800000	1600000	0.177	547.843
1000000	2000000	0.142	729.966

The memory burden of a copy is quite easy to understand: you double the amount of memory needed every time you copy.[1] The time burden of a copy is less obvious: from a naive perspective, you can assume that the time needed to copy an array is linear with its size. If you look at the table, sometimes the linear relationship breaks. This will be explained in chapter 6.

THE TAKEAWAY

As we have seen, views can save you both compute time and memory, so you should generally try to use views when possible. The biggest drawback of views is that they are not always an option; sometimes there is simply no alternative to copying. That said, NumPy's view mechanism is both powerful and flexible, so it can be used in plenty of situations. Let's have a deeper look at the view mechanism so we can see how to put it to use in a wide range of situations.

4.1.2 *Understanding NumPy's view machinery*

To be able to make the most of views for efficient processing, we first have to understand how they work. The flexibility of views comes mostly from two pieces of metadata: the first, which we have just seen, is the shape. The second is the strides; we'll get a more precise definition of strides in a moment. First, let's look at a few examples illustrating different shape and stride values.

Let's start by allocating an array consisting of [0, 1, 2, 3, 4, 5, 6, 7, 8, 9], of 4-byte unsigned integers and look at its stride and shape. We will later reshape this simple linear array into a two-dimensional structure:

```
import numpy as np

linear = np.arange(10, dtype np.uint32)
```

The array will be allocated *contiguously* in memory. This means that 0 will be followed by 1; 1 by 2; 2 by 3, and so on. This might seem obvious at this stage, but as we will see, it is far from it.

---

[1] For very small arrays this doesn't hold as metadata would be an important portion of the allocation, but for large arrays, which are what we care about, it is a very good approximation as the 96 bytes of overhead from Python and NumPy are negligible.

> **WARNING** The contiguous allocation with NumPy presented in this example is an oversimplification—albeit a correct one for this case—for pedagogical purposes. From this point on, we will see examples of arrays that are not contiguous. But we will delay important details about allocation until chapter 6. As a suggestion, if this is the first time you're seeing a discussion about an array being contiguous, refrain from visiting that chapter immediately. Get the basic concepts right first.

Let's get a view as a 2×5 matrix of the same data. After that, let's create another view, a 5×2 matrix from a transposition of the 2×5 matrix. We want to understand the relationship between the original array and the new matrices:

```
m2x5 = linear.reshape((2, 5))
print(np.shares_memory(linear, m2x5))

print("2x5", m2x5.shape)
print("2x5 corners", m2x5[0, 0], m2x5[0, 4],
      m2x5[2, 0], m2x5[2, 4])

m5x2 = m2x5.T
print(np.shares_memory(m2x5, m5x2))
print("5x2", m5x2.shape)
print("5x2 corners", m5x2[0, 0], m5x2[0, 1],
      m5x2[4, 0], m5x2[4, 1])
```

The first thing we want to do is to make sure the matrices share memory (i.e., they are views, not copies). np.shares memory shows that both linear, m5x2, and m2x5 share memory, which is depicted in figure 4.3. We also print the corners of the newly declared matrices so that their boundaries are clear.

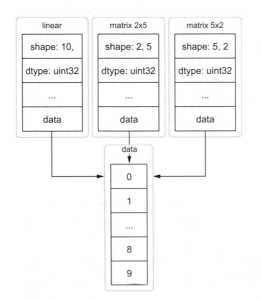

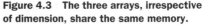

Figure 4.3   The three arrays, irrespective of dimension, share the same memory.

The question is, how can NumPy know how to find an element from the same memory? The shape may be enough to distinguish between the one-dimensional array and one of the matrices. But what about distinguishing between the two differently shaped matrices from the same memory? That is what strides are for:

```
print("linear", linear.strides)
print("2x5 strides", m2x5.strides)
print("5x2 strides", m5x2.strides)
```

The results will be `4`, `(4, 20)`, and `(20, 4)`.

The *stride*, then, is how many bytes you need to jump to get to the next element along a dimension. Let's make this concept clear by relating it to the three previous examples.

The stride for the `linear` variable is 4: this means that there is only one dimension and that to hop from one element to the next one, you need to jump 4 bytes, which is the size of the data type that we chose, `np.uint32`. In figure 4.4, every time you advance one position in the linear array, you advance 4 bytes in memory to get the value. The memory position for index `i` is then `stride * i` or `4 * i`.

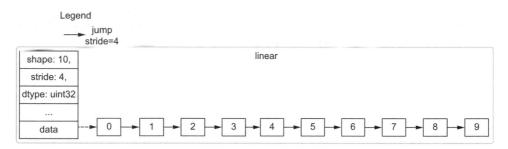

Figure 4.4 Jumping to adjacent elements in a one-dimensional array. This has a single stride: the number is the size of our data type.

Things get a little more complicated with two-dimensional arrays. For our 2×5 array, if you want to jump a column forward, then the element is adjacent, so a jump of one element—the current one—is required (figure 4.5). Given that our element size is 4 bytes, we end up with a stride of 4. But if you want to jump a row forward, then you have to skip the current element plus an extra 4 (given that each row has five elements), So 5 elements times the element size of 4 equals 20. In this interpretation of the memory, you can get to element `i,j` with the function `strides[0]*i + strides[1]*j` (`20*i + 4*j`).

The stride for the `m5x2` is `20, 4`: this means that there are two dimensions and that to go to the next row you need to hop 20 bytes (five columns at 4 bytes each). The next column is the next value, which is 4 bytes away.

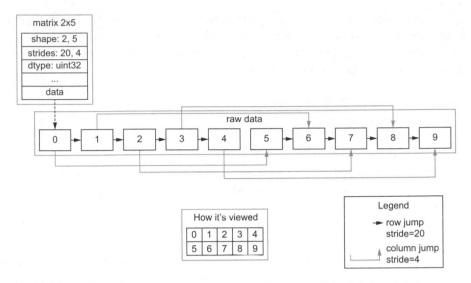

Figure 4.5 Jumping to adjacent elements in a 2 × 5 in a two-dimensional array. We will need two strides: one for each dimension.

Figure 4.6 should make this clear. (This will vary substantially with the inner representation of the array, something we will consider in chapter 6.)

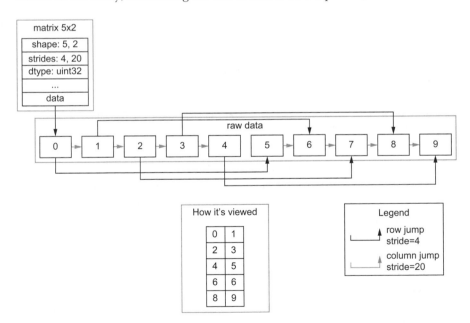

Figure 4.6 Jumping to adjacent elements in a 2 × 5 in a two-dimensional array. The stride for rows will depend on the number of columns.

Many NumPy operations are view transformations. For example, reversing an array can also be rendered as a view:

```
back = linear[::-1]
print("back", back.shape, back.strides, back[0], back[-1])
```

Note that the stride is now –4. NumPy can create views that go backward (figure 4.7).

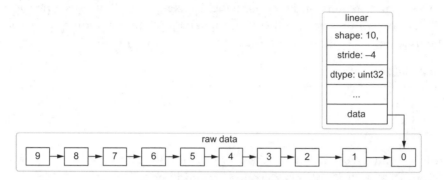

Figure 4.7   Reversing a one-dimensional array will invert the signal of the stride.

A similar approach can be used with two-dimensional arrays. What would be the strides for m2x5 and m5x2 if they were reversed?

The ability to render a transformation as a view is not always possible, as it depends on the ability to establish a linear relationship between the existing and new view. For example, let's take a 20 × 5 matrix and then choose a row out of three and a column of two, creating a matrix of 7 × 3. Finally, let's get a one-dimensional version of that 7 × 3 matrix:

```
a100 = np.arange(100, dtype=np.uint8).reshape(20, 5)
a100_step_3_2 = a100[::3, ::2]
print(a100_step_3_2.shape, a100_step_3_2.strides)
print(np.shares_memory(a100, a100_step_3_2))
a100_step_3_2_linear = a100_step_3_2.reshape(21)
print(np.shares_memory(a100_step_3_2, a100_step_3_2_linear))
```

The 7 × 3 matrix can still be rendered as a view using a stride of 15, 2. The apparently easier process of converting it to a one-dimensional representation is impossible to do as a view, and as such a copy is created.

NumPy's so-called fancy indexing is always rendered as a copy. Here is an example where we get five alternate values, top and down, from a 2 × 5 matrix:

```
import numpy as np

m5x2 = np.arange(10).reshape(2, 5)

my_rows = [0, 1, 0, 1, 0]
```

```
my_cols = [0, 1, 2, 3, 4]

alternate = m5x2[my_rows, my_cols]

print(m5x2)
print(alternate)
print(np.shares_memory(m5x2, alternate))
```

To refresh your memory on fancy indexing, it takes a list of indexes, one for each of the dimensions of the array, and returns the element corresponding to the positions on the lists. Let's see this in action with the matrix shown in table 4.2.

Table 4.2 Original matrix

0	1	2	3	4
5	6	7	8	9

We will have an `alternate` of `[0 6 2 8 4]` for the list of rows `[0, 1, 0, 1, 0]` and the list of columns `[0, 1, 2, 3, 4]`. `np.shares_memory` will be `False`.

THE TAKEAWAY

First, views can be substantially more efficient than copies. Second, views can be used in the ways that we just learned in this section. Let's apply those uses to our image processing code so we can see some advantages as well as some pitfalls of using views.

4.1.3   *Making use of views for efficiency*

We are now going to transform our example image by using operations that only require views. This is a good time to remember why we are doing this in the context of big data: for very large arrays, memory can be limited, and copying large arrays incurs a time cost as well.

Let's start by flipping the image vertically and horizontally:

> We can flip an image with an array reverse over a dimension. Remember that in the previous section we used Image.flipud to flip the image horizontally.

```
import numpy as np
from PIL import Image

image = Image.open("../manning-logo.png").convert("L")
width, height = image.size
image_arr = np.array(image)
print("original array", image_arr.shape, image_arr.strides, image_arr.dtype)
image.save("view_initial.png")

invert_rows_arr = image_arr[::-1, :]
print("invert rows", invert_rows_arr.shape, invert_rows_arr.strides,
      np.shares_memory(invert_rows_arr, image_arr))
Image.fromarray(invert_rows_arr).save("invert_x.png")

invert_cols_arr = image_arr[:, ::-1]
print("invert columns", invert_cols_arr.shape, invert_cols_arr.strides,
      np.shares_memory(invert_cols_arr, image_arr))
Image.fromarray(invert_cols_arr).save("invert_y.png")
```

At this stage, the code should be easy to read: for the 182 × 24 Manning logo, the original array has a shape of 45, 182 with a stride of 182, 1. We are dealing with a data type of unsigned integers of 1 byte, hence a single byte per pixel. When we flip the image horizontally (i.e., by rows), the only thing that changes is the second stride, which goes from 1 to -1. Conversely, when we flip the image vertically, the first stride goes from 182 to -182.

Let's now try to rotate the image. We will use three approaches: reshape, transpose (`.T`), and 90-degree rotation (`.rot90`). We are doing this to check the output for the three different strategies and how they are internally represented:

```
view_swap_arr = image_arr.reshape(image_arr.shape[1], image_arr.shape[0])

print("view_swap", view_swap_arr.shape, view_swap_arr.strides)
Image.fromarray(view_swap_arr, "L").save("view_swap.png")

trans_arr = image_arr.T
print("transpose", trans_arr.shape, trans_arr.strides)
Image.fromarray(trans_arr, "L").save("transpose.png")

rot_arr = np.rot90(image_arr)
print("rot", rot_arr.shape, rot_arr.strides)
Image.fromarray(rot_arr, "L").save("rot90.png")
```

The same thing can be done with the swapaxes method.

To check whether we have a view or a copy, we are printing the `memoryview` object, which will give us a hexadecimal number reflecting the memory position. All the memory locations will be the same so the operations created views.

Now, let's include a slice—just the word *Manning* from the logo, which, in this case, is also a view:

```
slice_arr = image_arr[15:, 77:]
print("slice_arr", slice_arr.shape, slice_arr.strides,
      np.shares_memory(slice_arr, image_arr))
Image.fromarray(slice_arr, "L").save("slice.png")
```

The shapes and strides are shown in table 4.3.

Table 4.3 Shapes and strides of axes swap, transposing, and rotation

Operation	Shape	Stride
swapaxes	182 45	45 1
transpose	182 45	1 182
rot90	182 45	-1 182
slice	30 105	182 1

Can you predict how the images will look, especially the axes swap, rotation, and the transposition? The results are shown in figure 4.8.

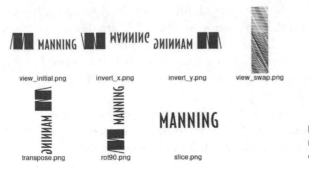

view_initial.png   invert_x.png   invert_y.png   view_swap.png

transpose.png   rot90.png   slice.png

Figure 4.8   The images resulting from using direct array manipulation of the original Manning logo

TIP   For ease of explanation we only used one- and two-dimensional arrays with views, but all this NumPy machinery can be used with higher-order arrays.

WARNING   It is possible to change the stride and shape values directly. Module `numpy.lib.stride_tricks` has a function called `as_strided` that takes an existing array, desired shape, and stride values and returns the results.

The fact that such a function is inside a module called `stride_tricks` should raise some flags. Also, the help page of the function starts with this text: "This function has to be used with extreme care."

The problem is that you can pass arbitrary values (i.e., wrong values) to the function. This is one of the rare cases where you can cause memory corruption in Python, as wrong values will be used to access wrong memory positions. Your program might crash or even expose sensitive information.

THE TAKEAWAY

Views can severely reduce computation and memory costs. While they cannot be used in all cases, NumPy's view machinery is quite flexible and can be used in many situations where data can be reinterpreted with NumPy machinery: shape and stride.

That's enough for now about views and copies from a performance perspective. Let's now look at ways to program NumPy more efficiently, and as you'll see, that means using more idiomatic NumPy.

4.2   *Using array programming*

Array programming is a programming model in which operations are applied to all values of an array at once. This model is used in scientific and high-performance programming. It has two main purposes: making code writing more declarative and more readable and making the code run more efficiently. It turns out that NumPy *can be* mostly done using array programming techniques.

We should make a distinction between *an array library* and *array programming*. A simple example will make this difference clear. (This example is just for teaching purposes, and I wouldn't expect anyone to use the non-array solution.)

NOTE While there is no expectation that anyone would use the non-array solution in this simple example, it is quite common to see NumPy code written using non-array dialects. In this example, the benefits of an array approach are obvious, but it is perfectly possible, and undesirable, to use NumPy in the less-efficient way as presented in the first solution. Probably one of the most important skills when using NumPy and many other similar libraries (e.g., pandas) is recognizing when array code can replace naive Python code.

Imagine that you want to compute the sum of two vectors. From a user perspective, here is the common, non-array programming version (the code is available in 04-numpy/ sec3-vectorize/array_and_broadcasting.py):

```
import numpy as np

def sum_arrays(a, b):  # Assumes both are the same size
    my_sum = np.empty(a.size, dtype=a.dtype)
    for i, (a1, b1) in enumerate(zip(np.nditer(a), np.nditer(b))):
        my_sum[i] = a1 + b1
    return my_sum.reshape(a.shape)
```

We explicitly wrote code to go through all elements. This implementation is riddled with problems, which we will discuss later. For now, let's just compare it to the array version:

```
a + b
```

The glaringly obvious advantage is that the array version is more succinct and declarative, and that, by itself, is enough to make the array idiom preferable. But from our high-performance perspective, there is something more relevant going on.

The array example is probably also orders of magnitude faster. The first example is Python code and has the already discussed inherent speed limits of native Python code. The array example in the overloaded + operator will be implemented as fast as possible. This means a non-Python implementation typically in C or Fortran, probably making use of vectorized CPU operations or even running over a GPU.

At this stage, we will not be overly concerned with how the + operator is implemented. We just need to grasp the potential performance advantages of using the array dialect.

4.2.1 *The takeaway*

Efficient code can be clean code. The myth that efficient code must always be dirty is, I hope, put to rest here. The array implementation is both more efficient and cleaner.

Now that I've advocated for the use of array programming, let's take the previous pure Python implementation to briefly introduce another NumPy concept: broadcasting. Broadcasting is important because it allows us to make more use of array programming and write clearer, more concise code.

4.2.2 *Broadcasting in NumPy*

To understand broadcasting, let's start by taking a deeper look at our pure Python implementation of adding two arrays. That code is repeated here:

```python
def sum_arrays(a, b):
    my_sum = np.empty(a.size, dtype=a.dtype)        # Assumes shape and type
    for i, (a1, b1) in enumerate(zip(np.nditer(a), np.nditer(b))):   from the first array
        my_sum[i] = a1 + b1
    return my_sum
```

Before we discuss the major problem of this code, it is worthwhile noting one redeeming feature of it: the use of `np.empty`. This function allocates the memory for the array but does not initialize it with any value. This can be a time-saver when you are creating a massive array. You have to be sure that you initialize the array later, as we do here, or you will end up with garbage. As such, this is not a general solution, but it can increase performance in many cases.

The major problem with the previous code is that it has no input checking, so it accepts arrays of any shape, including ones that can be potentially incompatible. The seemingly simple solution would be to impose the constraint that a and b would have to be of the same shape and to reshape the output accordingly. This would work but would be very clumsy to use. For example, if you add an array with 100,000 elements and would like to increase all elements by one you would have to do the following:

```python
array_100000 = np.arange(100000)
sum_arrays(array_100000, np.ones(array_100000.shape))
```

This would mean allocating and initializing a big array just to increment our original array by 1. This is both ugly and, with big data, can be too expensive.

Wouldn't it be nice if we could write something like `sum_arrays(array_100000, 1)`? It turns out that in NumPy we can! The following code is perfectly valid:

```python
array_100000 = np.arange(100000)        # As we will see later, this is not the same thing as
array_100000 += 1                        writing array_100000 = array_100000 + 1.
```

`array_100000` is an array with 100,000 positions while 1 is an atomic value (i.e., they have different types). This is an example of *broadcasting*, which is a set of sensible rules so that NumPy applies operators to arrays with different dimensions.

Following are a few practical examples of broadcasting rules being applied. We also compare them to functions that can be confused with broadcasting operators. Let's start with 1D arrays:

```python
a = np.array([0, 20, 21, 9], dtype=np.uint8)
b = np.array([10, 2, 25, 5], dtype=np.uint8)

print("add one", a + 1)
print("multiply by two", a * 2)
```

```
print("add a vector", a + [10, 2, 25, 5])
print("multiply by a vector", a * [10, 2, 25, 5])
print("dot (inner) product", a.dot(b))

print("matmul (inner product)", a @ b)
```

The + operator adds 1 to all elements of the array in the first print. It will add element by element on the second print: [0 20 21 9]] + [10, 2, 25, 5] = [10 22 46 14].

Notice that the * operator works similarly with arrays: the first case * 2 will multiply all values by 2. The second case will multiply element by element: [0 20 21 9]] + [10, 2, 25, 5] = [0 40 525 45].

The inner product is implemented by np.dot and the @ (np.matmul) operator (more on @ later).

Now let's see some matrix examples with broadcasting:

```
x = np.array([[0, 20], [250, 500], [1, 2]],
             dtype=np.uint8)
y = np.array([[1, 10], [25, 5]], dtype=np.uint8)

print("add a matrix to itself", x + x)
print("add a matrix with column size", x + [1, 2])
# print(x + [-1, -2, -3])
print("add a matrix with row size", (x.T + [-1, -2, -3]).T)
print("inner product", np.inner(a, b))
print("matrix multiplication", x.dot(y))
# print(x.T.dot(y))

print("matmul", x @ y)

x[:, 0] = 0
print("assignement broadcasting", x)
```

Adding a matrix to itself produces the expected result, as all values are doubled. You can also add a one-dimensional array to a matrix: it should have the size of the number of columns, and it will be applied row by row. You cannot do the converse (i.e., add a one-dimensional array with the number of rows). But a fast way of doing that (i.e., not involving excessive copying or non-array programming) can be achieved by transposing the matrix—remember, a very fast view operation—and then transposing the result.

> **TIP** NumPy operators do not map directly to standard mathematics expectations. For example, * is *not* a mathematical matrix multiplication; that would be np.dot.

THE TAKEAWAY

There's a lot more to learn about broadcasting, but here we have covered its essential uses from a performance perspective. The most important thing to remember about broadcasting from this perspective is that its implementation is normally vectorized, and as we discussed in the previous section, vectorized implementation can be orders of magnitude faster. We are now ready to go back to our image processing code, hopefully armed with enough motivation to consider array-based approaches.

4.2.3   *Applying array programming*

Let's now apply some of these array-based programming techniques to our image manipulation program. While we are doing this more efficient approach, we will have to learn how to deal with some pitfalls. Do not let these pitfalls discourage you from applying these approaches: array programming is more efficient and elegant than typical imperative programming based on `for` loops.

We will now try to brighten our image. Remember that we are using 1 byte per pixel—the `L` option when converting the image—varying between 0 and 255. We will increase the brightness using two different approaches: by adding 5 to every pixel and by doubling the value, like this:

```python
import numpy as np
from PIL import Image

image = Image.open("../manning-logo.png").convert("L")
width, height = image.size
image_arr = np.array(image)

brighter_arr = image_arr + 5
Image.fromarray(brighter_arr).save("brighter.png")
brighter2_arr = image_arr * 2
Image.fromarray(brighter2_arr).save("brighter2.png")
```

In an ideal world, our problem would be solved. But, if you look at the results in figure 4.9, something needs to be corrected.

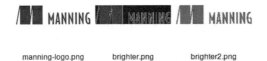

manning-logo.png   brighter.png   brighter2.png

Figure 4.9   Brightening the original image doesn't have the expected effect.

The doubling figure is *apparently* correct, but there is some problem with the one we increased by 5. Remember that the image is represented by 1-byte unsigned integers that range from 0 to 255. Because 5 is added to 255, you end up with an overflow: 260 becomes 4. Hence, the color becomes fairly black.

There is a more insidious problem—because it's unnoticed—with the doubling figure. The figure seems right but suffers from the very same problem. To understand what is going on, let's print the maximum value on the original image and on `brighter2`:

```python
print(image_arr.max(), image_arr.dtype)
print(brighter2_arr.max(), brighter2_arr.dtype)
```

The maximum value for the original image is 255 (total white) whereas the maximum value for the double image is 254, how so? Remember that in binary, 255 is 0x11111111 (8 bits, all 1s), 2 * 255 is 510 0x1111111110 (8 higher bits, all 1s with last bit 0) but the overflow cuts the right bit. We end up with 0x111111110 (i.e., 254). The image looks correct, but it is not.

> **WARNING** Be extremely careful when choosing your data type. When there are no memory or speed concerns, you can be lax and get something wide. But if you need to save as much memory as possible, make sure you do not choose a type that is too small. Unless you have memory and time to spare, there is no general rule other than having good test coverage for corner cases.

The simplest, although not more memory-efficient solution, is to use a larger data type. For example:

```
brighter3_arr = image_arr.astype(np.uint16)
brighter3_arr = brighter3_arr * 2
print(brighter3_arr.max(), brighter3_arr.dtype)
brighter3_arr = np.minimum(brighter3_arr, 255)    ←┐
print(brighter3_arr.max(), brighter3_arr.dtype)
brighter3_arr = brighter3_arr.astype(np.uint8)
print(brighter3_arr.max(), brighter3_arr.dtype)
Image.fromarray(brighter3_arr).save("brighter3.png")
```

Do not confuse minimum with min. min returns the minimum of the array; minimum chooses the smallest value with broadcasting.

We can assume that a value cannot be whiter than maximum white. So we convert all values greater than 255 to 255. We start by taking the original array and converting it to a 2-byte unsigned int; the array is then doubled. When we check the maximum, it is the correct value, 510. We then use np.minimum to choose the minimum from 255 and each element of the array, which is a prime example of broadcasting to create a copy. This makes the maximum value representable by a single byte. Finally, we recast to 8-bit unsigned int where the maximum is now correct. In the next section, we will look at a more memory-efficient approach to do this.[2]

There are more efficient ways of doing some of the casting, such as making the multiplication return a np.uint16 automatically, which we will see in the next subsection.

Finally, let's take another look at the way we double values. Previously, we used:

```
brighter3_arr = brighter3_arr * 2
```

This dialect creates an intermediary array that will be used to hold the result of the multiplication. The variable brighter3_arr is then replaced with the new one. But, for a short time—actually, until garbage collection is run—both arrays will exist in memory. This can be problematic for very large arrays both in terms of memory and time to create the new array. It turns out that we can do much better:

```
brighter3_arr *= 2
```

---

[2] There is a very simple solution to this problem that is not very useful from a pedagogical perspective. Can you think of it? As a tip, consider using the maximum instead of the minimum.

In this case, NumPy understands that the array is going to be mutated and does the multiplication *in place*. This means no doubling of memory and no time wasted in initialization and garbage collecting. The final result is the same, but from a performance perspective these two dialects are completely different. x = x * 2 uses double memory and more time. x *= 2 is more efficient and should be used whenever possible.

THE TAKEAWAY

Part of the problem when using libraries like NumPy or pandas is the tendency to return to non-array programming dialects, which are not efficient. This is not intentional, but we tend to maintain "normal" dialects unless we make a conscious effort to change. Let's continue to delve deeper into array programming as it has a lot more to offer when working on performance problems and also because we want to insist on the paradigm.

4.2.4   *Developing a vectorized mentality*

Vectorized *pure* Python code is not more efficient than nonvectorized code. The documentation of np.vectorize is quite explicit about this.

But we will be thinking in vectorized terms in many chapters of the book: when we discuss Cython, pandas, CPU vectorization, and, to an extreme level, GPU processing. It will probably make your learning curve in those chapters easier if you are exposed to these concepts in pure Python and NumPy before facing them in less familiar environments. In other words, the vectorization mentality stressed in this section will be very useful later.

To understand vectorization and NumPy's universal functions, we will return to a familiar example. From the previous subsection, we have seen that brighter_image = image * 2 can overflow. How would a function that doesn't overflow look? That is quite simple with a vectorized function:

```
def double_wo_overflow(v):
    return min(2 * v, 255)
```

We will now vectorize this function and apply it to our image:

```
import numpy as np
from PIL import image

vec_double_wo_overflow = np.vectorize(         We need to specify
    double_wo_overflow, otypes=[np.uint8])  ⊲┘ the output type.

brighter_arr = vec_double_wo_overflow(image_arr)
print(brighter_arr.max(), brighter_arr.dtype)
Image.fromarray(brighter_arr).save("vec_brighter.png")
```

np.vectorize takes a typical (i.e., nonvectorized) function and, in this case, allows it to be applied to each scalar. We then apply the new vec_double_wo_overflow to our image. It will compute element by element.

TIP While np.vectorize is essentially a for loop, it could, in theory, be called in parallel using all the cores of your machine so it could potentially speed things up. Grasping this mode of programming and its potential for parallelization gives you great insight into how a GPU works. If you learn the concept here, you will have a much easier time when we discuss GPU optimizations in chapter 10.

Just to drive the message home that this code is not faster, a %timeit of our function is in the millisecond range. For the *, we are in the *microsecond* range.

np.vectorize is substantially more sophisticated than this, as it allows the support of broadcasting rules. To exemplify this, let's take a color image as an example. We will use a NASA image, called "St. Patricks's Aurora" (https://images.nasa.gov/details-GSFC_20171208_Archive_e000760).

Let's start by reading the image, which has now a slightly different representation:

```python
import numpy as np
from PIL import Image

image = Image.open("../aurora.jpg")
width, height = image.size
image_arr = np.array(image)
print(image_arr.shape, image_arr.dtype)
```

The image size is 2040 × 1367. Because we are reading a color image, the default mode is RGB (i.e., three channels: red, green, and blue), and there will be an unsigned byte per channel. Each pixel now takes 3 bytes, not 1. We thus have a three-dimensional NumPy array in the shape of 2048 × 1367 × 3. Making an image grayscale is a trivial algorithm when we have a RGB image: we compute the mean of the three components and that becomes our gray intensity:

```python
def get_grayscale_color(row):          # This is the mean of the
    mean = np.mean(row)                # three RGB values.
    return int(mean)
                                       # The mean will be a float,
                                       # so we convert it to int.
vec_get_grayscale_color = np.vectorize(
    get_grayscale_color, otypes=[np.uint8],   # We override the default expectation for the
    signature="(n)->()")                      # signature of the function being vectorized.

grayscale_arr = vec_get_grayscale_color(image_arr)
print(grayscale_arr.max(), grayscale_arr.dtype, grayscale_arr.shape)
Image.fromarray(grayscale_arr).save("grayscale.png")
```

While by default np.vectorize will send a scalar to our function, we can change the signature to accept and return other kinds of objects. In our case, we want our function to accept an array (i.e., the three components) and return a scalar, hence the signature (n)•(). The final result is shown in figure 4.10.

Figure 4.10   The result of our simple grayscaling algorithm

WARNING It is worthwhile repeating here that we are showing solutions for the sake of illustrating vectorization, and they might not be the most efficient. In this case, by far the most efficient and *best* solution would be

```
grayscale_arr = np.mean(image_arr, axis=2).astype(np.uint8)
```

This will compute the means across the last axis (i.e., the one with the color channels). While an iterative solution is the worst choice, that doesn't mean creating your own vectorized function is always the best approach. In this case, the best approach is a good understanding of the use of *built-in* vectorized functions.

THE TAKEAWAY

From a performance perspective, pure Python vectorization is not really an option. But in other contexts, such as working with Cython and GPUs, vectorization can have an effect of several orders of magnitude on performance. So if you understand the vectorization approach in general, it will be much easier to understand the Cython and GPU chapters.

Now that we have considered the basics of NumPy programming for performance, we will take a look at NumPy internals and how we can optimize them for performance. It turns out that the choices that we make when we install NumPy can make quite a difference in terms of speed and multiprocessing choices.

4.3 *Tuning NumPy's internal architecture for performance*

In this section, we will delve into NumPy and learn how to make sure it is configured for maximum performance. We start with an overview of NumPy's internal architecture.

A lot of NumPy's internals that make it a highly performant library are not implemented in pure Python. This is not really a surprise, is it? The nonpure Python parts, especially the external libraries, can be configured, and those choices can have a massive effect on performance.

The subject of this next section might be, I have to be honest, a bit dry for programmers who are mostly concerned with the Python side of the equation. If you trust that your NumPy library is in good shape (or you have no control over it), then feel free to skip to the last subsection, Threads in NumPy, as it is very actionable from a Python side. If you have control over all your Python stack, you like systems-based problems, and you want to make sure you are extracting all performance possible, read on.

4.3.1 *An overview of NumPy dependencies*

Many scientific libraries, Python-based or not, depend on two widely used library APIs for linear algebra: BLAS (Basic Library Algebra System) and LAPACK (Linear Algebra PACKage).

BLAS implements a set of basic functions to deal with arrays and matrices. The BLAS library will implement functions like vector addition and matrix multiplication.

On top of that, LAPACK implements several linear algebraic algorithms. For example, SVD (singular value decomposition) is fundamental for principal components analysis. Figure 4.11 depicts NumPy's architecture.

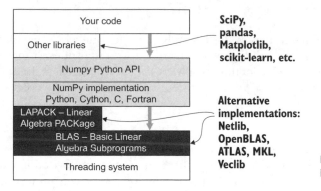

Figure 4.11 **The NumPy stack, including library dependencies**

There are many alternative implementations and the one you choose has operational consequences. For example, the standard LAPACK implementation available at netlib.org is nonthreaded and not very efficient on modern architectures. A common BLAS/LAPACK alternative is OpenBLAS, and another is Intel MKL; both are threaded. The way you use your computer resources can vary substantially if your NumPy implementation is threaded or not. For example, if you have a nonthreaded version, you can allocate as many processes as CPU cores as you want, but if the BLAS and LAPACK are multithreaded, you have to be careful not to overcommit CPU resources.

Thus, knowing which libraries your NumPy implementation depends on is important to understand the next optimization steps. In theory, you can detect dependencies by using:

```
import numpy as np

np.show_config()
```

In practice, you might have to go to your file system and package management system to understand what is going on. For example, when I link MKL using Anaconda Python, part of the output is:

```
lapack_opt_info:
    libraries = [
      'lapack', 'blas', 'lapack', 'blas', 'cblas', 'blas', 'cblas', 'blas']
    library_dirs = ['/home/tra/anaconda3/envs/book-mkl/lib']
    language = c
    define_macros = [('NO_ATLAS_INFO', 1), ('HAVE_CBLAS', None)]
    include_dirs = ['/home/tra/anaconda3/envs/book-mkl/include']
```

If you do this in your computer you might get lucky, but in my case, this is stupendously uninformative (book-mkl comes from the name I gave the environment; there is nothing to infer from it). To determine what I was using, I ended up doing `ls -l` `'/home/tra/anaconda3/envs/book-mkl/lib/libcblas.so*` and noticed this: `libcblas` `.so.3 • libmkl_rt.so`. Hence, MKL seems to be the linked library. You might have to research what libraries are being linked in your case.

> **TIP** NumPy not only uses BLAS and LAPACK but also provides a Python interface to them so that you can access them directly if you desire. Or rather, SciPy provides that interface.

SciPy is the sister library to NumPy, and they share a close historical relationship. SciPy implements higher-level functions than NumPy.

Because NumPy and SciPy share such a close relationship, you might be confused by their APIs. SciPy's documentation makes this very clear. Here is a verbatim copy of the SciPy linear algebra module, `scipy.linalg`, documentation:

```
See also: `numpy.linalg` for more linear algebra functions. Note that
although `scipy.linalg` imports most of them, identically named
functions from `scipy.linalg` may offer more or slightly differing
functionality.
```

So, sometimes SciPy imports, and re-exports, NumPy functions. Sometimes the APIs can be slightly different. Sometimes the implementations can be completely different.

If you want, you can access BLAS as LAPACK directly: you can find Python APIs in, respectively, `scipy.linalg.blas` and `scipy.linalg.lapack`. If you were thinking that it would make more sense to have this interface in NumPy and not SciPy, know that you are not alone.

You can thus make use of the libraries directly from Python, but it tends to be more useful, from a performance perspective, to use a library from a lower-level language. We will not discuss it here further, but we will revisit this in the Cython chapter.

Before we return to more practical concerns regarding NumPy internals, we still need to discuss the effect of our installation on performance by taking a look at Python distributions.

4.3.2   *How to tune NumPy in your Python distribution*

Here we'll explore some tips on how to make sure your NumPy is optimized for your distribution. It is impossible to cover all existing Python distributions against all operating systems so we will cover the standard Python one from python.org and Anaconda Python. We will be using Linux, given that this is also OS dependent. The comments will be made in a general way to be useful in other scenarios.

If you install NumPy on the standard distribution, you will most probably do it by using `pip install numpy`. This will only work if you have BLAS and LAPACK installed in your operating system. The problem becomes then *what* version is installed? The most common version is the original NetLib one, which is slow and not threaded. This will be terrible from a performance perspective. You will then have to make sure that (1) you install something more efficient like OpenBLAS or Intel's MKL, and (2) following the previously discussed np.show_config trail, you are linking the fastest BLAS/LAPACK version on your system.

If you use another distribution, it is quite possible that the packaging system of that distribution will take care of BLAS and LAPACK for you. Furthermore, the dependency install will be quite reasonable. For example, with Anaconda Python, when you do conda install numpy, at this point, you will probably be getting OpenBLAS, which is fine for most cases.

While the default installed with most scientific Python distributions is probably good enough, you might want to consider alternatives. Most distributions will allow you to do that. For example, with Anaconda, you can install NumPy with MKL by using:

```
conda create -n book-mkl blas=*=mkl
conda activate book-mkl
conda install numpy
```

We create a new environment called book-mkl just to be sure the current environment is untouched and maintains its defaults. We then install blas=*=mk, which specifies the MKL build of BLAS. With that at the core, we can go ahead and install NumPy.

> **TIP** For most use cases, you need to make sure you are not using the slow NetLib implementation of BLAS. In many situations, either OpenBLAS or MKL will be good enough. If you use other implementations, you will have to research them.

If you really need to squeeze the maximum performance possible out of your system, then you will have to benchmark the alternative implementations yourself. While there are some benchmarks available on the internet, you should devise a test for *your* specific code because different implementations have different strengths, and no size fits all in terms of benchmarking.

Now that you have your NumPy installation properly configured, let's make use of it.

4.3.3   *Threads in NumPy*

NumPY will be threaded or not depend on the BLAS/LAPACK implementations. Most implementations of BLAS/LAPACK libraries are threaded—the GIL is released by NumPy, so we are talking real parallelism here—and you can make use of them. But there are two caveats: (1) most, but not all, implementations are threaded, and (2)) you might actually prefer BLAS/LAPACK to be single-threaded.

Imagine the following scenario in our image processing application. You have thousands of images to process, and as such, you spawn 8 parallel processes on your eight-core machine. If your NumPy is threaded, you will end up with 8 processes, each running 8 threads for a total of 64 concurrent threads. We want the compound maximum to be just eight.

To be more efficient, it is quite common to have eight processes of one thread each rather than one process with eight threads. Remember that the non-BLAS code in each Python process will be single-threaded, so you only make use of the eight threads when you are inside NumPy/BLAS.

Sometimes we would like to reduce the number of threads used by BLAS and LAPACK, potentially to one. That should be easy, right? Unfortunately, there is no way to control the number of threads in NumPy directly. You have to configure the BLAS/ LAPACK implementation; hence, the code is not portable.

For NetLib, it is simple because it's single-threaded. However, you should avoid it anyway if you are looking for performance. OpenBLAS and Intel's MKL have different interfaces, as they can still have another lower-level dependency for doing the threading: they *might* be compiled and dependent on OpenMP. So you have to configure your BLAS/LAPACK implementation and *maybe* the multiprocessing library being used.

For OpenBLAS, before you call your Python code, do:

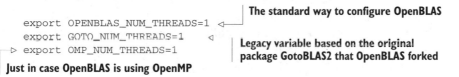

```
export OPENBLAS_NUM_THREADS=1
export GOTO_NUM_THREADS=1
export OMP_NUM_THREADS=1
```

The standard way to configure OpenBLAS

Legacy variable based on the original package GotoBLAS2 that OpenBLAS forked

Just in case OpenBLAS is using OpenMP

For MKL, you will need:

```
export MKL_NUM_THREADS=1
export OMP_NUM_THREADS=1
```

The standard way to configure MKL

Just in case OpenBLAS is using OpenMP

For other libraries, you will have to check yourself. Be careful with potential dependencies on lower-level threading libraries like OpenMP and their configuration requirements.

From a practical standpoint, there is still another problem: when you move your code from one computer to another—say, your development machine to production— the linked libraries might change. You can tune your initialization code to account for that or just set all variables for all libraries all the time, which is a more pragmatic solution.

THE TAKEAWAY

Perhaps looking into the details of NymPy's underlying libraries is not the most exciting takeaway from this book. But if you want an efficient use of NumPy and all the stack on top of it, it's important to investigate which libraries your NumPy implementation depends on, optimize NumPy for your Python distribution, and find out whether the underlying libraries use multithreading.

Summary

- Array views can be extremely efficient compared to copies, both in terms of memory and performance. They should be considered when possible.

- NumPy's view machinery is very flexible and can be used to render perspectives over existing data with very little computing and memory costs.

- Understanding shape (i.e., the number of elements across each dimension of an array) and strides (i.e., the number of bytes to step in each dimension to find the next element) is the basis of making the most use of views. Both shape and stride can be changed from view to view to present data differently.

- Array programming (i.e., doing declarative operations on whole arrays instead of using an imperative style element by element) can provide an orders of magnitude increase in performance. It should be used whenever possible.

- NumPy's broadcasting rules—the flexible way NumPy can use operators over arrays of different dimensions—allow for more efficient and elegant programming.

- The internal architecture of NumPy can be optimized for computing performance. NumPy depends on BLAS and LAPACK libraries, and there are different offerings available for those.

- Make sure you check that your NumPy implementation is using the most efficient libraries for your architecture.

- Parallel programming in NumPy can be tricky because the threading semantics of NumPy depends on the threading semantics of algebra libraries.

- Make sure you understand whether NumPy's underlying libraries make use of multithreading before you use Python-based multiprocessing on top of your NumPy implementation. If they don't use multithreading, you probably should change the underlying libraries. If they do, you should be careful not to use multiprocessing on top of NumPy calls that are themselves multithreaded.

- There is much more to be said about NumPy as it is *the* core of data analysis in Python. Given its importance, we will revisit the library in other chapters.

Part 2

Hardware

Part 2 of this book is concerned with developing Python solutions from the perspective of extracting maximum performance from commonly available hardware. We first discuss using lower-level languages that are closer to the hardware to extract more speed from the CPU. Namely, we concentrate on Cython, a superset of Python that generates efficient C code. We then focus on modern hardware architectures and how they sometimes require counterintuitive approaches to extract maximum performance. Our discussion includes how modern Python libraries, like NumExpr, are designed to take advantage of the hardware.

Re-implementing 5
critical code with Cython

This chapter covers

- How to re-implement Python code more efficiently
- Understanding Cython from a data processing perspective
- Profiling Cython code
- Using Cython to implement performant NumPy functions
- Releasing the GIL to implement true threaded parallelism

Python is slow. The standard implementation is slow, and the language's dynamic features pay a performance toll. Many Python libraries are performant precisely because they are partially implemented in lower-level languages, making available efficient data processing algorithms. But sometimes we will need to implement our own high-performance algorithms in *something* faster than Python. In this chapter, we will consider Cython, a superset of Python that is converted to C and is substantially more performant than Python.

There are plenty of alternatives other than Cython that can be integrated with Python for performance, so we will start with a brief overview of the available options. After that, we will delve into Cython properly.

If you never used Cython in the past, this introduction will give you enough background from a data analytics perspective and, hence, coupled with NumPy as it is the core library for data analysis. We will then discuss Cython profiling and optimization. We will also write Cython code in a way that allows NumPy to release the GIL and do parallel multithreading. We finish up with a general-purpose parallel threaded example where our Cython code will release the GIL itself.

But first, let's survey other alternatives to Cython. There might be an alternative that fits your profile better than Cython. This is especially true if you already know a low-level language like C or Rust.

5.1   *Overview of techniques for efficient code re-implementation*

Cython is one of the many alternatives to re-implement code in a more performant way. We will use it because it doesn't require us to learn substantially more than Python; Cython is a superset of Python. But you should be aware of alternatives, either because you might know some of them already or you have some constraint that requires you to use something else.

Alternatives come in four shapes (table 5.1):

- Existing libraries
- Numba
- Faster languages, such as Cython, C, and Rust
- Alternative Python implementations, such as PyPy, Jython, Iron Python, and Stackless Python

Table 5.1   Different approaches to efficient code re-implementation: libraries, faster languages, alternative Python implementations, and Numba

Libraries	Low-level languages	Alternative Python implementations	Just-in-time compilers
NumPy, SciPy, scikit-learn, PyTorch	C, Rust, Fortran, C++, Go, Cython	PyPy, IronPython, Jython, Stackless Python	Numba

NumPy is an example of an existing library that offers an efficient implementation of Python. There are many libraries implementing all kinds of functionality efficiently (e.g., pandas, scikit-learn). Before implementing your own code, be sure it's not done elsewhere in an existing library.

The second option worth considering is Numba. Numba is a just-in-time compiler that converts a subset of Python into fast native code. Numba is normally easier to use than another language, even Cython. There are Numba optimizations for a plethora of libraries, NumPy and pandas included, and to several architectures, including

GPUs. The reason we prioritize Cython in the book is that we have a *hidden agenda* of explaining how things work, and there is something *magical* about Numba. It tries to be intelligent with the code it generates. But in this book, we are trying to *understand* how more efficient code can be created; as such, we want to go a bit deeper than just a *magic* solution. In practical terms, you should not discard Numba; on the contrary, for most situations it might provide equal performance gains compared to Cython with less work. That being said, we will touch upon Numba throughout the book when it makes sense; indeed, appendix B is dedicated to it.

The path we follow in this chapter is re-implementing code in a lower-level language. It happens that the language, Cython, is very close to Python, but you have many alternatives. C is probably the most common, but the list is almost never-ending: C++, Rust, Julia, and so on. Cython makes your life easier in many ways because it is so tightly integrated with Python. If you decide to use another language, you will need to research how to link the code in the other language to Python. For C and C++, you might want to consider Python's built-in `ctypes` module or SWIG (https://swig.org).

Finally, you can consider using a Python implementation different from CPython. If you are tied to Java, you can consider Jython. If you are tied to .Net, then consider IronPython. The most realistic alternative to CPython is PyPy, which is faster because it is a just-in-time compiler. While PyPy is somewhat viable, it has limitations to which libraries work on it. At this stage, for most use cases, CPython is still the most realistic option.

Many of these alternatives can be used in conjunction with one another. The core for this chapter is tying an external library, NumPy, with a low-level language, Cython.

Now that you are aware of the most important alternatives, let's work on a concrete example using Cython. This will demonstrate how we can easily gain substantial computing performance with Cython.

5.2 *A whirlwind tour of Cython*

While this is not an introductory book, it's fair to assume there may be plenty of readers who have never used Cython. In this section, we'll use a small project to demonstrate the basics, with a focus on performance. We will avoid many details about Cython compilation that, while important, are not fundamental to understand performance problems. You will find plenty of tutorials on the internet covering topics such as Cython compilation and explicit memory management, and if you want to study the basics, Cython's project documentation is a good way to start (https://cython.readthedocs.io/en/latest/).

Here we will take the example from the previous chapter, image processing, and build a filter that takes an image, generates a grayscale version, and then darkens it according to a value on another image of the same size. Our first implementation might not necessarily be faster—we will get that later in the chapter—but it will introduce fundamental Cython concepts that are needed before we speed up the code. Figure 5.1 provides an example output to make this clear.

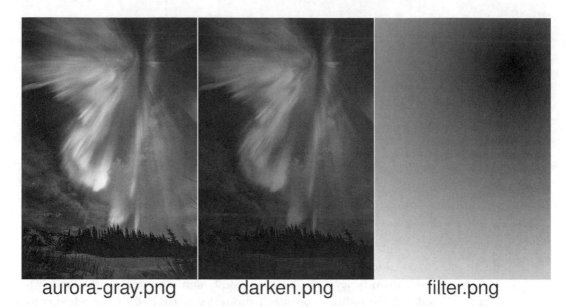

aurora-gray.png   darken.png   filter.png

Figure 5.1   The original image (here in grayscale), the processed image, and the filter applied

Let's go ahead and implement the filter code in Cython. For performance comparison, the code in the repository allows you to run a native Python implementation. For reference, the native Python code takes 35 s on my computer.

5.2.1   *A naive implementation in Cython*

Our image filter will use NumPy and Pillow for image processing as in the previous chapter. The image will be in color; hence, there will be three RGB components. The filter will vary between 0 to 255, with 0 being no darkening and 255 being completely black. Our code first converts each pixel to grayscale and then does the darkening.

We are now going to do the first implementation in Cython. We will divide the code into two parts: The Python code that *calls* the Cython code in a normal `.py` file and the Cython code proper, which is written in a file with a `.pyx` extension. `.pyx` comes from Pyrex, the project from which Cython was originally forked. The Python code is in `05-cython/sec1-intro/apply_filter.py`:

The only conceptually new piece in the previous code is related to `pyximport`. This will take care of compiling and linking the Cython code.

> ### Linking Cython code
>
> Remember that Cython is a superset of Python, which compiles to C, making the code available as a foreign extension. It's not as easy as simply importing a native Python module.
>
> There are several ways to take care of the whole process, as referenced in the Cython documentation. We won't go into all of them here, but I will point out three approaches of note:
>
> - The approach used here, `pyximport`, will take care of compiling the code and linking it in a way that is transparent and easy. Every time you import a Cython module, the code might be converted to C, compiled, and linked, and as such, you pay a performance price at startup, but only at startup. Just make sure that when you are profiling, you discount this time in some way.
> - If you are using Jupyter/IPython Notebook, the `%cython` magic is available. See either the Cython or IPython documentation for details.
> - Directly calling `cython` over the `.pyx` file. This approach will require us to do our own linking. We will use it later in the chapter, but just to take a peek at the generated code.
>
> If you are in Jupyter or more generally in IPython, `%cython` takes care of everything for you, and it's really easy; I recommend it if you are working with Jupyter or IPython. But if you plan to distribute the code to general Python users, you cannot use it.
>
> Calling `cython` directly is mostly useful to inspect the C code. There is no real pragmatic reason to do it for any other use case.
>
> When putting your code in production or preparing to distribute it to users, other alternatives should be used. Most probably you will have to precompile your Cython code for the target architectures, as requiring your users to have a complete C compiler stack is normally asking for too much. Preparing code for distribution is a fairly complex subject, which we will not address here, and for the purposes of this book, it's not very relevant.

The Cython code is, for now, *exactly the same* as the Python version. It is just in a pyx file (`05-cython/sec2-intro/cyfilter.pyx`):

```
#cython: language_level=3        ◁── The first line is not really a
                                     comment. It is instructing Cython
import numpy as np                   to compile for Python version 3.

def darken_naive(image, darken_filter):
    nrows, ncols, _rgb_3 - image.shape
    dark_image = np.empty(shape=(nrows, ncols), dtype=np.uint8)
    for row in range(nrows):
        for col in range(ncols):
            pixel = image[row, col]
```

```
        mean = np.mean(pixel)
        dark_pixel = darken_filter[row, col]
        dark_image[row, col] = int(mean * (255 - dark_pixel) / 255)
    return dark_image
```

Save for the first line and the function name, the code is the same as the Python version. If you call the Python top-level file, you will be sorely disappointed. On my computer, it took 33 s. Just 2 s less than the native Python version. In the next section, we will write something much faster and determine why the previous version is slow.

Cython as a compiled language

Cython is a compiled language, not interpreted as Python. That has many consequences; one of them regards where you find certain types of errors. For example, this code

```
def so_wrong():
    return a + 1
```

will fail *only* at run time in Python, so you can deploy it in production and be oblivious to the problem. But it will immediately fail when you try to compile it as a Cython program. In this regard, Cython helps a bit with catching bugs, but be prepared for the Cython compiler to nag you about errors that Python would not catch.

5.2.2   *Using Cython annotations to increase performance*

Before we dig into the reasons why the previous code is slow, let's produce a faster version so that we have something to compare with. The faster version depends on using the Cython annotation system:

```
#cython: language_level=3        We import
import numpy as np               C-level definitions
cimport numpy as cnp    ◁────┘   for NumPy.


def darken_annotated(
        cnp.ndarray[cnp.uint8_t, ndim=3] image, ◁
        cnp.ndarray[cnp.uint8_t, ndim=2] darken_filter):       ◁
    cdef int nrows = image.shape[0]    ◁
    cdef int ncols = image.shape[1]
    cdef cnp.uint8_t dark_pixel, mean
    cdef cnp.ndarray[np.uint8_t] pixel

    cdef cnp.ndarray[cnp.uint8_t, ndim=2]
      dark_image = np.empty(shape=(nrows, ncols), dtype=np.uint8)
    for row in range(nrows):
        for col in range(ncols):
            pixel = image[row, col]
            mean = (pixel[0] + pixel[1] + pixel[2]) // 3     ◁
            dark_pixel = darken_filter[row, col]
            dark_image[row, col] = mean * (255 - dark_pixel) // 255
    return dark_image
```

We import C-level definitions for NumPy.

We type the first parameter as a C-level NumPy array with three dimensions; remember that for a color image, we have three components (RGB) per pixel. The type is a C-level unsigned integer of 8 bits.

The second parameter is a two-dimensional array of 8-bit unsigned integers.

We also type all local variables. Tuple assignment is sometimes not possible with Cython, so we split the tuple assignment into two.

Typing of variables must be done at the beginning of the function, so we define the inner loop variables before we enter it.

This is a slightly more efficient way to compute a mean.

The really important difference in this code is the use of Cython annotations. For example, nrows becomes cdef int nrows: we inform Cython that the variable is of the type int. This definition will be operative at the C level as Cython code is converted to C. It is possible to have C-level definitions of external libraries like NumPy; that is exactly what cimport numpy as cnp imports. Then we can type arrays.

> **WARNING** Cython-level–type annotations are completely different from modern Python-level annotations, and the two have no relation to each other.

Note that save for the mean calculation and the tuple assignment split, the code is exactly the same. Namely, the two for loops have the same complexity.

Run time falls from ~30 s in the native Python version to 1.5 s—20 times faster. Now we are getting somewhere.[1]

> **TIP** Annotate *all* your Cython variables.

This code can still be made several times faster. We will discuss techniques for that later in the chapter. But for now, we will turn our attention to *understanding* why the annotations are so important.

5.2.3 *Why annotations are fundamental to performance*

Why are annotations so important for performance? To answer that, we need to look at the C-generated code for our functions. Even if you do not know C, there is no reason to be afraid: reading C is substantially easier than writing it, and you will get the gist of it easily.

We will use a trivial example: add 4 to a number. Here is the code with and without annotations (this code is in 05-cython/sec2-intro/add4.pyx):

```
#cython: language_level=3

def add4(my_number):
    i = my_number + 4
    return i

def add4_annotated(int my_number):
    cdef int i
    i = my_number + 4
    return i
```

Simple right? To be able to see the C-generated code, we will run Cython directly:

```
cython add4.pyx
```

---

[1] For details on how to measure time, see chapter 2. With IPython/Jupyter, you can use the %timeit magic. With standard Python, you can use the timeit module. Or, as I did in this case, I simply timed the run time of the process. In some cases, a rough approximation can be a good start.

This will generate a C file called add4.c. My version of Cython has almost 3,000 lines. No reason to panic: most of it is boilerplate, and Cython makes it very easy to find our code and learn what is generated. You can find every line of your code inside C comments so that you know what is being generated. For example, this is generated by Cython:

```
/* "add4.pyx":9
 *
 *
 * def add4_annotated(int my_number):
 *     cdef int i
 *     i = my_number + 4
 */
```

For each of our functions, Cython generates two C functions: A Python wrapper—responsible for interfacing between Python and C—and the function implementation proper.

So, for add4, we have a C wrapper, which is:

```
static PyObject *__pyx_pw_4add4_1add4(
  PyObject *__pyx_self, PyObject *__pyx_v_my_number)
```

If you think in terms of Python, not C or Cython, this makes sense: the function returns a Python object, static PyObject *. self is also a Python object, PyObject *__pyx_self, and the parameter is PyObject *__pyx_v_my_number. Python only knows objects.

Here is the signature for the wrapper of add4_annotated:

```
static PyObject *__pyx_pw_4add4_3add4_annotated(
  PyObject *__pyx_self, PyObject *__pyx_arg_a) {
```

The types are *exactly the same*, and this makes sense: remember that Python only sees objects. Thus, at the Python interface level, the functions are the same.

Both wrappers do a lot of packing and unpacking and then call the implementations. Here is the signature for the implementation of add4:

```
static PyObject *__pyx_pf_4add4_add4(
  CYTHON_UNUSED PyObject *__pyx_self, PyObject *__pyx_v_my_number)
```

The types are mostly the same. This makes sense as we did not annotate the function and Cython to create code for the most general case.

Here is the function signature for add4_annotated:

```
static PyObject *__pyx_pf_4add4_2add4_annotated(
  CYTHON_UNUSED PyObject *__pyx_self, int __pyx_v_my_number) {
----
```

Note that the type my_number is now a native C type, not a Python object, int __pyx_v_my_number.

If you look at the wrapper for both functions, you will notice that the wrapper for the annotated function is more complicated, with a lot of packing and unpacking of types. The non-annotated wrapper can just pass parameters to the implementation as it deals with Python objects. But the annotated wrapper must manage the Python object to int conversions.

After all these preliminaries, we arrive at the fundamental problem: the implementation of i = my_number + 4. This is what we have for the non-annotated version:

```
__pyx_t_1 = __Pyx_PyInt_AddObjC(__pyx_v_my_number, __pyx_int_4, 4, 0, 0);
  if (unlikely(!__pyx_t_1)) __PYX_ERR(0, 5, __pyx_L1_error)
__Pyx_GOTREF(__pyx_t_1);
__pyx_v_i = __pyx_t_1;
__pyx_t_1 = 0;
```

This code is calling the function __Pyx_PyInt_AddObjC to add an integer to an object. This function is defined in the source code add4.c. You are invited to inspect that monstrosity. You will find a lot of calls to the CPython functions, a lot of C ifs, and, in some cases, even a goto call. Remember that all this is in service of adding 4 to a variable. It is extremely burdensome.

There is another serious problem with this code: because we are dealing with Python objects, Cython cannot release the GIL. Python code is GIL bound, but lower-level code can, in certain circumstances, release the GIL. As this code stands, the GIL cannot be released, and as such, we cannot have parallel threads.

In reality, the biggest problem is the former—the implementation of the sum—as it is mostly spent on managing Python objects. Even if we could, although we can't, make a parallel version of it, the loss from Python manipulation of the sum would be much bigger than the gain from using a handful of parallel cores.

Without further ado, here is the annotated version from add4_annotated:

```
__pyx_v_i = (__pyx_v_my_number + 4)
```

This is a simple C-level addition and, as such, should be *orders of magnitude faster* than the non-annotated version.

THE TAKEAWAY

Annotations help Cython to remove a lot of CPython infrastructure from the C version of your code. As such, annotated Cython will run faster than non-annotated Cython, and I recommend using annotated Cython whenever possible.

5.2.4 *Adding typing to function returns*

You can also type function returns like this:

```
cdef int add4_annotated_cret(int my_number):
    return my_number + 4
```

Notice that not only the int return type but also that the function are now defined using cdef and not def. This is a function that can only be called from C. If you try to call this from Python, it will not work because there is no wrapper. What is the advantage of this? For Cython functions that are called *only* from other Cython functions, it is possible to declare a function to be usable from Python and Cython (i.e., a different interface will be used if called from Python or Cython):

```
---
cpdef int add4_annotated_cpret(int my_number):
    return add4_annotated_cret(my_number)
----
```

In this case, you get both the wrapper and the low-level implementation.

So you have three ways of declaring a function: Cython only, which interfaces with cdef; both Python and Cython, which interface with cpdef; and Python only, which interfaces with def. Any time you need to go through a Python native interface, you are sure to pay a performance price. When you go through a Cython-only interface, your burden will be smaller. (As we have seen in the previous section, a def function generates both levels, but that is an implementation detail that is not assured if you use def.)

Why not always use cpdef instead of def and cdef? Sometimes you want to use def as cpdef and cdef to impose extra restrictions on the function implementation and sometimes you have an explicit need to add annotations. cdef is needed when you are using types that Python cannot understand, for example, C pointers written in Cython code.

THE TAKEAWAY

Always annotate types with Cython; the upside is tremendous with no downside other than the hassle of writing the annotations. If possible, use cdef. If it's not possible, consider having the code refactored so that you have the Python linked part in a def/cpdef and the computationally intensive part in a cdef.

Now that we have a deeper understanding of *why* annotations are important for performance, let's continue to fine-tune our code by profiling our Cython code. ,

5.3   *Profiling Cython code*

Let's get back to our Cython-based image filtering code. While it is substantially faster than the pure Python implementation, it still *feels* a bit slow. After all, it's more than 1 s to apply a trivial filter. While our intuition serves us well to suspect there is a problem, as we noted in chapter 2, gut feelings with performance analysis tend to deliver bad results, so we will revisit profiling from a Cython perspective to rigorously find remaining bottlenecks.

Cython profiling is well integrated with that of native Python. The profiling techniques of chapter 2 can readily be used here. As such, we will line profile our function to find the sources of delay.

5.3.1 *Using Python's built-in profiling infrastructure*

We will start with using the built-in profiling infrastructure. The first thing we need to do is to annotate our Cython code, so we generate profilable code. This is quite simple to do. Here are the annotations for our darkened annotated function (the code is in `05-cython/sec3-profiling/cython_prof.py`):

```
# cython: profile=True        ◁──────  We tell Cython that we want
import numpy as np                     our code to be profiled.

cimport cython
cimport numpy as cnp

def darken_annotated(
        cnp.ndarray[cnp.uint8_t, ndim=3] image,
        cnp.ndarray[cnp.uint8_t, ndim=2] darken_filter):
    cdef int nrows = image.shape[0]
...
```

It is as simple as adding the global directive in the code. If, for some reason, you don't want to instrument a specific function in your file, just add `@cython.profile(False)`.

As a variation from the profiling example in chapter 2, let's use the built-in `pstat` module to get profiling statistics. Here is our caller function (see `code/05-cython/sec3-profiling/apply_filter_prof.py`):

```
import cProfile    ◁──────  We will take care of running the
import pstats      ◁──────  profiling code from within.
import pyximport
                           The pstats module processes
import numpy as np         the output of the profiler.
from PIL import Image

pyximport.install(
    setup_args={
        'include_dirs': np.get_include()})

import cyfilter_prof as cyfilter

image = Image.open("../../04-numpy/aurora.jpg")
gray_filter = Image.open("../filter.png").convert("L")
image_arr, gray_arr = np.array(image), np.array(gray_filter)

# We just want to profile this                                              We call the
cProfile.run("cyfilter.darken_annotated(image_arr, gray_arr)",             profiler on
  "apply_filter.prof")                      ◁──────────────                 our function.
s = pstats.Stats("apply_filter.prof")
s.strip_dirs().sort_stats("time").print_stats()  ◁───  We use the pstats module to
                                                       print the collected statistics.
```

With regard to profiling, there is nothing in this code that is Cython specific. The output is:

```
Tue May 10 14:43:03 2022     apply_filter.prof

        5 function calls in 0.707 seconds

   Ordered by: internal time

   ncalls  tottime  percall  cumtime  percall filename:lineno(function)
        1    0.707    0.707    0.707    0.707 cyfilter_prof.pyx:9
                                             (darken_annotated)
        1    0.000    0.000    0.707    0.707 {built-in method
                                               builtins.exec}
        1    0.000    0.000    0.707    0.707 <string>:1(<module>)
        1    0.000    0.000    0.707    0.707
                                     {cyfilter_prof.darken_annotated}
        1    0.000    0.000    0.000    0.000 {method 'disable' of
                                             '_lsprof.Profiler' objects}
```

Details about the output are discussed in chapter 2. As we saw in chapter 2 as well, built-in profiling is sometimes not as informative as we would like. With this in mind, let's revisit line profiling, now in the context of Cython.

5.3.2 *Using line_profiler*

We will use the `line_profiler` module, just like in chapter 2. For that, we have to instruct Cython to instrument our code for line profiling (see `05-cython/sec3-profiling/cython_lprof.py` in the repository for details):

```
# cython: linetrace=True      ◁───┐   We need Python-like
# cython: binding=True         ◁───┘   bindings.
# cython: language_level=3
import numpy as np                       We tell Cython to generate
cimport cython                           line-tracing code.
cimport numpy as cnp

cpdef darken_annotated(
        cnp.ndarray[cnp.uint8_t, ndim=3] image,
        cnp.ndarray[cnp.uint8_t, ndim=2] darken_filter):
    cdef int nrows = image.shape[0]  # Explain
    cdef int ncols = image.shape[1]
    cdef cnp.uint8_t dark_pixel
    cdef cnp.uint8_t mean  # define here
    cdef cnp.ndarray[cnp.uint8_t] pixel
    cdef cnp.ndarray[cnp.uint8_t, ndim=2]
      dark_image = np.empty(shape=(nrows, ncols), dtype=np.uint8)
    for row in range(nrows):
        for col in range(ncols):
            pixel = image[row, col]
            mean = (pixel[0] + pixel[1] + pixel[2]) // 3
            dark_pixel = darken_filter[row, col]
            dark_image[row, col] = mean * (255 - dark_pixel) // 255
    return dark_image
```

The only change we need is to instruct Cython to generate the line-tracing instrumentation. We use the directive `# cython: linetrace=True` to accomplish that. You can also activate line tracing on a function-by-function basis by not using the directive and instead annotating each function that you want to profile:

```
@cython.binding(True)
@cython.linetrace(True)
```

You might remember from chapter 2 that line tracing is very slow. For that reason, Cython requires that you not only annotate your Cython code with `linetrace` but also that you explicitly request tracing when you *use* the code. To see this in action, let's check the code that calls this function (i.e., the Python side):

```
import pyximport
import line_profiler        ◁──── We import line_profiler.

import numpy as np
from PIL import Image

pyximport.install(
    language level=3,
    setup_args={
        'options': {"build_ext":        We need to compile the C code
          {"define": 'CYTHON_TRACE'}},  ◁─┘ with the CYTHON_TRACE macro.
        'include_dirs': np.get_include()})

import cyfilter_lprof as cyfilter

image = Image.open("../../04-numpy/aurora.jpg")
gray_filter = Image.open("../filter.png").convert("L")
image_arr, gray_arr = np.array(image), np.array(gray_filter)

profile = line_profiler.LineProfiler(        We will explicitly call line_profiler here.
   cyfilter.darken_annotated)  ◁───────
profile.runcall(cyfilter.darken_annotated, image_arr, gray_arr)
profile.print_stats()
```

We must not forget to activate the C code that does the instrumentation. The C code is wrapped in C macros and is only compiled if the directive `CYTHON_TRACE` is passed to the compiler. We do this by instructing pyximport via the distutils system. Both the C macro system and the Python building infrastructure are beyond the scope of this book. But you have to make sure that the `CYTHON_TRACE` macro is defined in whatever system you use to compile your C code—remember, pyximport is one of several options.

Here we instrument the `line_profiler` machinery directly from our code; in chapter 2, we used a different approach by calling our code with `kernprof`. We create the `LineProfiler` object, call `darken_annotate` inside it, and print the statistics. As an exercise, before we look at the result, think about *your expectations* of where the bottleneck is. Then have a look at the following figure.

```
Total time: 3.58894 s
File: cyfilter_lprof.pyx
Function: darken_annotated at line 11

Line #      Hits         Time  Per Hit   % Time  Line Contents
==============================================================
    11                                           cpdef darken_annotated(
    12                                               cnp.ndarray[cnp.uint8_t, ndim=3] image,
    13                                               cnp.ndarray[cnp.uint8_t, ndim=2] darken_filter):
    14         1          2.0      2.0      0.0       cdef int nrows = image.shape[0]  # Explain
    15         1          0.0      0.0      0.0       cdef int ncols = image.shape[1]
    16                                               cdef cnp.uint8_t dark_pixel
    17                                               cdef cnp.uint8_t mean   # define here
    18                                               cdef cnp.ndarray[cnp.uint8_t] pixel
    19         1          7.0      7.0      0.0       cdef cnp.ndarray[cnp.uint8_t, ndim=2] dark_image = np.empty(shape=(nrows, ncols), dtype=np.uint8)
    20         1          0.0      0.0      0.0       for row in range(nrows):
    21      2048        337.0      0.2      0.0           for col in range(ncols):
    22   2799616    2151338.0      0.8     59.9               pixel = image[row, col]
    23   2799616     481380.0      0.2     13.4               mean = (pixel[0] + pixel[1] + pixel[2]) // 3
    24   2799616     477328.0      0.2     13.3               dark_pixel = darken_filter[row, col]
    25   2799616     478551.0      0.2     13.3               dark_image[row, col] = mean * (255 - dark_pixel) // 255
    26         1          1.0      1.0      0.0       return dark_image
```

The run time for our function is 3.5 s; this is substantially more than the 1.5 s for the whole run before. Remember that line profiling is very expensive and incurs overhead. We should not compare the *absolute* timings of standard profiling with line profiling, as they are expected to be different. We also need to be a bit more patient while profiling.

The apparently innocent assignment `pixel = image[row, col]` is taking 60% of the time. Was this what you expected?

The easiest way to understand what is slowing us down is again to do `cython cyfilter_lprof.py` and have a look at the generated code. This C-analysis case is easier than the first example presented; in that case, we can use a web report produced by Cython with `cython -a cyfilter_lprof.py`. An HTML file is created—cyfilter_lprof.html—and can be opened with any web browser. Figure 5.2 shows the main view for our function. You can click each line and see which C code is generated for it. The grayed-out lines (in the browser version they would be in yellow) hint at interactions with the Python machinery: if the Python machinery is required you can bet that performance will suffer.

```
Generated by Cython 0.29.21

Yellow lines hint at Python interaction.
Click on a line that starts with a "+" to see the C code that Cython generated for it.

Raw output: cyfilter_lprof.c

+01: # cython: language_level=3
 02: # cython: linetrace=True
 03: # cython: binding=True
+04: import numpy as np
 05: cimport cython
 06: cimport numpy as cnp
 07:
 08:
 09: @cython.binding(True)
 10: @cython.linetrace(True)
+11: cpdef darken_annotated(
 12:         cnp.ndarray[cnp.uint8_t, ndim=3] image,
 13:         cnp.ndarray[cnp.uint8_t, ndim=2] darken_filter):
+14:     cdef int nrows = image.shape[0]  # Explain
+15:     cdef int ncols = image.shape[1]
 16:     cdef cnp.uint8_t dark_pixel
 17:     cdef cnp.uint8_t mean   # define here
 18:     cdef cnp.ndarray[cnp.uint8_t] pixel
+19:     cdef cnp.ndarray[cnp.uint8_t, ndim=2] dark_image = np.empty(shape=(nrows, ncols), dtype=np.uint8)
+20:     for row in range(nrows):
+21:         for col in range(ncols):
+22:             pixel = image[row, col]
+23:             mean = (pixel[0] + pixel[1] + pixel[2]) // 3
+24:             dark_pixel = darken_filter[row, col]
+25:             dark_image[row, col] = mean * (255 - dark_pixel) // 255
+26:     return dark_image
```

Figure 5.2   **The web output for cyfilter_lprof.html. The lines that are grayed out (in the browser version they would be in yellow) hint at interactions with Python.**

If you expand line 22—our "innocent" assignment of `pixel = image[row, col]`—you will see that there is much more there than just an assignment. There are many C calls that raise many performance flags: `__Pyx_PyInt_From_int`, `PyTuple_New`, `__Pyx_PyObject_GetItem`, and `__Pyx_SafeReleaseBuffer` all seem to be invoking a lot of potentially slow stuff for something that should be a simple assignment, at least at the C level.

THE TAKEAWAY

While we informed Cython of lower-level types with our previous Cython annotations, the profiling process indicates that it is still manipulating NumPy arrays. If the code operations are interacting with Python objects like NumPy arrays, the whole Python machinery is still required to run the code. Involving that machinery is a sure way to drag down your performance rates.

The question then becomes: can we look at these arrays more efficiently and make the code for an innocent assignment simpler? It turns out we can.

5.4 *Optimizing array access with Cython memoryviews*

To accelerate our code, we need to reduce the interaction with Python objects to the least amount possible—ideally, zero. We need to remove Python built-ins *and* Python views of NumPy arrays. In our current example, we still have our arrays as Python objects, and we need to change that.

It turns out that Cython has a concept of memoryview for NumPy arrays, which is somewhat similar to the equally named concept that we explored in the previous chapter. It is possible for Cython to directly access the raw array representation without using Python's object machinery. We will separate our Cython code into two functions: one to deal with Python objects, which cannot ever be that fast, and another to work at C-level speeds. So one receives the NumPy arrays and prepares the memoryviews, and the other applies the image filter (see `05-cython/sec4-memoryview` in the repository). Let's start with the function that takes NumPy arrays and prepares memoryviews:

```
cpdef darken_annotated(
        cnp.ndarray[cnp.uint8_t, ndim=3] image,
        cnp.ndarray[cnp.uint8_t, ndim=2] darken_filter):
    cdef int nrows = image.shape[0]
    cdef int ncols = image.shape[1]
    cdef cnp.ndarray[cnp.uint8_t, ndim=2] dark_image =
      np.empty(shape=(nrows, ncols), dtype=np.uint8)
    cdef cnp.uint8_t[:,:] dark_image_mv
    cdef cnp.uint8_t [:,:,:] image_mv
    cdef cnp.uint8_t[:,:] darken_filter_mv
    dark_image_mv = dark_image
    darken_filter_mv = darken_filter
    image_mv = image
    darken_annotated_mv(image_mv,
      darken_filter_mv, dark_image_mv)
    return dark_image
```

This declares a memory view that will point to dark_image raw data.

Here we make Cython resolve the view to the raw data of the NumPy array.

Finally, we call a new function, darken_annotated_mv, that deals with views only.

Notice the syntax to declare memoryviews: it has a C type and the dimensionality needs to be known (e.g., `[:,:,:]` for the three dimensions of `image`). Cython will make sure that the memoryview variables point to the raw data of the array with correct strides and shapes.

Lets now look at the new inner function:

```
cpdef darken_annotated_mv(
        cnp.uint8_t[:,:,:] image_mv,       ◁———  We change the type of the
        cnp.uint8_t[:,:] darken_filter_mv,        input parameters from
        cnp.uint8_t[:,:] dark_image_mv):   ◁———   Numpy arrays to views.
    cdef int nrows = image_mv.shape[0]
    cdef int ncols = image_mv.shape[1]            ◁——— The output is now a parameter.
    cdef cnp.uint8_t dark_pixel
    cdef cnp.uint8_t mean   # define here
    cdef cnp.uint8_t[:] pixel
    for row in range(nrows):
        for col in range(ncols):
            pixel = image_mv[row, col]
            mean = (pixel[0] + pixel[1] + pixel[2]) // 3
            dark_pixel = darken_filter_mv[row, col]
            dark_image_mv[row, col] = mean * (255 - dark_pixel) // 255
```

The code ends up being very similar to the original version. The input types are changed from arrays to memoryviews, and just to have a cleaner version, we are passing the output view as a parameter.

The performance gets a bit better from line profiling, as shown in the following figure.

```
Total time: 1.82865 s
File: cyfilter_mv.pyx
Function: darken_annotated_mv at line 10

Line #      Hits         Time  Per Hit   % Time  Line Contents
==============================================================
    10                                           cpdef darken_annotated_mv(
    11                                               cnp.uint8_t[:,:,:] image_mv,
    12                                               cnp.uint8_t[:,:] darken_filter_mv,
    13                                               cnp.uint8_t[:,:] dark_image_mv):
    14         1          2.0      2.0      0.0     cdef int nrows = image_mv.shape[0]
    15         1          2.0      2.0      0.0     cdef int ncols = image_mv.shape[1]
    16                                             cdef cnp.uint8_t dark_pixel
    17                                             cdef cnp.uint8_t mean   # define here
    18                                             cdef cnp.uint8_t[:] pixel
    19         1          0.0      0.0      0.0     for row in range(nrows):
    20      2048        358.0      0.2      0.0         for col in range(ncols):
    21   2799616     469718.0      0.2     25.7             pixel = image_mv[row, col]  <1>
    22   2799616     452761.0      0.2     24.8             mean = (pixel[0] + pixel[1] + pixel[2]) // 3
    23   2799616     452165.0      0.2     24.7             dark_pixel = darken_filter_mv[row, col]
    24   2799616     453647.0      0.2     24.8             dark_image_mv[row, col] = mean * (255 - dark_pixel) // 255
```

It is now 50% faster, and the "innocent" assignment `pixel = image_mv[row, col]` is now more innocent in the sense that it requires no Python object management code. However, insight suggests that it still takes way too much time for a simple image manipulation.

It turns out that a lot of Python interactions are still happening in this code. If we run `cython -a`, generating a web page for the code that colors each code line with the amount of Python interactions, we get a lot of marked interactions as shown in figure 5.3.

```
+09: cpdef darken_annotated_mv(
 10:         cnp.uint8_t[:,:,:] image_mv,
 11:         cnp.uint8_t[:,:] darken_filter_mv,
 12:         cnp.uint8_t[:,:] dark_image_mv):
+13:     cdef int nrows = image_mv.shape[0]
+14:     cdef int ncols = image_mv.shape[1]
 15:     cdef cnp.uint8_t dark_pixel
 16:     cdef cnp.uint8_t mean    # define here
 17:     cdef cnp.uint8_t[:] pixel
+18:     for row in range(nrows):
+19:         for col in range(ncols):
+20:             pixel = image_mv[row, col]
+21:             mean = (pixel[0] + pixel[1] + pixel[2]) // 3
+22:             dark_pixel = darken_filter_mv[row, col]
+23:             dark_image_mv[row, col] = mean * (255 - dark_pixel) // 255
 24:
```

Figure 5.3 The web output for our memoryview-based function. The lines that are grayed out (in the browser version they would be in yellow) hint at interactions with Python.

5.4.1 The takeaway

It is generally worth the time to create memoryviews of NumPy arrays, which will allow Cython to interact with raw array representations and avoid the Python machinery. The performance improvements can be significant. But further profiling indicates we are still interacting with the machinery, thus still performing suboptimally.

Our next question then is: can we get rid of the remaining (Python) interactions to substantially optimize our code? The answer again is, yes we can.

5.4.2 Cleaning up all internal interactions with Python

There are three types of interactions that are responsible for `cython -a`, marking the lines in figure 5.3, still going on:

- We have a `cpdef` function that generates a C function *with* a Python stub. We can replace that with a `cdef`.
- The function is implicitly returning a `None` object as expected from all Python functions. This means managing a Python object, even if only a `None`.
- The NumPy memoryview is still trying to help you with bounds checking (i.e., if you put an index that is not valid the Python exception machinery will be activated).

Let's sort out all these problems in one fell swoop. We simply need to change the function definition:

```
                                    ┌─── We deactivate bounds checking.
@cython.boundscheck(False)  ◄───────┘
cdef void darken_annotated_mv(  ◄─────────┐  We have a cdef (i.e., no Python stub), and
        cnp.uint8_t[:,:,:] image_mv,      │  we declare the return type as C void.
        cnp.uint8_t[:,:] darken_filter_mv,
        cnp.uint8_t[:,:] dark_image_mv) nogil:  ◄───┐
                                                    │ We can now tell Cython that this
                                                    │ function can release the GIL.
```

We will revisit bounds checking later; in a general case, your code can now crash without the bounds-checking guard rails. It is not a problem in this case, but later in the chapter, we will see how this can be a problem.

The `nogil` annotation is optional; there is nothing to be gained at this stage. This will allow us to have real parallelism, a subject we will return to later in the chapter. Cython would complain if you have this annotation and have not removed all Python connections. So it's only possible to do it because of all the other changes we have done.

On my computer, a laptop with an Intel i5 CPU at 1.6GHz, this now takes 0.04 s. Remember that we started with 35 s for a native Python implementation and 18 s for a naive Cython one.

THE TAKEAWAY

To remove the last lingering interactions between Cython and Python, we can change the function definition to avoid making or returning calls with a Python function. By combining this process with annotating Cython code, adding typing to function returns, and using memoryviews instead of raw NumPy arrays, we have a strategy for eliminating the interactions between the faster Cython and the slower Python.

Later, we will discuss bounds checking and other NumPy optimizations. We will also discuss parallelism, but for now, we will visit implementing NumPy universal functions in Cython. This can be quite useful as universal functions are amenable to NumPy broadcasting rules.

5.5   *Writing NumPy generalized universal functions in Cython*

We are now going to use an alternative solution to the image filtering problem by writing a universal function in Cython. Remember from the previous chapter that the universal function machinery makes life easier by providing goodies like broadcasting. Universal functions come with all these extra perks and, as we will see later, are somewhat akin to the programming paradigm GPU. However, remember that they are not universal computing solutions, and we will see such an example in the next section.

We also learned in chapter 4 that universal functions operate on an element-by-element basis. In our case, that will mean pixel by pixel. Our code will be composed of two parts: the universal function and the code to register it. Let's start with the universal function (code is available in the repository in `05-cython/sec5-ufunc`):

```
# cython: language_level=3
import numpy as np
cimport cython
cimport numpy as cnp


cdef void darken_pixel(
        cnp.uint8_t* image_pixel,
        cnp.uint8_t* darken_filter_pixel,
        cnp.uint8_t* dark_image_pixel) nogil:
```

Notice the usage of pointer notation (*).

```
cdef cnp.uint8_t mean
mean = (image_pixel[0] + image_pixel[1] + image_pixel[2]) // 3
dark_image_pixel[0] = mean * (255 - darken_filter_pixel[0]) // 255
```

We are now operating on a pixel-by-pixel basis so the code is simpler as we do not have the for loops over the whole array/image.

The fundamental difference is that instead of passing a number, cnp.unit8_t, a *pointer* to a number is passed, cnp.uint8_t *. This concept may be new to you if you are not used to lower-level languages like C. For our practical purposes, this doesn't have many consequences, but for more complex examples, you are directed to Cython's documentation. The only consequence of significance is that the output will be written to an "input variable." Finally, the function is marked as nogil, allowing it to run in parallel: no Python objects are being referred, so the GIL can be released by a parallel executor.

Our universal function, as was the case in the previous chapter, is a *general* universal function because the first parameter, image_pixel, is not a primitive type but an array: the pixel in color has three RGB components.

We now need to *wrap* our (general) universal function. Sadly, the boilerplate is a bit long and slightly complicated:

```
cdef cnp.PyUFuncGenericFunction loop_func[1]        We need a variable to specify the
cdef char all_types[3]              ◁───            types of all inputs and outputs.
cdef void *funcs[1]          ◁───────
                                                    All functions that implement
                                                    the universal function
loop_func[0] = cnp.PyUFunc_FF_F

all_types[0] = cnp.NPY_UINT8    ◁─────      We specify the types for our two
all_types[1] = cnp.NPY_UINT8                input and one output parameters.
all_types[2] = cnp.NPY_UINT8
                                            The list of functions that implements
                                            the universal function
funcs[0] = <void*>darken_pixel     ◁────

darken = cnp.PyUFunc_FromFuncAndDataAndSignature(   ◁──┐   Creates the wrapped
    loop_func, funcs, all_types,                          universal function
    1,
    2,    ◁───
    1,    ◁───
    0,          Number of output parameters
    "darken",
    "Darken a pixel", 0
    "(n),()->()"    ◁──────   The Numpy signature
)
```

(Annotations: "Number of input types" points to the `1,`; "Number of input parameters" points to the `2,`.)

We need to specify the data types of all parameters, which is coded all_types. Also, the general universal function signature, (n),()→(), means (n) is an array with the three color components of our initial pixel, (), a primitive value representing the grayscale darkening pixel, and the output, (), another primitive type with the grayscale pixel.

The most confusing part is the ability to have several functions to render the implementation; notice that we have a list of functions in `funcs`, not a single function. In our case, we only need a single function, `darken_pixel`, but we could have different functions for different input or output parameters—say, one for `NPY_UINT8` and another for `NPY_UINT16`.

This can now be used as any other universal function. In our case:

```
import pyximport

import numpy as np
from PIL import Image

pyximport.install(
    language_level=3,
    setup_args={
        'options': {"build_ext": {"define": 'CYTHON_TRACE'}},
        'include_dirs': np.get_include()})

import cyfilter_uf as cyfilter

image = Image.open("../../04-numpy/aurora.jpg")
gray_filter = Image.open("../filter.png").convert("L")
image_arr, gray_arr = np.array(image), np.array(gray_filter)

darken_arr = cyfilter.darken(image_arr, gray_arr)
```

5.5.1   *The takeaway*

Writing NumPy universal functions in Cython is often both possible and preferable, especially since they come with some built-in time-saving features. However, in some cases, NumPy universal functions are not enough to implement an algorithm—for example, when you need to inspect the state of other places in the array, not just your current position. To deal with that and other problems with array processing in Cython, we will now consider a new example: the Game of Life.

5.6   *Advanced array access in Cython*

In this section, we will solidify our understanding of Cython and NumPy interactions by going deeper into optimizing array access. Specifically, we will do low-level multi-threaded parallelism finally bypassing the GIL's limitation on running a single Python thread at a time.

We'll work on a new example project to see these processes in action: we will create a color version of Conway's game of life (see https://conwaylife.com/ for details). Conway's Game of Life is a zero-player game that evolves automatically from its initial state; devising interesting initial states is part of the fun. The state of the game is composed of a grid of arbitrary size, and each cell can have two states: alive or dead. As time advances, each cell will change its state according to the following rules:

- Any live cell with two or three neighbors survives.
- A dead cell with three neighbors becomes live.
- All other cells die or stay dead.

The world wraps around in the sense that the left-most column will look at the right-most column to compute neighbors, and vice versa. The same applies to the top and bottom rows.

Figure 5.4 shows three examples over time. The first example is a dash that eternally changes direction from vertical to horizontal. The second is a box that is stable, and the third dies off completely.

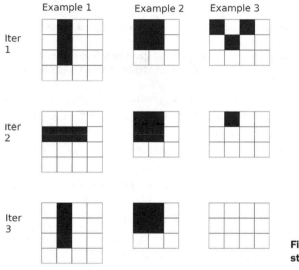

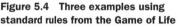

Figure 5.4 Three examples using standard rules from the Game of Life

We will be using an extension called QuadLife,[2] where each live cell can have four different states: red, green, blue, and yellow. I prefer this extension simply because it looks cooler. It includes two new rules:

- If a color is present in the majority of neighbors, that color becomes the color of the new cell.
- If all three live neighbors are different, the new cell takes the remaining of the four possible colors.

As with previous Cython examples, our implementation will include two components: calling Python code, with the computationally expensive part implemented in Cython.

The Python part should be familiar and simple by now. It is available in the repository (05-cython/sec6-quadlife). It is provided here with annotated explanations:

---

[2] You can find a lot of information about game variants and the Game of Life in general on the LifeWiki (https://conwaylife.com/).

```
import sys

import numpy as np
import pyximport            We set up pyximport
pyximport.install(          to include NumPy.
    language_level=3,
    setup_args={
        'include_dirs': np.get_include()})

import cquadlife as quadlife
                            We read parameters
                            from the command line.
SIZE_X = int(sys.argv[1])
SIZE_Y = int(sys.argv[2])
GENERATIONS = int(sys.argv[3])
                                        We use a function
                                        (defined later) to create
                                        a random world.
world = quadlife.create_random_world(SIZE_Y, SIZE_X)
for i in range(GENERATIONS):
    world = quadlife.live(world)        We apply the Quadlife algorithm for the
                                        number of generations specified by the user.
```

We call this script by passing the desired X and Y resolution along with the number of generations. The script doesn't output anything for now, it just runs the game; later we will do some cool stuff with the results.

To start, we will generate a random world with `create_random_world`, which is good enough for testing; later we will consider better-looking alternatives. We will use a NumPy array of the dimension SIZE_Y, SIZE_X, as specified by the user. It will be filled with random values between 0 and 4. Zero represents a dead cell. We then run the simulation function called `live` for GENERATIONS: the first call gets the random world, and its output is then fed to itself in succession. There is nothing conceptually new presented in the code and it should be easy to understand.

We now consider our Cython code. Creating the initial random world doesn't really need to be optimized as it is called only once at the beginning:

```
#cython: language_level=3
import numpy as np

cimport cython
cimport numpy as cnp


def create_random_world(y, x):
    cdef cnp.ndarray [cnp.uint8_t, ndim=2] world =
      np.random.randint(0, 5, (y, x), np.uint8)
    return world
```

Now the fun starts. Our implementation will include conceptually new techniques, but we will be piling up on what we have learned in the previous sections.

5.6.1 *Bypassing the GIL's limitation on running multiple threads at a time*

First, we want to make sure our inner loop can be GIL-free. For that, we create a Cython top-level `live` function that mostly converts NumPy arrays into memoryviews:

```
def live(cnp.ndarray[cnp.uint8_t, ndim=2] old_world):
    cdef int size_y = old_world.shape[0]
    cdef int size_x = old_world.shape[1]
    cdef cnp.ndarray[cnp.uint8_t, ndim=2] extended_world =
        np.empty((size_y + 2, size_x + 2), dtype=np.uint8)    # empty
    cdef cnp.ndarray[cnp.uint8_t, ndim=2] new_world =
        np.empty((size_y, size_x), np.uint8)
    cdef cnp.ndarray[cnp.uint8_t, ndim=1] states = np.empty((5,), np.uint8)

    live_core(old_world, extended_world, new_world, states)
    return new_world
```

The conversion to memoryviews will be forced by the `live_core` function signature (see following discussion), but we still need a layer that can convert Python objects into potentially GIL-free representations. `old_world` is the input world; `new_world` will have the output. `extended_world` and `states` are `live_core` internal variables that we will pre-allocate here. Before we present the core algorithm in `live_core`, let's discuss how we will algorithmically optimize part of it.

In the Game of Life, the extremes of the board are connected; for example, the left-most column cells will "look" at the states of the right-most cells to compute their new states. To avoid a lot of corner case testing, which would add a lot of `if` statements and thus increase the time to compute, we will implement a temporary extended world in the previously mentioned variable `extended_world` of dimensions (y+2, x+2). The extended boundaries copy what happens on the other side, as in figure 5.5.

Figure 5.5 The extended board used to compute the new world

The purpose of this algorithm is to allow a slightly more efficient approach when computing the new board: we do not need `if` statements for boundary conditions. This is done at the cost of memory: we now need to store a new and bigger version of the board. Making these kinds of tradeoffs (i.e., memory versus computation) is our bread and butter across high-performance computing problems. It's difficult to come up with generalized guidelines to decide on the tradeoff. It will depend on the computational and memory cost of a specific algorithm and the resources that you have available.

Following is the code that implements this extended world. Notice that the code has no boundary tests, thus reducing the computation time of using `if` statements:

```
@cython.boundscheck(False)          Uses deactivate bounds,
@cython.nonecheck(False)            None, and wrap checks
@cython.wraparound(False)
cdef void get_extended_world(       We use cdef to avoid the GIL.
        cnp.uint8_t[:,:] world,
        cnp.uint8_t[:,:] extended_world):   We type everything on
    cdef int y = world.shape[0]             the function signature.
    cdef int x = world.shape[1]
    extended_world[1:y+1, 1:x+1] = world
                                            The copy of world
    extended_world[0, 1:x+1] = world[y-1, :]    # top       in the middle of
    extended_world[y+1, 1:x+1] = world[0, :]     # bottom    extended_world
    extended_world[1:y+1, 0] = world[:, x-1]     # left      can be potentially
    extended_world[1:y+1, x+1] = world[:, 0]     # right     expensive.

    extended_world[0, 0] = world[y-1, x-1]    # top left
    extended_world[0, x+1] = world[y-1, 0]    # top right
    extended_world[y+1, 0] = world[0, x-1]    # bottom left
    extended_world[y+1, x+1] = world[0, 0]    # bottom right
```

The copy of world in the middle of extended_world can potentially cost a steep computation and memory price, but the computational part might be compensated by the easier core algorithm.[3] But at least for pedagogical purposes, it makes the core algorithm substantially simpler, which is important for learning purposes.

You might notice that many lines on the previous function look like they could be written in a more expedient notation. For example, perhaps

```
extended_world[1:y+1, 1:x+1] = world
```

could maybe be written as:

```
extended_world[1:-1, 1:-1] = world
```

It turns out, however, that we cannot do these kinds of rewrites because when we deactivate wrap-around to avoid paying the price of the generated C code, we must spend time on wrap verification. In addition, deactivating wrap-around means we cannot use negative indexes. The tradeoff—i.e, not being able to write certain idioms—is worth it, though: wrap-around requires the CPython machinery, which slows things down, so our implementation without it is substantially faster, *and* we need to deactivate it to release the GIL as the wrap-around uses the Python machinery.

> **WARNING** Not doing wrap-around or bounds checking may result in segmentation faults of your code. If you see those errors, make sure to deactivate the decorator during development. Your code must be robust enough to tolerate removing this and the other checks.

---

[3] To determine whether it is compensated or not would require careful profiling, which you now know how to do.

We also use optimizations discussed previously: a cdef, complete typing of parameters and variables, and use of memoryviews instead of NumPy arrays. If you use cython -a cquadlife.pyx, you will see no yellow lines in the browser version of the previous code denoting Python interaction lines.

The main implementation that changes the state makes use of the extended world. The code following implements the QuadLife game rules. Because it is quite long we will carefully annotate it, including problems that we might have addressed previously.

```
                                          We deactivate a lot of checking
                                          machinery: bounds and None,
                                          checking along with wrap-around.
@cython.boundscheck(False)
@cython.nonecheck(False)
@cython.wraparound(False)      We use a cdef to avoid passing standard
cdef void live_core(           Python objects. We also declare the return
    cnp.uint8_t[:,:] old_world,   type as void, which is C for nothing at all.
    cnp.uint8_t[:,:] extended_world,
    cnp.uint8_t[:,:] new_world,
    cnp.uint8_t[:] states):          Some internal variables (states
    cdef cnp.uint16_t x, y, i        and extended_world) are
    cdef cnp.uint8_t num_alive, max_represented   allocated outside, and we use
    cdef int size_y = old_world.shape[0]    the memory made available.
    cdef int size_x = old_world.shape[1]
    get_extended_world(old_world, extended_world)
                                         Everything is pre-allocated when
                                         we call get_extended_world.

    for x in range(size_x):
        for y in range(size_y):
            for i in range(5):
                states[i] = 0
            for i in range(3):
                states[extended_world[y, x + i]] += 1
                states[extended_world[y + 2, x + i]] += 1
            states[extended_world[y + 1, x]] += 1
            states[extended_world[y + 1, x + 2]] += 1

            num_alive = states[1] + states[2] +
              states[3] + states[4]
            if num_alive < 2 or num_alive > 3:
                # Too few or too many neighbors
                new_world[y, x] = 0
            elif old_world[y, x] != 0:
                # Stays alive
                new_world[y, x] = old_world[y, x]
            elif num_alive == 3:  # Will be born
                max_represented = max(states[1],
                  max(states[2], max(states[3],
                  states[4])))
                if max_represented > 1:
                    # majority rule for color
                    for i in range(1, 5):
                        if states[i] == max_represented:
                            new_world[y, x] = i
                            break
```

We type all parameters.

We type all local variables.

Implements sum(states[:1])

Implements max(states[:1])

Implements states[1:].index(max_represented)

```
            else:
                # diversity - use whichever color doesn't exist
                for i in range(1, 5):
                    if states[i] == 0:     ◁——— Implements states[1:].index(0)
                        new_world[y, x] = i
                        break
        else:
            new_world[y, x] = 0   # stays dead
```

This function is complicated, but many of these techniques used were introduced before; here, they are combined in a more realistic example. So read the code and the annotations carefully, and you will understand it all.

You might see a few oddities in the code—namely, the replacement of `sum` and `index` by less declarative versions. We do this because `sum` and `index` would make use of the CPython machinery, and we want to avoid that. A similar argument is valid for the `max` function, but in that case, a replacement version can't compare all values in a single call. When you are using general functions, you might want to profile them and maybe replace them with optimized nongeneral functions.

> **NOTE** Because the Game of Life produces nice evolving visualizations, we will make a simple GUI. We will be using the Python built-in `tkinter` module for the GUI along with the external library Pillow for image manipulation. We will not discuss the code here because it falls outside of the scope of this book, but you can find it in the repository in `05-cython/sec6-quadlife/ gui.py`.

Our implementation is complete, but now we want to gauge the performance gain that we got from our code.

5.6.2 *Basic performance analysis*

You can find the native Python version in the repository. We will use this version to make some basic comparisons with the Cython one. Running the Python version at a resolution of 1000×1000 for 200 generations on my computer takes slightly less than 1000 s, which is below 17 min. The Cython code takes 2.5 s.

> **WARNING** Our implementation is memory-intensive. Be very careful if you test it with large resolutions. In fact, a running theme in the book is the consideration of amount of memory used by algorithms: if they can be in-memory, they will be much faster than if they require disk storage for ongoing computations. Whenever possible, we will try to use in-memory algorithms. If not, we normally will have to optimize storage for processing to happen efficiently.

Let's now consider a very large map of $400 \times 900,000$ run for only four generations. On my computer, it takes 44 s. Now, if we run the transposed map of $900,000 \times 400$ for the same four generations, how much time do you think it will take? It's the same number of total cells for the same number of generations. It turns out that it's not the same amount of time, not even close. It's only 20 s. What is apparently the same problem in theoretical terms has very different results. The answer to this mind-boggling difference will be explored in chapter 6. To make things even weirder, the relationship that you get on *your* computer might be completely different from the one I got on *my* computer.

Before we address the final topic of this chapter, GIL-free multithreading with Cython, let's take a quick detour and generate a cool video from the Game of Life. This process will allow us to consider computational complexity and think about the role of theory in helping us to write more efficient programs.

5.6.3 A spacewar example using Quadlife

In the repository, you will find code that will generate a video using a starting state that includes "spaceships" and "defenses." The code itself is not very relevant for optimization purposes so we won't discuss it here. If you want to replicate it, you will need Python's Pillow library for image processing and ffmpeg to generate videos. You can find the main shell script to generate it in `05-cython/generate_video.sh`. Figure 5.6 shows the starting state, with color inverted.

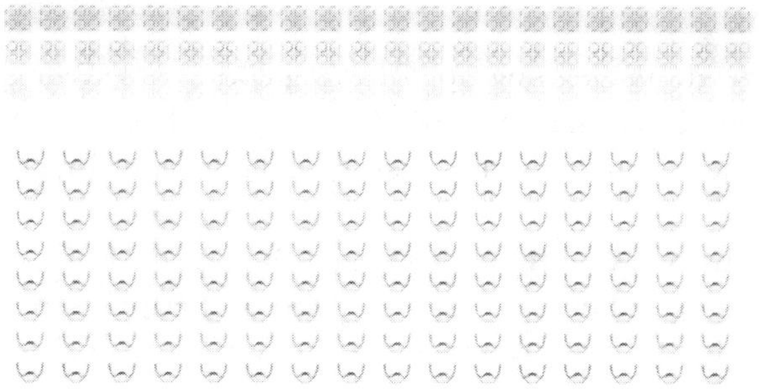

Figure 5.6   The video starting state for our QuadLife simulation

A video is available at https://www.youtube.com/watch?v=E0B1fDKU_MI. A library (www.conwaylife.com) also allows you to get patterns like the ones used in the video.

You can use the code in the repository (`05-cython/patterns.py`) to generate similar kinds of movies. This code will run the Game of Life on the spaceship model for 400 generations on a map of 400 × 250, which takes less than 1 s. An HD resolution of 1920 × 1080 with the same 400 generations takes around 11 s; 800 frames takes 22 s; and 400 frames at the 4K resolution of 3840 × 2160 takes 48 s. At 10 frames per second, a 4K game of 90 min would take roughly 196 min to generate. The silver lining is that the same video would take 54 days to generate in a pure Python solution.

The role of computational complexity

While this is not a theoretical book, it is impossible to deny the importance of computational complexity and its underlying theory. That is the study of resources consumed by an algorithm—commonly, but not only, time and memory.

> *(continued)*
> For example, the time cost of our system increases linearly with the number of generations that we compute. But if we are computing a world that is square and has a lateral size of n, the growth is quadratic: a square of 20 is not two times slower than a square of 10; it's actually four times slower. Also, a square of size 200 is a whopping 400 times slower (not 20 times) than a 10 × 10 square. In this case, the algorithm is also quadratic for the memory required.
>
> In the world of ever-increasing big data, this means that some algorithms will scale very poorly and eventually might need to be replaced by completely different solutions. In this book, we will not formally discuss computational complexity theory, but sometimes we will have to address some intuitions behind it.

We still have plenty of motivation to do better. Because our code does not interact with Python objects, we can release the GIL and do real parallelism with multiple threads. Let's do that in the final section.

5.7   *Parallelism with Cython*

With all the preparation we've done cleaning up GIL-tying code, introducing a multiprocessing solution is now quite straightforward. Our approach will make use of Cython's internal parallel functionality, and the code (available in `05-cython/sec7-parallel`) is quite simple.

Cython provides declarative parallel functions based on OpenMP. OpenMP is a multiplatform library providing parallelism primitives. One of the functions provided is a parallel range function, which will multithread the content of a `for` loop; using it is quite easy:

```
from cython.parallel import prange     ◁——— We import the prange function.
@cython.boundscheck(False)
@cython.nonecheck(False)
@cython.wraparound(False)
cdef void live_core(
    cnp.uint8_t[:,:] old_world,
    cnp.uint8_t[:,:] extended_world,
    cnp.uint8_t[:,:] new_world,
    cnp.uint8_t[:] states) nogil:     ◁——— nogil is now compulsory.
    cdef cnp.uint32_t x, y, i
    cdef cnp.uint8_t num_alive, max_represented
    cdef int size_y = old_world.shape[0]
    cdef int size_x = old_world.shape[1]
    get_extended_world(old_world, extended_world)

    for x in prange(size_x):     ◁——— We simply replace range with prange.
        for y in range(size_y):
...
```

It's as simple as that. Of course, remember that by cleaning all GIL-related code, we did most of the work well before arriving at this step. We also need to remember to annotate the `get_extended_world` function:

```
@cython.boundscheck(False)
@cython.nonecheck(False)
@cython.wraparound(False)
cdef void get_extended_world(
        cnp.uint8_t[:,:] world,
        cnp.uint8_t[:,:] extended_world) nogil:
    ...
```

Cython provides a few functions over OpenMP to make parallel code easier to write. This can be extremely handy in most cases. The fundamental requirement is to clear all GIL-related calls.

We are mostly concerned with the interactions between GIL's Python and threaded parallelism. We are also concerned with Cython's primitives, based on OpenMP, to write parallel code. The elephant in the room is the whole field of parallel processing. Here we provide the fundamental building blocks to unleash true parallel threaded processing in the Python space. But parallel programming techniques in general are a separate subject for which you should consult other resources.

Note that with Cython you are, in fact, inside a C-paradigm. While there is no reason to ignore Cython's OpenMP functionality, remember that you are not tied to it. You can use other C-based parallelisms libraries: it's just that you have to go an even lower level yourself.

Summary

- Native Python, CPython, is not enough to implement the fastest code for complex operations.
- There are many options to accelerate your Python-based code: using optimized libraries, lower-level languages, Numba, or even other Python implementations such as PyPy.
- Cython is a superset of Python that compiles to C and provides C-like speeds without having to learn a new language.
- Cython can be profiled in similar ways to Python code.
- Writing efficient Cython code requires annotating Cython variables to provide type hints, which are different from the hints of standard mypy, and sometimes analyzing the generated C code from Cython.
- The C code browser provided by Cython allows you to easily identify lines that interact with the Python interpreter and thus are potential candidates for being rewritten more efficiently.
- You should remove as many interactions with CPython as possible, to the point that you should consider re-architecting your code so that the expensive inner

loop for your implementation is free of CPython interactions. This can easily accelerate your Cython code by numerous orders of magnitude.

- Cython integrates with NumPy, allowing for the efficient manipulation of arrays. Resources, like memoryviews, are available that allow direct communication between Cython and NumPy, thus removing the inefficient Python interpreter as a middleman.

- CPython-independent code is the first step for GIL-independent code. If we can release the GIL, we can use parallel multithreading from our Cython code.

- Remember to consider Numba as an alternative to Cython: in many cases, it is easier to use, although not as customizable as Cython.

Memory hierarchy, storage, and networking

6

This chapter covers

- Making efficient use of CPU cache and main memory
- Using Blosc to access compressed array data
- Using NumExpr to accelerate NumPy expressions
- Designing client/server architectures for very fast networks

It goes without saying that hardware affects performance. But how hardware interacts with performance is not always so obvious. The goal of this chapter is to help you get a better grasp of how, exactly, your machinery can affect your speed and what you can do on the hardware end to improve performance. To that end, we will take a close look at the effects of modern hardware and network architectures on efficient data processing with Python.

There are many counterintuitive implications for software development stemming from hardware considerations. For example, there are quite a few cases where working with compressed data is *faster* than dealing with uncompressed data.

Conventional wisdom suggests that the cost of both decompressing and analyzing data would be much more expensive than just analyzing data. After all, when we decompress, we are adding more computations. So how can this be computationally more efficient? It turns out that modern hardware architectures can play tricks with "obvious" observations.

To make the most of modern hardware performance, we need to understand what makes some default assumptions so counterintuitive. To gain this understanding, we will start with a introduction to modern computer architectures from a performance perspective. The topic itself would merit a book, but we will concentrate on the less intuitive features: we will study memory hierarchy, from CPU caches to wide area networks, going through RAM, hard disks, and local networks.

We are interested in making computing faster and storage processing more efficient, both from a size and a speed perspective. After we understand some of the implications of modern hardware architectures, we will see how some Python libraries make the most of hardware. We'll first explore how Blosc, a high-performance library to compress binary data, can be used to generate compact representations of NumPy arrays that can be accessed in about the same time as uncompressed arrays. As we break down this process, you will see how intelligent use of CPU caches can make the compression and decompression times virtually irrelevant. Then, we will look at how NumExpr can accelerate NumPy expressions over very large arrays by, again, being intelligent about processing data in a cache-minded way.

Finally, we will change gears and discuss the effect of performing computations on clusters or clouds based on very fast local networks. Much of the code that we use to conduct data analysis is run on clusters or clouds, which may be implemented on these types of networks, so it is useful for you to know how this is done.

Interpreting performance

Because this is a hardware-dependent chapter, the results that you get may be *qualitatively* different from the ones I present, given that your hardware is different from mine. What might fit in the cache of my machine might not fit into yours. Furthermore, if you run this code on the machine with a user interface, cache usage will be mostly unpredictable due to all the other processes running concurrently with your code.

All the benchmarks presented here were run on a server without a user interface or other large processes running. The specifications are: Intel Xeon 8375C CPU @ 2.90GHz, 32 cores, L1 Cache 2 MB, L2 Cache 40 MB, L3 cache 54 MB, DRAM 16 GB. We will give a concrete example of how results can vary tremendously with your hardware in the NumExpr section.

Let's start with a review of modern hardware architecture, focusing on the problems that may have counterintuitive consequences on efficient Python coding. This chapter will require the installation of Blosc (`conda install blosc`). If you use Docker, the main image includes everything you need.

6.1 How modern hardware architectures affect Python performance

In this section, we will survey the current landscape of hardware architectures, focusing on their less intuitive, but crucial, implications for efficient Python development. Hardware architecture includes what's inside the computer—CPU, memory, and local storage—as well as the network. When we look at local storage, and especially network architecture, we will also sometimes dabble in system software architecture problems: namely, file systems and network protocols. Again, the topics here could easily fill several books, so we will narrow our concentration to problems that have a direct effect on Python performance and for which there are Python libraries to address those problems.

We will start with a seemingly trivial example that will serve as motivation and, I hope, convince you of the very real benefits of understanding how these hardware and system problems affect performance—and what you can do about it. If you are interested in having performance gains of up to two orders of magnitude on some operations where you were expecting to have none, read on.

6.1.1 The counterintuitive effect of modern architectures on performance

Our trivial example with be simply taking a NumPy square matrix and duplicating the value of a row and the value of a column. From a performance perspective, doubling a row should take exactly the same time as doubling a column, given that the matrix is square. It's obvious! Or is it?

To find out, let's evaluate the performance cost of doubling a row and of doubling a column:

```
import numpy as np

SIZE = 100

mat = np.random.randint(10, size=(SIZE, SIZE))
double_column = 2 * mat[:, 0]
double_row = 2* mat[0, :]
```

> IPython on Jupyter allows us to conduct a performance analysis by adding %timeit before the last two lines.

We create a random matrix with values between 0 and 9. We start with a size of 100. Later, we'll vary this, using 1000 and 10,000.

Again, notice that the matrix is square. That means that double_column and double_row will require the same number of operations. Common sense suggests that this is a trivial problem (i.e., not worth our time), and that the time cost of doubling a column or doubling a row should be mostly the same. In this case, common sense is wrong.

Let's start with the previous code, a square matrix of size 100—hence, 10,000 elements. Given that the default integer representation is 8 bytes, we have 80 KB. On my computer, doubling a column takes a mean time of 750 ns; doubling a row takes 715 ns. Not a big difference, and given the granularity of the operation, the difference may be caused by the instrumentation to profile this. So far, so obvious.

Let's increase the size of our matrix to 1000, thus 1 million elements and 8 MB. We now have 1.99 μs and 1.5 μs respectively. Again, nothing really striking.

Let's increase the size to 10,000. Such a matrix will take approximately 800 MB, so make sure you have enough memory to perform this. Doubling a column takes 4.51 µs; doubling a row, 74.9 µs!

For this bigger matrix, it is 16 times faster to double a column than to double a row. Let this sink in: there is *something* regarding the hardware architecture and NumPy's internal representation that makes two apparently equal operations have a difference in performance of more than one order of magnitude!

There are two problems here at work. One is the relationship between the CPU cache and the main memory. The other is the internal representation of the matrix. They conspire to cause the difference in performance. We will delve into both these problems later in this chapter.

6.1.2 *How CPU caching affects algorithm efficiency*

Let's first consider transient memory. We typically think in terms of DRAM, but computation happens in CPU registers (i.e., the lowest level of memory) and passes through several layers of CPU caches. Table 6.1 shows an example of what a modern machine might look like.

Table 6.1   Memory hierarchy with sizes and access times for a hypothetical, but realistic modern desktop

Type	Size	Access time
CPU		
L1 cache	256 KB	2 ns
L2 cache	1 MB	5 ns
L3 cache	6 MB	30 ns
RAM		
DIMM	8 GB	100 ns

L1 cache times are near the cycle speed of modern CPUs. Remember that 2 GHz means 2×10^9 cycles/s, and a nanosecond is 10^{-9} seconds.

If the data that the CPU needs can be found in the L1 cache (hit rate), then the speeds will match. However, using DRAM means that the CPU will be idle for a long time: it's not impossible that 90% of the time, it's just waiting for data to be fetched.

Now we can explain our original example: why the doubling of a column in a square can have a completely different time cost than doubling a row. So, if you have a matrix like

l11	l12	l13	l14
l21	l22	l23	l24
l31	l32	l33	l34
l41	l42	l43	l44

it will have to be represented in memory sequentially:

I11	I12	I13	I14	I21	I22	I23	I24	I31	I32	I33	I34	I41	I42	I43	I44

When you access element I11, the CPU will bring a few more elements into the memory, not just a single one. So, if you do 2*I11, 2*I12, 2*I13, 2*I14, there will only be a single move from memory to cache. But if you do 2*I11, 2*I21, 2*I31, 2*I41, because they are not contiguous, every time you do an operation there will be a memory move, which is comparatively a very expensive operation. So, the first case is four doubling operations with one memory move, whereas the second case is four doubling operations with four memory moves.

Our example is, of course, a simplification. Depending on the size of the matrix and the size of the caches, it might be possible that the CPU brings all the data in a single move; that is why we don't see a difference with very small matrices, But if the matrix is large enough, the effect becomes so pronounced that it can make one operation one order of magnitude more expensive than the other.

TIP There is another problem to take into account with the representation of matrices: we can have each row contiguously represented or have each column contiguously represented. The former is common in C-based code, whereas the latter is common in Fortran-based code. This is quite important for us because the backend of NumPy can be implemented in both languages, so we must be mindful of the backend implementation to devise how to access data.

The next two sections will demonstrate how to use two libraries, Blosc and NumExpr, to make efficient use of CPU caches.

6.1.3 Modern persistent storage

Another potential problem area is persistent storage. The most common is local storage, either hard disk drives (HDDs) or solid-state drives (SDDs). Persistent memory is orders of magnitude slower to access than transient memory: SSDs have access times in the microsecond range, and HDDs, in the millisecond range. While we are not going into this topic further here (although some of these topics will resurface in a different form in chapter 8), note that techniques for transient memory like the one presented in the next section are equally valid for storage. For example, there are cases where it is faster to work with compressed files than with raw files; the cost of decompressing can be substantially lower than reading more (raw) data from disk.

In addition to transient memory and local persistent memory, we have remote storage and remote computation. In theory, remote storage and remote computation are substantially slower than local storage. For example, access times when you are accessing a storage server on the Internet are long and unpredictable. That being said, modern local computation clusters can have very fast backbones. How fast? It can be faster to access a remote server than to get data from a local disk! We will discuss the implications of that in the last section of the chapter. As you will see, standard network protocols that we use to access long-distance web services might not be fast enough when we are working on a local fast network.

THE TAKEAWAY

What I hope you take away from this section is the realization that some old assumptions about computation and memory locality can be wrong. As we've seen, the apparently same operation can have dramatically different costs, depending on how memory is allocated. Therefore, if we want to be CPU-efficient, we need to make sure that the information that the algorithm needs is as close to the CPU as possible. Furthermore, DRAM proximity is not enough, as accessing it can cause CPU starvation and cause the CPU to be idle for multiple cycles. Having data available in the L1 cache is our aim whenever possible.

But the rabbit hole goes deeper: sometimes it can be faster to decompress data on the fly (i.e., use expensive decompression algorithms) than to use raw data. This is exactly what Blosc allows us to do and we will explore it in the next section.

6.2   *Efficient data storage with Blosc*

Blosc is a high-performance compressor framework that is designed to make processing compressed data faster than processing its uncompressed counterpart. How is that even possible? Remember from the previous section that the CPU can be starved most of the time if the data that it needs to process is located far away in DRAM. If the number of CPU cycles that we use to (un)compress data is small enough that they occur during the starvation time of the CPU, then compression is actually "free."

6.2.1   *Compress data; save time*

To see how dealing with compressed data can be faster than raw data in some cases, we will look at three alternative ways to create NumPy arrays and then store and retrieve them from the disk using NumPy and Blosc. We will be looking at the time and disk space implications of each approach. This is a substantially more complex task than it seems.

Let's start with array creation and support functions:

```
import os
import blosc
import numpy as np

random_arr = np.random.randint(
➥ 256, size=(1024, 1024, 1024)).astype(np.uint8)

zero_arr = np.zeros(shape=(1024, 1024, 1024)).astype(np.uint8)


rep_tile_arr = np.tile(
    np.arange(256).astype(np.uint8),
    4*1024*1024).reshape(1024,1024,1024)
```

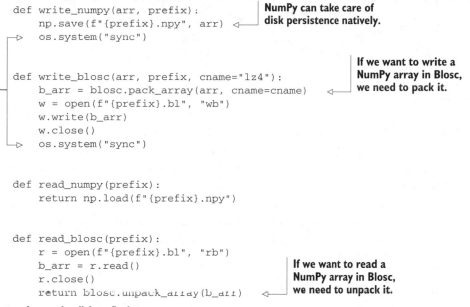

```
def write_numpy(arr, prefix):            NumPy can take care of
    np.save(f"{prefix}.npy", arr)        disk persistence natively.
    os.system("sync")


                                         If we want to write a
                                         NumPy array in Blosc,
def write_blosc(arr, prefix, cname="lz4"):   we need to pack it.
    b_arr = blosc.pack_array(arr, cname=cname)
    w = open(f"{prefix}.bl", "wb")
    w.write(b_arr)
    w.close()
    os.system("sync")



def read_numpy(prefix):
    return np.load(f"{prefix}.npy")



def read_blosc(prefix):
    r = open(f"{prefix}.bl", "rb")
    b_arr = r.read()                     If we want to read a
    r.close()                            NumPy array in Blosc,
    return blosc.unpack_array(b_arr)     we need to unpack it.
```

sync forces the disk to flush.

We start by creating three arrays: one has only zeroes, another has tile values of up to 256, and one has random values. We use these three array types because they represent very different situations regarding compression: a zero-array is trivial to compress, a tiled array takes an average amount of time to compress, and a random one is mostly impossible to compress.

We then create a set of helper functions to read and write arrays to the disk. This is not trivial on the write side: because we want to fairly benchmark the total cost of the writing function, we need to force the operating system to flush buffers—hence, the use of sync. sync is not available on Windows.

Let's now benchmark the write part:

```
os.system("sync")
%time write_numpy(zero_arr, "zero")
%time write_blosc(zero_arr, "zero")
%time write_numpy(rep_tile_arr, "rep_tile")
%time write_blosc(rep_tile_arr, "rep_tile")
%time write_numpy(random_arr, "random")
%time write_blosc(random_arr, "random")
```

We start by calling sync, which will clean the operating system IO buffers as much as possible. We then use %time to time the write functions. While it might be safe, at least for the write part, to use %timeit, we want to avoid any possibility that the operating system optimizes our calls, which would make the benchmarks difficult to interpret. Table 6.2 provides the time results.

Table 6.2 Writing time in seconds of different array times using NumPy and Blosc

Array	NumPy	Blosc
zero	7.49	0.53
rep_tile	7.49	0.53
random	7.5	8.13

For the zero and rep_tile arrays, Blosc is around 15 times faster. For the random array, NumPy is slightly faster. Which case is more common? The most distant case from reality is the random one: data in tables tends to have some sort of pattern. It is not overly optimistic to assume the zero and rep_tile cases.

So, unintuitively, Blosc proves more efficient in terms of time. But what about disk space occupation? This is another important metric for very large datasets where we expect Blosc to outperform. rep_tile is 200 times smaller, zero is 250 times smaller, and random has the same size.

6.2.2 *Read speeds (and memory buffers)*

Now we will check read speeds. In theory, this is a question of just reading the files, right? Well, given that we have written them to disk, the operating system might have them in intermediate memory buffers, thus providing a biased view of performance. In other words, caches can make profiling unreliable. To have a fair comparison, we need to make sure we are *really* reading from disk and not from temporary memory buffers, which would be much faster. So we have to flush the buffers.

A brutal way to solve this problem is to reboot the computer. Another way is to tell the operating system to invalidate all caches. Unfortunately, this is OS-dependent. Here I will give you a way to do this on Debian/Ubuntu and derivatives. This does not work on Windows or Macs or in some other Linux distributions. If you are in such a situation, you will have to investigate how it can be done with your operating system.

As the root, use the command:

```
sync; echo 3 > /proc/sys/vm/drop_caches
```

Now we can read with the expectation that the data is not in transient buffer memory:

```
%time _ = read_numpy("zero")
%time _ = read_blosc("zero")
%time _ = read_numpy("rep_tile")
%time _ = read_blosc("rep_tile")
%time _ = read_numpy("random")
%time _ = read_blosc("random")
```

The times are provided in table 6.3.

Table 6.3   Reading time in seconds of different array times using NumPy and Blosc

Array	NumPy	Blosc
zero	7.02	0.63
rep_tile	7.04	0.61
random	7.37	8.58

This is a similar pattern to the write times. For nonrandom data, Blosc clearly outperforms NumPy, which means that you should consider it for large data sizes.

Up to this point, we haven't cared much about which compression algorithm we are using; we just accepted the default. But Blosc allows you to choose from many algorithms.

6.2.3   *The effect of different compression algorithms on storage performance*

The objective here is not to make an exhaustive survey of existing algorithms and their benchmark speeds. Instead, I simply want to make you aware that different algorithms exist and more may be added in the future. These algorithms vary in speed and efficiency, depending on how and when they are used. With this awareness, you should be able to choose the one that best suits your particular data and needs. To illustrate the potential variation in performance, let's compare two algorithms: LZ4 and Zstandard.

At this stage, we will stop writing data to disk, as it should be clear by now that it is cumbersome to benchmark it. We will perform only in-memory operations; namely, we will compress the data with BLOSC because we've already seen its superior performance. First, we'll use LZ4 and then Zstandard:

```
%timeit rep_lz4 = blosc.pack_array(rep_tile_arr,
    cname='lz4')
rep_lz4 = blosc.pack_array(rep_tile_arr, cname='lz4')
%timeit rep_std = blosc.pack_array(rep_tile_arr,
    cname='zstd')
rep_std = blosc.pack_array(rep_tile_arr, cname='zstd')
print(len(rep_lz4) // 1024)
```

We create an in-memory representation using LZ4 as a compression algorithm.

We create an in-memory representation using Zstandard as a compression algorithm

Table 6.4 provides the time and size results.

Table 6.4   Compression time and size using LZ4 and Zstandard

	LZ4	Zstandard
Time (ms)	527	919
Size (KB)	5204	366

If you recall from the previous section, the LZ4 representation is 200 times smaller than the standard NumPy representation. This means that the Zstandard compression is 2800 times smaller than NumPy (200 times 14—the ratio between LZ4 and Zstandard).

Blosc still has an extra trick up its sleeve: not only does it offer a variety of algorithms, but it also allows you to change the representation of your input on the fly. And this can further reduce the size of the compressed data. Let's see how that works.

6.2.4   *Using insights about data representation to increase compression*

Imagine that you know that your data has some patterns of regularity; for example, numbers in sequence are common. Say your data includes the following sequence of 8-bit encoded numbers:

```
3,4,5,6
```

This will be encoded typically in binary as:

```
00000011/00000100/00000101/00000110
```

Now imagine that you take the highest order bit of each number and encode it, then the second highest, and so on until the 8 bit of each number. This will end up looking like:

```
0000000000000000000011110011010
```

The second pattern looks much more regular. This is exactly what enables compressors to be efficient. Blosc allows you to do precisely this:

```
for shuffle in [blosc.BITSHUFFLE, blosc.NOSHUFFLE]:
        a = blosc.pack_array(rep_tile_arr, shuffle=shuffle)
        print(len(a))
```

The shuffled version comes at 4,600,034 bytes, whereas the unprocessed version comes at 5,345,500. Shuffle is marginally slower at 596 ms versus 524 ms.

THE TAKEAWAY

Intelligent use of memory hierarchy and CPU processing can speed up some basic array operations. Blosc allows us, in many cases, to access compressed stored representations of data faster than using raw data. This is in addition to the usual benefit of having smaller persistent datasets.

Let's take this a step further and use similar techniques while analyzing data. For that, we will explore the NumExpr library.

6.3   *Accelerating NumPy with NumExpr*

Blosc is one example of how we can make intelligent use of memory hierarchy to accelerate data processing. But we can take this approach much further by accelerating NumPy expressions with NumExpr.

NumExpr is a numerical expression evaluator for NumPy, which can be faster than NumPy. It takes an expression—say, a + b—and computes its result. But wait: what is the point of it? Isn't that what NumPy does anyway? Indeed, NumExpr replaces some of NumPy's functionality with an engine that tries to reorganize computation more efficiently when working with large datasets. One technique used by NumExpr relies on *not* generating full intermediate representations for parts of an expression: computation is made in chunks that are designed to fit into the L1 cache.

6.3.1 Fast expression processing

Now let's see a few examples of how NumExpr changes the performance of evaluating expressions:

```
import numpy as np
import numexpr as ne

a = np.random.rand(100000000).reshape(10000,10000)
b = np.random.rand(100000000).reshape(10000,10000)
f = np.random.rand(100000000).reshape(10000,10000)
  .copy('F')                          ◄─────────  This matrix is represented
                                                  using Fortran standard.
%timeit a + a
%timeit ne.evaluate('a + a')          ◄──── NumExpr provides the
%timeit f + f                               evaluate function to
%timeit ne.evaluate('f + f')                process an expression.
%timeit a + f
%timeit ne.evaluate('a + f')
%timeit a**5 + b
%timeit ne.evaluate('a**5 + b')
%timeit a**5 + b + np.sin(a) + np.cos(a)
%timeit ne.evaluate('a**5 + b + sin(a) + cos(a)')
```

We first create three square matrices to support our performance evaluation. The last one has a Fortran organization. The output of the `%timeit` benchmarks is summarized in table 6.5.

Table 6.5 Comparison of execution times between NumPy and NumExpr. Values are in milliseconds.

Expression	Mean Numpy time	Mean NumExpr time	Speed up
a + a	224	58	3.8
f + f	224	58	3.8
a + f	577	153	3.7
a**5 + f	1690	87	19.4
a**5 + f + sin(a) + cos(a)	3840	153	25.1

In our hardware setup, NumExpr is more efficient. Take a look at the operations involving matrices represented in different formats, C versus Fortran. These are more expensive than when all the arrays are homogeneous in format. As expressions become more complex, the benefit of NumExpr increases as more space becomes available for optimization techniques to be used.

The examples, however, paint an excessively rosy picture of NumExpr. There are some cases where NumExpr can decrease performance. The rest of this section will showcase some downsides. We will start with the qualitative variations in performance caused by the hardware.

6.3.2 How hardware architecture affects our results

As I alluded to at the start of this chapter, your results can vary widely from the ones shown here. To make this clear, I will compare the machine that I am using to write this text (i.e., a machine that is running a Linux GUI with a text editor). I will not put the cache sizes of my CPU here because that might be misleading: there are so many processes hitting the cache simultaneously that it is completely impossible to estimate the L1 cache anyway. Table 6.6 compares the performance speedup of using NumExpr on our arithmetic operations on the server versus my laptop.

Table 6.6 The effect of hardware architecture on performance: Speedup as a function of hardware

Expression	Server speedup	Laptop speedup
a + a	3.8	0.7
f + f	3.8	0.8
a + f	3.7	1.3
a**5 + f	19.4	11.5
a**5 + f + sin(a) + cos(a)	25.1	6.7

The performance benefit from using NumExpr is severely reduced. Indeed, for some of the operations, the NumExpr implementation suddenly becomes *slower* than the NumPy one. One of the main reasons is related to the unpredictable availability of the CPU cache on a typical local because many processes are running and competing for it.

> **TIP** Don't expect to have large speedups based on cache optimization on local machines that are running a lot of other applications (e.g. all the UI-based apps like your text editor or your browser). There will be massive competition for the CPU cache, and the results can vary widely from run to run. These techniques will shine on the server but not on a typical development machine. Hence, when testing the advantages of using any techniques that make use of the CPU cache, test on the server.

As the previous example demonstrates, not all scenarios are appropriate for NumExpr. Let's elaborate on when, where, and why NumExpr isn't the best choice.

6.3.3   *When NumExpr is not appropriate*

There are several scenarios where NumExpr can be deleterious. Let's discuss them.

The most important factor is the size of your arrays: NumExpr tends to perform better with larger arrays. Let's repeat some of the previous examples but with small arrays:

```
small_a = np.random.rand(100).reshape(10, 10)
small_b = np.random.rand(100).reshape(10, 10)

%timeit small_a + small_a
%timeit ne.evaluate('small_a + small_a')
%timeit small_a**5 + small_b + np.sin(small_a) + np.cos(small_a)
%timeit ne.evaluate('small_a**5 + small_b + sin(small_a) + cos(small_a)')
```

The addition is 15 times slower with NumExpr, whereas the complex expression is still 30% slower if you use NumExpr. However, this is not a serious problem: in most cases, you will not be trying to optimize small arrays: big data, not small data, is our problem.

Another source of performance degradation for NumExpr is when you perform benchmarks on machines, like your own local machine, that have other processes running. NumExpr performs better on servers, especially if you can control the number of applications running. This means that on shared clusters, which are common in academia, NumExpr performance will vary. Finally, NumExpr only supports a subset of NumPy's operators, so some operations cannot be boosted by NumExpr.

Now that we have discussed several ways of optimizing the use of transient memory, we will change our focus completely and discuss local networks. Modern local networks can be faster than accessing local persistent storage, and that fact, once again, turns some common assumptions upside down.

6.4   *The performance implications of using the local network*

When we code for the network, we are dealing with an infrastructure that can have completely different properties. Many times we assume that the network is something far away—with speed, latency, and resilience problems. But in many high-performance scenarios, when we use the network locally, these assumptions do not apply. Modern network switches can support up to 2 Tb/s of backbone communication with up to 56 Gb/s per network port. As a reference, most local disks support 6 Gb/s per second. Think about this for a second: in a high-performance local network, it is faster to talk with another computer than it is to talk with a local disk. If you are in a situation where you have a fast network between your nodes, read on.

The typical software network framework for communication is wholly inappropriate to deal with the speed of a modern local network. Do you think interrogating your local disk using a REST call over HTTPS will be efficient? Given that high-performance local networks are faster than local disk access, we have to find a more efficient way to communicate.

Before we devise a solution, let's understand why a standard approach will not be efficient. In this section, we will implement the backend of a pastebin service *not* based on REST. A pastebin service allows you to store pieces of text to share with others over the internet. We will write a client that sends text for storage and requests texts for reading. We will also write the server, which stores the texts and serves those on request. For an example of a real-life service like this, see https://pastebin.com/. We will assume that our client and server will be run on a very fast local network.

6.4.1   The sources of inefficiency with REST calls

Before we devise an efficient solution, let's understand the performance bottlenecks of typical REST implementations. Client/server communication in REST is typically done using JSON payloads over HTTPS. JSON is a text format and thus requires computing time for parsing and a lot of space. HTTPS augments the HTTP protocol with authentication and encryption using public key cryptography. HTTPS thus adds substantial processing on top of HTTP.

The HTTP protocol does all its work on top of an Internet protocol called Transmission Control Protocol (TCP). TCP establishes a connection abstraction between two endpoints—in our case, the client and the server. The connection assures that the data arrives in order with no loss. But the protocol is heavy, at least for our very fast network: just establishing a connection will require at least three data packets to go backward and forward between the client and the server.

After we have our TCP connection established, the security part of HTTP needs to be done, which delegated to the Transport Layer Security (TLS) protocol. This protocol performs a handshake, which requires several packets to go backward and forwards between the client and the server. Given that it involves cryptography, it will be computationally intensive. Note that the computational time cost is relative: in a very fast network, it will be a big fraction of the computation; if you are computing with a server on the other side of the world, the same computing time will be negligible in the overall computation.

Now we are ready to send our payload, a verbose JSON payload that will require text parsing. Finally, we will have to close the connection at both the HTTPS and TCP levels.

From a message perspective, the communication will require at least 20 network packets to be exchanged, probably more. Given the speed of the local network, the overwhelming majority of the exchanges will be spent on protocols. Let's implement this using just two packets: the bare minimum—one for the request and another for the response.

6.4.2   A naive client based on UDP and msgpack

Our implementation will be quite simple. More important than understanding the code is understanding the tradeoffs that our implementation imposes.

Let's start with the client. Our client will post a text to the pastebin server and then retrieve it. It starts like this:

```
import socket

host = '127.0.0.1'
port = 54321

sock = socket.socket(socket.AF_INET, socket.SOCK_DGRAM)
```
Creates a new UDP,
SOCK_DGRAM socket

Instead of using the whole HTTPS over TCP stack, we dispense with application protocols altogether and replace TCP with UDP, the User Datagram protocol. UDP doesn't establish connections; it just sends packets. Think of UDP as the postal service, whereas TCP is the phone service. In the postal service, letters can be lost, delivered in the wrong order, and routed wrongly. In a phone call, the stream is delivered in order with no lost information. From an overhead perspective, UDP (postal) is less burdensome than TCP (phone call).

The previous code snippet uses the low-level module socket to create a UDP communication endpoint. We specify that the server address is 127.0.0.1—in this case, the address of the local machine—and we will use port 54321.

This solution implies a couple of assumptions, which you need to be sure are acceptable for your case:

- *By not using an encrypted channel, we are opening our implementation to eavesdropping and data changing.* When communicating in a local high-performance network, this is less of a problem than over the internet. Quite pragmatically, if a security threat can access the backbone of your network, you have bigger problems than access to the data: you have a compromised infrastructure.

- *The UDP protocol doesn't ensure that packets are delivered.* This means that our solution might lose data between the client and the server. This problem is substantially rarer in a high-performance local network than on the internet. That being said, it can realistically occur, and we will address it in the last subsection of this chapter.

Let's now complete our client by sending a text to the server and retrieving it:

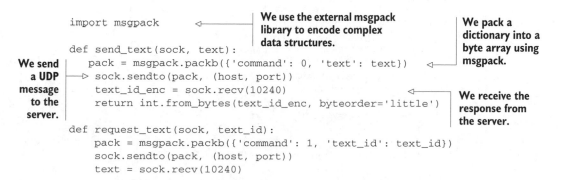

```
import msgpack

def send_text(sock, text):
    pack = msgpack.packb({'command': 0, 'text': text})
    sock.sendto(pack, (host, port))
    text_id_enc = sock.recv(10240)
    return int.from_bytes(text_id_enc, byteorder='little')

def request_text(sock, text_id):
    pack = msgpack.packb({'command': 1, 'text_id': text_id})
    sock.sendto(pack, (host, port))
    text = sock.recv(10240)
```

We use the external msgpack library to encode complex data structures.

We send a UDP message to the server.

We pack a dictionary into a byte array using msgpack.

We receive the response from the server.

```
        return text

text_id = send_text(sock, 'trial text')
returned_text = request_text(sock, text_id)
```

We use a function called `send_text` to send text to the server. The request includes the command 0, which means it stores a text and the text proper. We could have encoded the command more explicitly, for example, by using the string "store text," but that would be more verbose and thus less efficient. We send the text as-is, but given what we have seen in the previous sections, compressing the text might be a viable option, especially if we expect that large texts will be transferred.

The answer that we get from the server is not encoded with msgpack. Given that we will get the numeric id with which the text was stored, we use something even simpler: a reconstruction of an integer from a stream of bytes. This should be even faster than msgpack.

The `request_text` function has a command code of 1 and a numeric id that is packaged with msgpack. After sending the message, we receive the text.

Finally, we send a text to the server and then get the text back by using the text id. Now, we will implement the server side. After that, we will revisit the client to make it more robust to message losses.

6.4.3 *A UDP-based server*

The server code is based on the built-in module `socketserver`, which provides utility classes to write servers based on sockets:

```
import os
import socketserver

import msgpack
```

We implement our server processing code inside a handler class.

```
class UDPProcessor(socketserver.BaseRequestHandler):  ◁────┘
    def handle(self):  ◁────
        request = msgpack.unpackb(self.request[0])
        socket = self.request[1]
        if request['command'] == 0:
            text = request['text']
            w = open(f'texts/{self.server.snippet_number}.txt', 'w')
            w.write(text)
            w.close()
            socket.sendto(self.server.snippet_number.to_bytes(
              4, byteorder='little'), self.client_address)
            self.server.snippet_number += 1
        elif request['command'] == 1:
            text_id = request['text_id']
            f = open(f'texts/{text_id}.txt')
            text = f.read()
            f.close()
            socket.sendto(text.encode(), self.client_address)
```

The handler class requires the creation of the handle method to implement functionality.

```
host = '127.0.0.1'
port = 54321

try:
    os.mkdir('texts')
except FileExistsError:
    pass

with socketserver.UDPServer((host, port), UDPProcessor)
   ⊳  as server:
        server.snippet_number = 0    ⟵
        server.serve_forever()
```

We create a UDP server.

**We initiate an internal
variable for text ids.**

The handle function starts by getting the command to decide which operation to perform. A storage request will take the supplied text and write it to disk. A retrieve
request will get the text pertaining to the supplied id.

The performance-related concepts of this code were introduced in the previous
subsection: they use msgpack and UDP. Now that we have a server and a client, let's
make the client more robust.

6.4.4   *Dealing with basic recovery on the client side*

Our original client sends a message and waits for a response. UDP doesn't assure
packet delivery, so we need to add a timeout mechanism. That being said, in a high-
performance local network, UDP packet loss should be a rare event.

Here is our implementation, using a decorator:

```
import functools

def timeout_op(func, max_attempts=3):
    @functools.wraps(func)
    def wrapper(*args, **kwds):
        attempts = 0
        while attempts < max_attempts:
            try:
                return func(*args, **kwds)
            except socket.timeout:
                print('Timeout: retrying')
            attempts += 1
        return None
    return wrapper


@timeout_op
def send_text(sock, text):
    ...


@timeout_op
def request_text(sock, text_id):
    ...
```

```
sock = socket.socket(
    socket.AF_INET,
    socket.SOCK_DGRAM)
sock.settimeout(1.0)    ⊲——— We set a timeout for the socket.
```

We simply apply our decorator to `send_text` and `request_text`. By default, the socket is blocking; that is, it waits until a message is received, so after `socket`, we use `settimeout` to make it nonblocking and return after 1.0 s if no message is received. This simple timeout mechanism should be enough to deal with the client side precisely because the network should be reliable enough to ensure most UDP packets won't be lost.

It would also make sense to do something similar on the server side. On the server side, there is a problem with the semantics of repeating an operation: if you end up saving a pastebin twice, you are expending disk resources. As a general rule, be careful with the semantics of the operations that you are creating. They may not be repeatable without causing harm.

6.4.5   *Other suggestions for optimizing network computing*

Our implementation uses UDP to substantially reduce message overhead, but sometimes you might need to use TCP, or even HTTPS or other protocols on top of TCP. Here are a few tips if that is the case:

- *If your client will send several requests to a server, try to use the same connection for all the requests.* This way, you only pay the price of setting up and tearing down the connection once.

- *Sometimes it is possible to pre-open TCP connections before peak usage.* This would allow the cost of establishing a connection to be paid outside a critical time path. This technique, as well as the previous technique, is commonly used with database connections and is called *connection pooling*.

- *If UDP is too simple and TCP is too heavy, consider using the new QUIC protocol.* QUIC originally stood for "quick UDP internet connections." As the old name indicates, it attempts to bridge the gap between having the advantages of connections on top of UDP.

Summary

- Being mindful of the memory hierarchy is fundamental to the design of efficient programs. Most programmers are at least somewhat aware of the effect of RAM, disk storage, and network access, but are often less aware of the effect of the relationship between CPU cache and transient RAM memory.

- DRAM memory access causes CPU starvation, making the CPU idle for many cycles. Making sure that as much data is available in the CPU cache as possible can significantly increase processing speed.

- Algorithms that avoid CPU starvation will potentially be more efficient but sometimes in unintuitive ways. For example, it might be faster to process compressed data than raw data as the cost of the (de)compression algorithm might be less than the cost of getting (larger) uncompressed data from RAM.

- In many cases, Blosc allows you to access compressed stored representations of data faster than using the raw data counterpart. This is in addition to the usual benefit of having smaller persistent datasets.
- NumExpr can process NumPy-like expressions in less time and with less memory than NumPy itself. NumExpr makes use of smart L1 cache, among other techniques, to speed up evaluation, sometimes more than one order of magnitude.
- Some modern local networks are so fast that accessing other computers over the network can be faster than accessing local disks.
- The standard REST APIs are too slow and inefficient to make performant use of fast local networks.
- Network communication can be made faster by introducing changes at several levels: selecting the best transport protocol (TCP versus UDP), not using HTTPS, and using faster ways than JSON to serialize data.

Part 3

Applications and Libraries for Modern Data Processing

Part 3 of the book is most directly applied to data problems, as it covers widely used Python analysis libraries. We first discuss the ever-present pandas library to process data frames. We also look at Apache Arrow, a modern library that can, among other tasks, help speed up pandas processing. We then discuss libraries designed to extract maximum performance from persistence. We examine Zarr for N-dimensional arrays and Parquet for data frames. The topic of dealing with larger-than-memory datasets is also introduced.

High-performance pandas and Apache Arrow

This chapter covers

- Optimizing memory usage with pandas' data frame creation
- Decreasing computational cost of pandas operations
- Using Cython, NumExpr, and Numpy to accelerate pandas operations
- Optimizing pandas with Apache Arrow

Data analytics is essentially synonymous with using pandas. pandas is a data frame library, or a library to process tabular data. pandas is the de facto standard in the Python world to process in-memory tabular data. In this chapter, we will discuss approaches to optimize pandas usage. This will be a two-pronged approach: we will optimize pandas usage directly, and we will also optimize it using Apache Arrow.

Apache Arrow provides language-agnostic functionality to efficiently access columnar data, to share these data across different language implementations, and to transfer data to different processes and even to different computers. It can complement pandas from a performance perspective by introducing faster

157

algorithms to perform basic operations, such as reading CSV files, translating pandas data frames to the format of lower-level languages for faster processing, and enhancing serialization mechanisms to transfer data frames across different computers.

We will start by considering some techniques to optimize pandas usage. Here, we'll divide our attention between time and memory. Given that pandas is an in-memory library, we want to make sure we have the smallest memory footprint possible, which allows us to not only do complex analytics over data but also load as much data as possible before we need to consider on-disk implementations (we'll talk more about disk implementation in chapter 10).

Next, we will use previously studied libraries—NumPy, Cython and NumExpr—to optimize the processing of pandas data frames. As pandas is based on NumPy, it is actually quite easy to use Cython and NumExpr to optimize pandas.

Then we will get to know Apache Arrow and discuss it from two points of view. First, we'll see how Apache Arrow provides alternative implementations of standard algorithms to pandas. For example, is there any performance advantage to reading a large CSV file in Arrow and converting it to pandas as opposed to reading it directly in pandas? Second, we will use Arrow to efficiently transfer data frames to other, lower-level programming languages so we can speed up the processing by using more efficient implementations of algorithms.

Let's start with optimizing data loading with standard pandas. If you are using conda, you should install PyArrow: at the moment I am writing this book, `pip install pyarrow` seems to be the most functional solution. If you use Docker, please use the image `tiagoantao/python-performance-dask`.

7.1 *Optimizing memory and time when loading data*

Our first task is to optimize memory usage and the speed of pandas data frame loading. In the next section, we will optimize data analysis operations. For our example, we will use the records of trips by the famous yellow cabs of New York City. The New York City Taxi and Limousine Commission (TLC) makes available a public dataset of trips at http://mng.bz/516D. We'll use the Yellow Car data for January 2020. We have information available for each cab ride, including start and end times, the number of passengers, fare amount, tip, and more.

We will start by downloading the data once locally. While pandas can download directly from a remote source, we do not want to wait every time we load the data frame from the network, as this would cost a lot of time; nor do we want to consistently access the data server. Our objective will be twofold: determine how much memory pandas requires to load the whole table and different columns and reduce memory usage. You can download the 566 MB of data by using wget (https://tiago.org/yellow_tripdata_2020-01.csv.gz).

7.1.1 *Compressed vs. uncompressed data*

Let's start by loading the data (the code in this section is available in `07-pandas/sec1-intro/read_csv.py`):

```
import pandas as pd

df = pd.read_csv("yellow_tripdata_2020-01.csv")
```

On my computer, this takes around 10 s. As you have seen in previous chapters, compressing the data may have a positive effect on time to process. Let's try to compress the file with xz and load it. You will need to have xz installed, and then you can use `yellow_tripdata_2020-01.csv`:

```
df = pd.read_csv("yellow_tripdata_2020-01.csv.xz")
```

pandas is smart enough to infer the compression type by extension, although you can override it. On my computer it took 15 s. While the number is worse than the uncompressed version, the file size is now only 74 MB, a seven-fold reduction. In this case, we were unable to reduce the time, so we will need to make a compromise between disk space and time to open the file. How you balance the two will depend on the requirements of your specific problem. We will revisit this with Apache Arrow; for now, table 7.1 provides the times and sizes for different algorithms. Times, of course, are dependent on the hardware on which this is run, but the relationship between different compression programs is what matters. Depending on your use case, you might need to read as fast as possible, or maybe size on disk is most important.

Table 7.1   Effect of CSV data compression on file size and time to open with pandas

Application	Time to read (s)	Size (MB)
None	10	566
gip	12	105
bzip2	26	103
xz	15	74

Do not take the relative size of the files across compression algorithms as a holy grail, however. Be sure to test with your data to see which ratios you get.

THE TAKEAWAY

With this example and throughout this chapter, the important takeaway is not the relative numbers presented, but the insight that different implementations and algorithms can have substantially different results. Two points are crucial to remember about optimizing memory and time (or, realistically, memory or time) when loading data. First, having an understanding of the underlying algorithms, rather than looking at them as a black box, will allow you to develop appropriate expectations of performance. Second, of course, you should profile for your specific conditions and determine whether it's more important to conserve time or memory.

7.1.2   *Type inference of columns*

When you load the data, you will get the following warning, at least with pandas version 1.0.5:

```
DtypeWarning: Columns (6) have mixed types. Specify the dtype option on
➥ import or set low_memory=False
```

This message indicates that the data loader was not able to correctly infer the types of all columns.

> **WARNING**   Resist the temptation to set `low_memory=False` as suggested in pandas's warning; with large data, that your code will very likely run out of memory and crash.

The warning message is typically a smoking gun for the fact that some columns are being loaded with data types that are too general. For instance, a column that is an integer is promoted to an object, with the equivalent increase in memory required. We will look at concrete examples later in this chapter.

Before going into each column, let's start by determining how much memory the whole data frame uses. pandas provides a more specific method than the general ones presented in previous chapters:

```
df.info(memory_usage="deep")
```

The abridged output is:

```
<class 'pandas.core.frame.DataFrame'>
RangeIndex: 6405008 entries, 0 to 6405007
Data columns (total 18 columns):
 #   Column                 Dtype
---  ------                 -----
 0   VendorID               float64
 1   tpep_pickup_datetime   object
 2   tpep_dropoff_datetime  object
 3   passenger_count        float64
 4   trip_distance          float64
 5   RatecodeID             float64
 6   store_and_fwd_flag     object
 7   PULocationID           int64
 8   DOLocationID           int64
 9   payment_type           float64
...
 17  congestion_surcharge   float64
dtypes: float64(13), int64(2), object(3)
memory usage: 2.0 GB
```

We get information for each column type, the number of entries, and memory usage. In our case, our 566 MB file is expanding to 2 GB! Given that we are talking about an input in text format, this seems oddly excessive.

Let's check the occupation of each column along with the number of unique values:

```
def summarize_columns(df):
    for c in df.columns:
        print(c, len(df[c].unique()),
            df[c].memory_usage(deep=True) // (1024**2), sep="\t")

summarize_columns()
```

The abridged output is:

```
tpep_pickup_datetime    2134342 object   464
passenger_count         11      float64  48
trip_distance           5606    float64  48
RatecodeID              8       float64  48
store_and_fwd_flag      3       object   401
PULocationID            261     int64    48
payment_type            6       float64  48
fare_amount             5283    float64  48
improvement_surcharge   3       float64  48
total_amount            12488   float64  48
congestion_surcharge    8       float64  48
```

Columns of type object occupy more the 400 MB each (for details about the size, see chapter 2). `float64` requires 64 bits per float—hence, 8 bytes per value and thus 48 MB. The same is valid for `int64`. Can we reduce memory occupation by changing the types of columns? Yes, we can—dramatically.

Let's start with `tpep_pickup_datetime` and `tpep_dropoff_datetime`. Their values are, as the names imply, dates with times. You can inspect these with `df["tpep_pickup_datetime"].head()`. Let's convert these columns to `datetime` format:

```
df["tpep_pickup_datetime"] = pd.to_datetime(df["tpep_pickup_datetime"])
df["tpep_dropoff_datetime"] = pd.to_datetime(df["tpep_dropoff_datetime"])
```

Just this simple change reduced each column from 464 to 48 MB and the data frame from 2 GB to 1.2 GB. I hope this is enough to convince you of the importance of loading the correct data types.

Also, several variables are discrete and have a small number of possible values. For example, `payment_type` can only have six numeric values but is implemented with an 8-byte `float64`. Let's recode it to a single byte:

```
import numpy as np
df["payment_type"] = df["payment_type"].astype(np.int8)
```

The type for 8-bit signed integers comes from NumPy. pandas is, of course, dependent on NumPy.

Unfortunately, this attempt will fail. If you inspect the column, you will see that there are a few missing data (NA) values along with the numeric values. We can recode the NAs as 0 because the value 0 is not otherwise used; if 0 is used, we would need to choose another value:

```
df["payment_type"] = df["payment_type"].fillna(0).astype(np.int8)
```

This change reduces the columns from 48 to 6 MB as expected—for 8 bytes per value to 1 byte per value. We have six columns that can be downsized from 64 to 8 bits and two that require 16 bits. This means another 450 MB cut. We are now down to roughly 750 MB.

Don't be fooled by how easy it was to solve that example; encoding and dealing with missing values is a complex problem and generally not so easily solved. While this example was easy to address, not all of the columns are that simple.

store_and_fwd_flag is one example of a more complex column. It is a Boolean flag indicating whether the fare was held in vehicle memory because the server that stores fares was unavailable. For the many records that are missing values, it is unknown (i.e., we do not know whether it is true or false). If no values were missing, we could represent the column as a boolean, which would take 1 bit per value. Given that we need to represent the third state, we have to use the next available data container which is 8-bit wide. Thus, dealing with the missing values costs us an eight-fold increase in memory allocation for this column. We end up doing:

```
df["store_and_fwd_flag"] = df["store_and_fwd_flag"].fillna(" ").apply(ord)
    .apply(
    lambda x: [32, 78, 89].index(x) - 1).astype(np.int8)
```

We convert NAs to spaces and get the ASCII code value of each character: 32 for space, 78 for N, and 89 for Y. With the index function, we can code NAs(32) as -1, N(78) as 0, and Y(89) as 1.

THE TAKEAWAY

We will revisit the complex topic of the representation of missing values throughout the remainder of the book, especially in the next chapter when we discuss persistence and the Parquet file format. For now, it's enough to know that a common waste of memory (and thus the speed of operations) is columnar data of a more general type than necessary: the broader the data type, the bigger the memory footprint, and the slower the speed of operations. Changing the column types is not always a simple task, but it can dramatically reduce the memory footprint.

7.1.3 *The effect of data type precision*

Another technique that we can use to reduce the memory footprint is using the same data type but with lower precision. For example, we can convert some of the cash values from float64 to float32 (i.e., double to single precision) for a 50% reduction in memory usage:

```
df["fare_amount_32"] = df["fare_amount"].astype(np.float32)
```

Now we need to assess the effect of lowering precision on our ability to represent values. A simple approach here could be:

```
(df["fare_amount_32"] - df["fare_amount"]).abs().sum()
```

We can compute the difference between the double and single precision. We must be careful to get the absolute values before adding them together to avoid cancellations. The total error on the whole data frame is a whopping $0.063:

```
df = pd.read_csv(
    "yellow_tripdata_2020-01.csv.gz",        We specify different types per column.
    dtype={
        "PULocationID": np.uint8,            We restrict some columns
        "DOLocationID": np.uint8             from 64-bit to 8-bit integers.
        },
    parse_dates=[
        "tpep_pickup_datetime",              There is a slightly different
        "tpep_dropoff_datetime"],            way to specify date types.
    converters={
        "VendorID":
            lambda x: np.int8(["", "1", "2"].index(x)),   We are explicitly
        "store_and_fwd_flag":                              converting VendorID
            lambda x: ["", "N", "Y"].index(x) - 1,         to np.int8.
        "payment_type":
            lambda x: -1 if x == "" else int(x),
        "RatecodeID":
            lambda x: -1 if x == "" else int(x),
        "passenger_count":
            lambda x: -1 if x == "" else int(x)

        }
)
```

We create several converters, mostly to recode NAs.

At this stage, `df.info(memory_usage="deep")` will report a memory usage of 757.4 MB. Notice, however, that most numeric types will report a 64-bit length, including `VendorID`, which we wrapped in a `np.int8` call—clearly to no avail.

We have several columns that clearly could still be smaller. Because we choose to be less precise, we will reduce all 64-bit floats to 16-bit ones. We will also reduce all 64-bit integers to 8-bit ones, as the range -128 to 127 of 8-bit integers is sufficient *in this specific case*.

```
for c in df.columns:
    if df[c].dtype == np.float64:
        df[c] = df[c].astype(np.float16)
    if df[c].dtype == np.int64:
        df[c] = df[c].astype(np.int8)
```

Our memory footprint is now down to 250.4 MB. Remember, we started with 2 GB. Not bad.

7.1.4   *Recoding and reducing data*

If you really need, you can try to reduce the operation even further. For example, several numeric columns make use of a small number of different values. Let's try to find those:

```
for c in df.columns:
    cnts = df[c].value_counts(dropna=False)      ⟵  value_counts returns the number
    if len(cnts) < 10:      ⟵                        of times each value is repeated.
        print(cnts)
```

We print all columns that have less than 10 distinct values.

Here we choose to print all columns that have less than 10 distinct values—10 is an arbitrary value that you can change. We already improved some of these columns, but two are represented by 16-bit floating points and can be reduced. `improvement_surcharge` has only three distinct values: 0, 0.3, and -0.3. These can easily be recoded to, say, 0, -1, and 1 and then reconverted. `congestion_surcharge` only has the values -2.5, -0.75, 0.5, 0.0, 0.5, 0.75, 2.0, 2.5, and 2.5. Although you can make a table of some sort, if you multiply all the values by 4, they become integers. You can use an 8-bit integer representation and encode them by multiplying by 4 and decode them by dividing equally by 4.

Finally, there is the ultimate solution to conserve memory: avoid loading the parts of the data that we do not need. For our next task, we will be fine if we only load pickup and drop-off date times along with the congestion surcharge. We can do this easily with pandas:

```
df = pd.read_csv(
    "yellow_tripdata_2020-01.csv.gz",
    dtype={
        "congestion_surcharge": np.float16,
        },
    parse_dates=[
        "tpep_pickup_datetime",
        "tpep_dropoff_datetime"],
    usecols=[
        "congestion_surcharge",
        "tpep_pickup_datetime",
        "tpep_dropoff_datetime"],
)
```

This code only requires 109.9 MB, around 5% of the original 2 GB requirement. We did this by reducing the number of columns and converting the load of some of them.

The false safety of using `inplace=True`

Most pandas methods have the ability to change the existing data structure in place, rather than returning a new data frame/series. You can save half of the memory at the expense of losing the original data. For example, you can drop all rows with NAs with

```
new_df = df.dropna()
```

> but you end up with three data frames, occupying twice the memory. Alternatively, you can use:
>
> ```
> df.dropna(inplace=True)
> ```
>
> This will change the state of the original data frame so it won't work in all situations, but in many cases, it can be a simple solution to reduce memory consumption by half.
>
> Be careful though: during the execution of the operation, pandas will allocate space for both arrays. So, during the execution, memory requirements will double. In a sense, this is mostly a convenience functionality that you can replicate with a `del` after using the default call without `inplace`.
>
> Arrow provides a much more interesting approach to lean memory management with the `self_destruct` parameter, which we will discuss later in the chapter.

The code in this section demonstrates the effect of making the right choices for the data representation of columns. In practice, the pandas reader can do all this at the start:

```
df = pd.read_csv(
    "yellow_tripdata_2020-01.csv.gz",        We can specify the desired
    dtype={                          ◁──────  type of some columns.
        "VendorID": np.int8,
        "trip_distance": np.float16,
        "PULocationID": np.uint8,
        "DOLocationID": np.uint8,
        },                           Dates are handled separately
    parse_dates=[         ◁────────  from other types.
        "tpep_pickup_datetime",
        "tpep_dropoff_datetime"],
    converters={              ◁────── We can convert on load.
        "VendorID":
            lambda x: np.int8(["", "1", "2"].index(x)),
        "store_and_fwd_flag":
            lambda x: ["", "N", "Y"].index(x) - 1,
        "payment_type":
            lambda x: -1 if x == "" else int(x),
        "RatecodeID":
            lambda x: -1 if x == "" else int(x),
        "passenger_count":
            lambda x: -1 if x == "" else int(x)

    }
)
```

Note that integer and float types will always be of the larger type, so you might need to downcast. Now that we have loaded the data in a memory efficiently, let's see what can speed up data analysis with pandas.

THE TAKEAWAY

We have gone through these exercises to demonstrate that careful choices of data types can decrease the amount of memory used. Narrowing the data type and broadening the precision are two approaches with relatively few tradeoffs.

There's more to understand about these general approaches, and we will return to them later. Reducing the amount and representation of data will be a big part of the last chapter of this book.

The good news about changing data types is that generally you don't need to convert the data after loading, as pandas will do that for you. In the next example, we will use `read_csv` to do most of the conversions on loading.

7.2 *Techniques to increase data analysis speed*

Let's now access records of NYC trips to do some statistical analysis. For example, we will determine the fraction of the payment that is a tip. We are not going to concentrate on the statistical analysis per se, as this is not a book about data science. Instead, we want to figure out how to access information efficiently so we can perform that kind of analysis if we choose. Here we will consider data frame indexing techniques and strategies to iterate over rows.

We start by loading the data. We just need three fields (the code is in `07-pandas/sec2-intro/index.py`):

```
df = pd.read_csv(
    "yellow_tripdata_2020-01.csv.gz",
    dtype={
        "congestion_surcharge": np.float16,
        },
    parse_dates=[
        "tpep_pickup_datetime",
        "tpep_dropoff_datetime"],
    usecols=[
        "congestion_surcharge",
        "tpep_pickup_datetime",
        "tpep_dropoff_datetime"],
)
```

7.2.1 *Using indexing to accelerate access*

Let's access all records with a certain pickup time:

```
df[df["tpep_pickup_datetime"] == "2020-01-06 08:13:00"]
```

For my machine, `timeit` reports a mean of 17.1 ms. We can try to sort the data frame by the pickup column:

```
df_sorted = df.sort_values("tpep_pickup_datetime")
df_sorted[df_sorted["tpep_pickup_datetime"] == "2020-01-06 08:13:00"]
```

Unfortunately, from a timing perspective, the result is on the same order of magnitude: pandas ignores column sorting to fetch rows. We can expect a completely different execution time if we use the index:

```
df_pickup = df.set_index("tpep_pickup_datetime")
df_pickup_sorted = df_pickup.sort_index()
df_pickup.loc["2020-01-06 08:13:00"]
df_pickup_sorted.loc["2020-01-06 08:13:00"]
```

In this case, we index the data frame on `tpep_pickup_datetime`. If we do not sort the data frame, as is the case in `df_pickup`, nothing is gained. But for `df_pickup_sorted`, which is now indexed *and* sorted by `tpep_pickup_datetime`, we go to 395 *micro*seconds, which is more than 40 times faster.

This solution comes with plenty of caveats, the obvious one being that it can only be used on the index. So, if you want to use another field, you would have to index on the other column or have an index with multiple columns. Thus, using the index is not a general solution, but our example suggests that you should carefully choose how you construct your index for performance. When you rely on the index—much pandas usage ignores the index—you are trading consistency of querying for potential speed gains. For example, if you want to know all rides that paid the congestion surcharge you can use this code:

```
df[
    (df["tpep_pickup_datetime"] == "2020-01-06 08:13:00") &
    (df["congestion_surcharge"] > 0)]
```

Notice that the query language treats both columns with the same language.

But if one is indexed, you can, for example, use this code:

```
my_time = df_pickup_sort.loc["2020-01-06 08:13:00"]
my_time[my_time["congestion_surcharge"] > 0]
```

> **TIP** All the arguments presented here for indexes can be used when joining frames (`df.join`) with an even greater effect on performance.

Now that we have a notion of the effect of using indexes, let's actually use the whole dataset to compute the mean fraction of the amount paid that is a tip.

7.2.2 *Row iteration strategies*

We will now consider different approaches to traverse a data frame. We will compute the fraction of the total amount paid that is a tip for our dataset, which will require going over all records to get the tip and total amounts.

We will start by reading the data and removing all total amounts that are zero (see `07-pandas/sec2-speed/traversing.py`):

```
df = pd.read_csv("../sec1-intro/yellow_tripdata_2020-01.csv.gz")
# ^^ replace

df = df[(df.total_amount != 0)]
df_10 = df.sample(frac=0.1)
df_100 = df.sample(frac=0.01)
```

Notice that we subsample the main data frame at 10% and 1%, which will help us later with performance testing.

Let's start by using a conventional Python technique (i.e., not using pandas- or NumPy-based approaches like vectorization): a `for` loop over all records:

```
def get_tip_mean_explicit(df):
    all_tips = 0
    all_totals = 0                        A typical Python for loop
    for i in range(len(df)):         ◁——  using the number of rows
        row = df.iloc[i]             ◁———— Accesses the row by position
        all_tips += row["tip_amount"]
        all_totals += row["total_amount"]
    return all_tips / all_totals
```

This code represents what a Python developer with no pandas or NumPy experience would typically write. The performance is, quite frankly, horrendous: measured in *minutes* on my computer as reported by `timeit`.[1]

There are two `for`-based approaches that provide better results. The first one is based on the `iterrows` method of a data frame:

```
def get_tip_mean_iterrows(df):
    all_tips = 0
    all_totals = 0
    for i, row in df.iterrows():
        all_tips += row["tip_amount"]
        all_totals += row["total_amount"]
    return all_tips / all_totals
```

This code is still a `for` loop, but in this case, we are using a pandas iterator that returns the current position and a row. The time is slightly better but still really bad.

> **TIP** If you are just starting with pandas and NumPy, it is perfectly normal for you to be used to a `for`-loop approach to perform many computations. While your medium-term approach should consider other techniques like vectorization (we will see a few examples later), in the short term, while you are not used to more efficient approaches, consider avoiding both the explicit and `iterrows`-based idioms. Of all the `for`-based approaches, `itertuples` will most probably save you the most time while still using an approach that you are comfortable with. You should, in any case, train yourself to use explicit iteration with pandas as soon as possible.

---

[1] If you plan on running this example, consider using the subsampled data frames `df_10` and `df_100`: you will still get a feeling for the time required without waiting so long.

Our final `for`-based approach is based on `itertuples`, where we use an iterator that returns one tuple per row:

```
def get_tip_mean_itertuples(df):
    all_tips = 0
    all_totals = 0
    for my_tuple in df.itertuples():
        all_tips += my_tuple.tip_amount
        all_totals += my_tuple.total_amount
    return all_tips / all_totals
```

While the idiom is still the same, the mean time falls to 18 s!

We are now going to consider pandas-based dialects. We will start by using `apply`, which is conceptually similar to using a map function, where each row is processed individually:

```
def get_tip_mean_apply(df):
    frac_tip = df.apply(
        lambda row: row["tip_amount"] / row["total_amount"],
        axis=1
    )
    return frac_tip.mean()
```

We use the data frame mean function to compute the final value.

Apply can be called for each column, which is the default, or for each row, which is what we will be using. The default axis of 0 will do column processing, and the axis of 1 will do row processing.

Using `apply` reduced the time to 9.5 s, which is twice as fast as the previous solution—good but not great.

Before we discuss the vectorization-based solution, let's try a slightly different dialect for `apply`:

```
def get_tip_mean_apply2(df):  # df_10: 14.9s
    frac_tip = df.apply(
        lambda row: row.tip_amount / row.total_amount,
        axis=1
    )
    return frac_tip.mean()
```

The difference here is that we use `row.tip_amount` and `row.total_amount` instead of `row["tip_amount"]` and `row["total_amount"]`. Our object attribute–based approach is actually slower compared to the dictionary approach. The mean cost on my computer is 14 s.

> **TIP** With different pandas versions, the performance relationship between different methods might change, as there is no guarantee that algorithms stay the same. This is valid both for accessing values on row objects, as well as for different algorithms. So, if performance is not good enough, always benchmark different algorithm approaches (`for`, `apply`, vectorization, etc.) and object access patterns (object attribute lookup versus dictionary lookup). Do not take the relationships presented in this book as gospel.

Now let's see the effect of using pandas best practices for computation. We will start with a vectorization approach:

```
def get_tip_mean_vector(df):
    frac_tip = df["tip_amount"] / df["total_amount"]
    return frac_tip.mean()
```

We take the `tip_amount` series from the data frame and divide it by the `total_amount` series. We then use the mean. The time required fell by several orders of magnitude: it now takes a mean time of 32 ms.

Remember, the example we worked on here is a simple one, to illustrate the importance of different strategies for iterating over rows. For more complex computations, try to come up with a vectorized approach. If that is not possible, you may be able to split the computation into parts, so you have isolated a vectorized (i.e., fast) part. Then you can reduce the nonvectorized part to the smallest cost possible.

THE TAKEAWAY

The data-loading process is often overlooked as a task that can contribute to memory usage and thus speed of operations further on down the line. Correct typing of columns is the main way to optimize memory while loading, although broadening precision parameters can also help. pandas can handle the typing as it loads so you don't have to do it afterward.

Accessing data once it is loaded is another process that can be examined for potential time-savings during operations. There are two general strategies for improving efficiency while accessing data. First, using indexing can be helpful but it also comes with a number of drawbacks. You can use row iteration. Some methods of iterating over data frames are faster than others. The general rule of thumb is that row-based analysis should usually be approached in a declarative way: vectorizing if possible but at least avoiding explicit iteration. Now that we have considered some pandas-native approaches to optimization, let's consider alternatives using lower-level techniques.

7.3   *pandas on top of NumPy, Cython, and NumExpr*

For the next few sections, we will draw on discussions we've had in previous chapters about NumPy (chapter 4), Cython (chapter 5), and NumExpr (chapter 6), so here we will just do a whirlwind tour of these technologies as they apply to Python. If you need any reminders of the basics, please feel free to turn back to those chapters at any point necessary.

The goal of this section is to investigate NumPy, Cython, and NumExpr from a pandas perspective and to see how they can improve performance for data analysis. To conduct this investigation, we will revisit the example we used in the previous section: computing the portion of the paid amount of each fare that is a tip.

7.3.1   *Explicit use of NumPy*

The approaches we used in the previous section are all, implicitly, NumPy approaches, in the sense that pandas sits on top of NumPy. It is also possible to use NumPy explicitly.

We start by getting the NumPy underlying representation of a series and then using a NumPy operation (see `07-pandas/sec3-numpy-numpexpr-cython/traversing.py`):

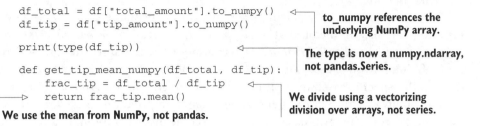

```
df_total = df["total_amount"].to_numpy()        ◁——  to_numpy references the
df_tip = df["tip_amount"].to_numpy()                  underlying NumPy array.

print(type(df_tip))                         ◁——  The type is now a numpy.ndarray,
                                                  not pandas.Series.
def get_tip_mean_numpy(df_total, df_tip):
    frac_tip = df_total / df_tip            ◁——
    return frac_tip.mean()                        We divide using a vectorizing
▷                                                 division over arrays, not series.
We use the mean from NumPy, not pandas.
```

The NumPy-based vectorized code runs in 11 ms on my computer, compared to 35 ms on the vectorized pandas version. The previous operation works on NumPy arrays, but not pandas series.[2]

> **TIP** The `to_numpy` method returns a reference to the underlying pandas array. If you prefer a copy because you might want to make changes that are not reflected on the original, then use the `to_numpy(copy=True)` method. Remember, if you copy, memory usage will double and there will be a time cost for doing the copy.

7.3.2   pandas on top of NumExpr

We can use NumExpr to query the data instead of using pandas' querying engine. NumExpr is an expression evaluator that can perform substantially better than NumPy, due not only to its highly efficient multithreaded implementation, but also because of its judicious use of intermediate memory, allowing many computations to be done mostly based on CPU cache. For more details, see the previous chapter.

Here is a simple implementation of the fraction of payment as the tip:

```
def get_tip_mean_numexpr(df):
    return df.eval("(tip_amount / total_amount).mean()", engine="numexpr")
```

As expected, pandas expands NumExpr's language with support for data frames and series. In the previous case, we refer to the columns `tip_amount` and `total_amount` in our evaluation string, which are resolved to the related pandas columns. It is also possible to use pandas' eval in the local namespace. For example, the previous code could be implemented as:

```
def get_tip_mean_numexpr(df):
    return pd.eval("(df.tip_amount / df.total_amount).mean()", engine="numexpr")
```

This would allow you to refer to more than a single data frame in an eval call. You could also use non-pandas variables; for details, see the eval documentation on the pandas website (http://mng.bz/aMAX).

---

[2] Of course, from a Python perspective, the difference is only conceptual: if you passed a series to the function, it would work as well, but with pandas objects. We are making an implementation point here, even if the language is more flexible.

What about performance? It is in the same league as the vectorized pandas solution—around 35 ms—hence substantially slower than the NumPy solution at 11 ms. What is going on?

First, we pay a price by parsing the string into executable code. As we saw in the previous chapter, this means that *NumExpr is only useful when the amount of data to process is large enough to justify the overhead*. Determining what is "large enough" will require some evaluation on a case-by-case basis: you will have to do some profiling of your data. In this specific case, we are using a large enough dataset. What is going on then?

The ability of NumExpr to generate efficient computation strategies *increases* with the complexity of the formula, as cache hits become more common. Let's consider the, arguably contrived, example of summing the fraction that we are using four times:

tip_amount / total_amount + tip_amount / total_amount + tip_amount / total_amount + tip_amount / total_amount

Here are the NumPy and NumExpr implementations:

```
def get_tip_mean_numpy4(df_total, df_tip):
    frac_tip = (
        df_total / df_tip +
        df_total / df_tip +
        df_total / df_tip +
        df_total / df_tip )
    return frac_tip.mean()


def get_tip_mean_numexpr4(df):
    return df.eval(
        "tip_amount / total_amount +"
        "tip_amount / total_amount +"
        "tip_amount / total_amount +"
        "tip_amount / total_amount", engine="numexpr").mean()
```

The only thing that changed was the complexity of the formula. The NumPy solution jumps, slightly worse than linearly, to a mean of 55 ms. NumExpr stays exactly the same at 35 ms! This is not to imply that the performance of NumExpr makes the complexity of the formula irrelevant, but it strongly suggests what we observed in the previous chapter: if our implementation can rely on the CPU cache as much as possible and avoid going to DRAM, then we can get substantial performance increases that are apparently counterintuitive.

THE TAKEAWAY

NumExpr is more efficient with lots of data *and* complex formulas, which means it will be helpful in the most complicated cases. As you have seen, in our first approach, NumExpr underperformed NumPy and pandas. This is yet another example suggesting that you should not always use the "best" technique, but instead, evaluate for your dataset and algorithm to determine the most efficient solution. One size doesn't fit all, and the most sophisticated and elegant solution presented in this book, which NumExpr arguably is, should not be taken as gospel. Let's now see how we can use Cython with pandas to improve the performance of our exercise.

7.3.3   *Cython and pandas*

We are now going to re-implement the tip analysis code using Cython and profile the potential performance benefits. We will keep this subsection deliberately short because there is really no such thing as a *direct* relationship between Cython and pandas. In this case, our ability to use Cython is completely based on NumPy, as depicted in figure 7.1. So, if you have read the Cython chapter, you should be mostly comfortable with the following code. Here we will recreate our ongoing example with Cython: we will be using Cython best practices from the get-go.

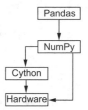

Figure 7.1   pandas using Cython via NumPy

The Pure Python calling code is (see `07-pandas/sec3-numpy-numpexpr-cython/traversing_cython_top.py`):

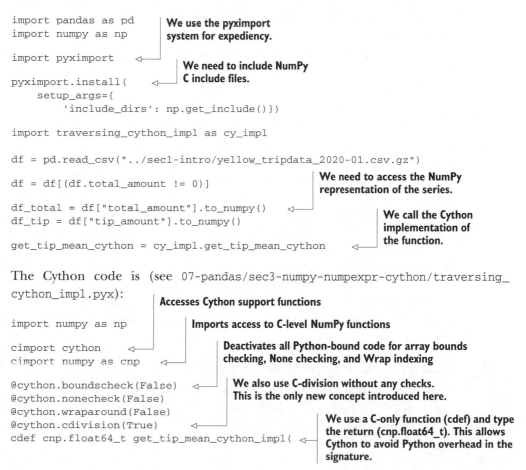

```
import pandas as pd
import numpy as np

import pyximport          ◁        We use the pyximport
                                   system for expediency.

pyximport.install(        ◁        We need to include NumPy
    setup_args={                   C include files.
        'include_dirs': np.get_include()})

import traversing_cython_impl as cy_impl

df = pd.read_csv("../sec1-intro/yellow_tripdata_2020-01.csv.gz")

df = df[(df.total_amount != 0)]              We need to access the NumPy
                                             representation of the series.
df_total = df["total_amount"].to_numpy()  ◁
df_tip = df["tip_amount"].to_numpy()                We call the Cython
                                                    implementation of
get_tip_mean_cython = cy_impl.get_tip_mean_cython ◁ the function.
```

The Cython code is (see `07-pandas/sec3-numpy-numpexpr-cython/traversing_cython_impl.pyx`):

```
                          Accesses Cython support functions

import numpy as np        Imports access to C-level NumPy functions

cimport cython          ◁
cimport numpy as cnp    ◁    Deactivates all Python-bound code for array bounds
                             checking, None checking, and Wrap indexing

@cython.boundscheck(False)  ◁     We also use C-division without any checks.
@cython.nonecheck(False)          This is the only new concept introduced here.
@cython.wraparound(False)
@cython.cdivision(True)     ◁     We use a C-only function (cdef) and type
cdef cnp.float64_t get_tip_mean_cython_impl( ◁  the return (cnp.float64_t). This allows
                                                Cython to avoid Python overhead in the
                                                signature.
```

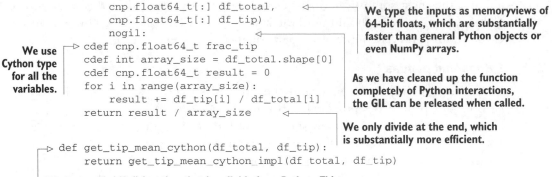

We use Cython type for all the variables.

```
        cnp.float64_t[:] df_total,
        cnp.float64_t[:] df_tip)
    nogil:
  cdef cnp.float64_t frac_tip
  cdef int array_size = df_total.shape[0]
  cdef cnp.float64_t result = 0
  for i in range(array_size):
      result += df_tip[i] / df_total[i]
  return result / array_size
```

We type the inputs as memoryviews of 64-bit floats, which are substantially faster than general Python objects or even NumPy arrays.

As we have cleaned up the function completely of Python interactions, the GIL can be released when called.

We only divide at the end, which is substantially more efficient.

```
def get_tip_mean_cython(df_total, df_tip):
    return get_tip_mean_cython_impl(df_total, df_tip)
```

We have a "bridge" function that is callable from Python. This will implicitly convert the NumPy array to memoryviews.

For completeness, I annotated all the code with the practices that we studied in the Cython chapter (chapter 4). The only new feature here is the usage of the `cdivision` annotation, which will not raise Python errors with a denominator of 0 and be more efficient. The code will crash if there is a division by 0. Remember, we carefully removed all rows with a `total_amount` of 0 in the native Python code, so for our case, we will be fine.

If you change the code, remember to use `cython -a` to generate an HTML report of potential interactions with the Python interpreter (i.e., potential performance bottlenecks). Performance? 8.51 ms. The best of the pack!

THE TAKEAWAY

Since pandas is built on top of NumPy, using NumPy is implicit when we use pandas. Still, if we explicitly require NumPy data structures, we can further improve performance speed. Cython can also be used with the NumPy data structures in pandas to improve performance speed. When working with very large data frames and complex algorithms, NumExpr is often your best bet for speed. Because of the many variables, including hardware, software, data, and both long-term and short-term goals, it is impossible to rank these solutions against each other. What works best for my situation and my needs may not be the best solution for yours. Understanding and experimenting with these different approaches should give you the insights you need to select an appropriate strategy for specific projects.

Next, we will consider another approach to optimize pandas. We will use Apache Arrow to increase the performance of some common operations, such as reading data from the disk.

7.4   *Reading data into pandas with Arrow*

In this section, we will accelerate data loading into a pandas data frame using Apache Arrow to do the loading. But before we get started on that, let's take a step back and understand the somewhat confusing relationship between pandas and Arrow.

> **NOTE** This section is intended to be a primer on how pandas and Arrow work together, not on Arrow per se, although we will indulge in some minor analytics at the end of the section. For more information on Arrow itself, see https://arrow.apache.org/.

7.4.1 The relationship between pandas and Apache Arrow

Apache Arrow is essentially a language-independent memory format for columnar data. It is language-independent, which means it is not tied to Python/pandas or any other language. It is, at its core, a set of libraries to perform basic operations in very fast low-level languages like C, Rust, or Go, although sometimes implementations exist in higher-level languages like JavaScript. For slower languages, the faster implementations are wrapped around in a layer. For example, the Python "implementation" of Arrow is actually a wrapper for the C++ implementation.

Here we will consider Arrow as a subsidiary to pandas: we want Arrow to accelerate certain parts of pandas data analysis, not replace pandas wholesale. Maybe in the future, as its analytics implementation grows, Arrow can work as a complete pandas replacement, but that is not yet the case.

In this section, we will replace pandas persistence mechanism (i.e., the reading of CSV files with Arrow) and briefly touch on Arrow analytics. In the next section, we will discuss Arrow's efficient Interprocess Communication (IPC) mechanism using the supplied IPC server, Plasma. In both cases, our objective is to determine whether we can increase speed.

Arrow has more functionality available. We will study the persistence part in more detail in the next chapter, especially in terms of file formats and their effects on efficiency. Arrow is also able to deal with several different persistent backends. In addition, there is functionality for remote procedure calls (RPC) to send data across different computers. A general overview of the current Arrow architecture is depicted in figure 7.2.

On top of Python is a Python wrapper for the C Arrow implementation. The C part is composed of several components—chief among them, a fledgling analysis engine that can make use of GPU computing and a persistence layer that can deal with several backends like the file system, Amazon S3, and Hadoop, and with several file formats such as CSV, Parquet, and JSON. Finally, there is interprocess and intermachine functionality to allow efficient communication with other processes, potentially running on other machines. Most important, the underlying Arrow data format is transversal to many programming languages and hardware architectures.

Figure 7.2 The internal architecture of PyArrow

Now let's see how efficient Arrow is at data reading compared to pandas.

7.4.2 *Reading a CSV file*

In the first section of this chapter, we used pandas to read a CSV file for information about taxi rides in New York City. One of the problems that Apache Arrow modernizes, compared to pandas, is file reading. It has a multithreaded reader and is substantially more intelligent at inferring column types. As stated in the beginning of this section, features of both pandas and Arrow will probably evolve after this book is published, and the relationship may change. At the time of this writing, Apache Arrow has a more modern architecture and it's difficult to see how pandas, with its need to support a long, successful legacy of applications, can catch up.

Let's load the same CSV file and study memory occupation of the loaded data (see 07-pandas/sec4-arrow-intro/read_csv.py):

```
from pyarrow import csv    ◁──── We import the CSV processor from PyArrow.

table = csv.read_csv("../sec1-intro/yellow_tripdata_2020-01.csv.gz")

tot_bytes = 0
for name in table.column_names:    ◁──┐  We traverse all columns to
    col_bytes = table[name].nbytes     │  get type and allocation.
    col_type = table[name].type
    print(name, col_bytes // (1024 ** 2))
    tot_bytes += col_bytes
print("Total", tot_bytes // (1024 ** 2))
```

The operation goes from 12 s to 2 s on my computer, a six-fold decrease. Here is an abridged version of the output:

```
VendorID int64 48
tpep_pickup_datetime timestamp[s] 48
passenger_count int64 48
trip_distance double 48
store_and_fwd_flag string 34
total_amount double 48
Total 865
```

Without any help, Arrow's memory consumption is 865 MB, compared with 2 GB from pandas. If we help pandas, then we get down to 250 MB, although using the naive Arrow to help pandas is not really fair. That being said, how does Arrow fare?

Arrow fares pretty well: without domain knowledge, an automated system could potentially do better, but not much. VendorID has only three values (1, 2, and null) and could be reduced to int8, which is valid for most integers. But in regard to using doubles for floats, Arrow could not know that we would be OK with a smaller representation.

> **NOTE** Arrow types are different from Python and NumPy/pandas, although conversion is easy from one to the other. While it is simple from a programmatic perspective, there are important differences in the way types are represented.

You may have noticed that VendorID, which includes null, is coded as an integer. This would be impossible in pandas/NumPy, unless we recode the NA. Arrow implements missing values in a completely different way from NumPy/pandas: there is an *extra* bit array with one entry per row indicating whether the value is missing. This means that, at the expense of a modest memory cost for most types, missing values do not require any representation on the type per se. Hence, an integer can be represented by an integer, without any recoding for missing values.

With Arrow's representation of missing values, we can substantially reduce the memory requirements of many columns, but we still have to inform Arrow in a few cases. For that, PyArrow provides the ConvertOptions class:

```
convert_options = csv.ConvertOptions(
    column_types = {
        "VendorID": pa.bool_()
    },
    true_values=["Y", "1"],
    false_values=["N", "2"])
table = csv.read_csv(
    "../sec1-intro/yellow_tripdata_2020-01.csv.gz",
    convert_options=convert_options
    )
print(
    table["store_and_fwd_flag"].unique(),
    table["store_and_fwd_flag"].nbytes // (1024 ** 2),
    table["store_and_fwd_flag"].nbytes // 1024
)
```

Arrow can infer the type of store_and_fwd_flag as a boolean from true_values and false_values but, given that VendorID is numeric, Arrow needs to explicitly state its type.

We inform Arrow that Y and 1 are to be converted to true. This will only be used in columns that are boolean. We perform a similar operation for false values.

We pass the conversion options to the CSV reader.

VendorID is technically not a boolean, but as it has only two possible values, we recode it as such to save memory.

Because missing values are handled separately, the memory cost of columns with a small number of possible states but that include missing values is much more efficient, with boolean being the most extreme case.

For store_and_fwd_flag, we display the three values, along with memory occupation. Because it is below 1 MB, we also print the value as 790 KB.

Unfortunately, we will have to convert from Arrow to pandas for analysis, as the internal formats are different. As such, we pay a memory and time price.

```
table_df = table.to_pandas()
```

As expected, the pandas version requires more memory. For example, store_and_fwd_flag is now an object. Even if you convert it to a more efficient type, it will be less compact than what is possible with Arrow's representation of missing values.

At this stage, it appears that many of the gains that we made from using Arrow are lost, but that is not so. There are two points to consider: the time cost of converting the data and the memory occupation. Both can be addressed.

The time cost of the conversion is a fraction of the gain from reading the file in Arrow: reading in pandas is around 12 s. Reading in Arrow is around 2 s to which the conversion time is added. That time is 23 ms on my computer, thus negligible when compared with the read gains.

The memory problem is real, and with the current approach, at one point, we need twice as much memory. Fortunately, Arrow provides a solution. You can ask Arrow to self-destruct the Arrow structure during conversion. This will not increase memory consumption at any point in time, at the expense of destroying the Arrow version:

```
mission_impossible = table.to_pandas(self_destruct=True)
```

THE TAKEAWAY

As this example should make clear, Arrow provides modern functionality with improved efficiency in both time and space when compared to pandas. As of now, Arrow is very far from offering the same analytics capabilities as pandas, so it is best used integrated with pandas. But let's take a few minutes to see what data analysis with Arrow looks like and get a taste of what is possible, and probable, with future versions of Arrow.

7.4.3   *Analyzing with Arrow*

Since this book is about what you can do right now to increase efficiency, what interests us about Arrow is how it works in service of pandas. But the fact is, Arrow can do data analysis on its own. Although it is seriously lacking in features for analysis, especially compared with pandas, as time goes by, its analytical capabilities will only improve.

To see how Arrow does data analysis, we will return, once again, to our analysis of tips for taxi drivers:

```
import pyarrow.compute as pc

t0 = table.filter(
    pc.not_equal(table["total_amount"], 0.0))

pc.mean(pc.divide(t0["tip_amount"], t0["total_amount"]))
```

The details of the code and, by extension, the design philosophy differ significantly from pandas. First, at this stage, the interface is lower level: if you try to perform the not_equal operation using an integer (0) and not a float (0.0), the code will fail, as the types are different. Second, the interface is substantially more functional than object-oriented; note that we call functions with array parameters and not methods on top of arrays. Finally, error reporting is based on error codes, not throwing exceptions. Irrespective of API preferences, there are potential benefits to being minimalist by mapping the underlying C Arrow library with the least Python idiom on top, one advantage being speed.

The time cost of the computation of the tip fraction is ~15 ms on my computer. This time is about half of the equivalent pandas version (`get_tip_mean_vector`).

We've seen how Arrow can efficiently load data into pandas. But there is a second way we can make use of Arrow and pandas together, and we turn to that next. Let's see how Arrow can help with interoperation between different languages; remember, Arrow provides a standard memory format across implementations.

7.5 Using Arrow interop to delegate work to more efficient languages and systems

One of the advantages of Arrow is its standard in-memory format, which allows data structure representation to be shared across implementations over many different languages. It does this sharing with zero-copy, or at the very least, it transfers data structure representations efficiently. In this section, we will explore why the Arrow architecture is more efficient than the alternatives. We will also implement an example using Arrow's Plasma server for interprocess communication.

The main objective of this section is to illustrate how Arrow can make interprocess communication more efficient. Given that Plasma is under heavy development and that you can actually implement memory sharing explicitly yourself across processes, take the content here as more of an illustration of a design pattern. That being said, the code is, of course, fully functional and usable.

7.5.1 Implications of Arrow's language interop architecture

Imagine a scenario where you are doing most of your processing in Python, but you need to use a piece of R code to do some analysis. There are many ways to conduct interprocess and interlanguage communication, but consider two typical non-Arrow scenarios and two typical Arrow scenarios, as shown in figure 7.3 and described as follows:

- The first approach would be to write our data in a file format in Python (e.g., CSV) and then read it in R. This could be very memory-efficient, but the time cost would be abysmal due to disk usage.
- The second approach would use rpy2,[3] which would require converting from pandas to R data frames, which are roughly the equivalent of pandas in the R world. This would entail at least doubling the cost of conversion, both in time and memory. It is actually worse than this as we will see in the following discussion.
- With Arrow, a third approach would be to take a pandas data frame, convert it to Arrow, pass it to R, convert it from Arrow, and process it. This requires time for two conversions (pandas to Arrow and Arrow to R). Memory-wise, the outcome will depend on whether you can be destructive, which adds no increase in consumption; if not, you will need to roughly double your memory during conversion.

---

[3] If you also use R—its pairing with Python is quite common in the data science world—consider integrating both by using the rpy2 package, which will embed an R process in Python and provide elegant primitives for Python/R communication.

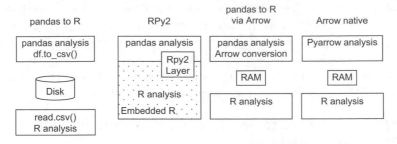

Figure 7.3   **Some alternatives for interoperability between Python and R**

- Finally, the best-case scenario with Arrow, if you are processing in *both* Python and R, is based on Arrow only (e.g., no pandas), then it is just a question of passing a memory pointer, which adds zero cost in terms of processing and of memory.

It might seem at first glance that solution 2, going from pandas' native format to R's, is more efficient than using solution 3, going from pandas to Arrow and from Arrow to R. However, that is not the case for a few reasons:

- The in-memory Arrow format is shared by all Arrow implementations, irrespective of language. This means that sharing an Arrow data structure is in essence just sharing a memory pointer.
- When converting from pandas to R, the converter has to occur on one side, either Python or R, which means that it will be nonnative and very inefficient in one of the formats (i.e., the one that is nonnative).
- Arrow converters are done in C/C++, multithreaded, and designed from scratch precisely to be as efficient as possible. You have seen the effect of that philosophy in the previous section about the performance of using CSV readers.

There is also another important reason: in a complex system, you will need 2^n converters. For example, if you use pandas, Java, R, and Rust, you will need pandas/Java, pandas/R, Java/R, Java/Rust, pandas/Rust, and R/Rust converters. But if you use Arrow as an intermediate format, then you will need only four: pandas/Arrow, Java/Arrow, R/Arrow, and Rust/Arrow. If you use more systems, the combinations explode.

It is beyond the scope of this book to delve into the use of languages other than Python, but feel free to experiment with other language options to get a measure of the performance effect of each one.

What we will do next, totally in Python, is demonstrate how to efficiently interprocess communication of data. In many real-world scenarios, one or more of your components would be implemented in a different language.

7.5.2   *Zero-copy operations on data with Arrow's Plasma server*

Let's go back to our old, familiar NYC taxi dataset and compute a set of statistics over the data. We will divide this into three processes: one reads the data and submits it for processing, another does the analysis, and a third just shows the results. There are two main reasons to consider this architecture: (1) There might be an implementation of an algorithm that we need that is available in a separate process that cannot be linked directly to Python, and (2) we might prefer to separate the more expensive processing code from the analysis code.

Arrow provides a server, called Plasma, that manages shared memory: it allows you to register, read, and write objects, along with all operations to consult the catalog of existing objects. This facilitates the way processes are able to find each other in a standard fashion. This server is local—that is, not accessible on the network but via a local socket. It mostly exists to facilitate sharing of memory, easily find existing objects, and allow for the sharing of memory across processes that do not overlap in the lifetime (i.e., a consumer process is started after the producer has died).

The first thing that we need to do is to start the Plasma server:

```
plasma_store -s /tmp/fast_python  -m 1000000000
```

This will use a UNIX socket, /tmp/fast_python, which is a form of interprocess communication, to allow processes to communicate. One gigabyte will be allocated as a shared space.

Our first process is responsible for loading a CSV file and putting it in Plasma: we connect to the Plasma socket, read a file with Arrow, and deposit it with Plasma (see 07-pandas/sec5-arrow-plasma/load_csv.py):

```
import os
import sys

import pyarrow as pa
from pyarrow import csv
import pyarrow.plasma as plasma

csv_name = sys.argv[1]
client = plasma.connect("/tmp/fast python")        ◁──┐  We connect to Plasma
                                                      └─ via the socket.

convert_options = csv.ConvertOptions(   ◁──┐  We are assuming that the CSV
    column_types={                         └─ is in the NYC taxi format.
        "VendorID": pa.bool_()
    },
    true_values=["Y", "1"],
    false_values=["N", "2"])
table = csv.read_csv(
    csv_name
    convert_options=convert_options
    )

pid = os.getpid()

plid = plasma.ObjectID(
  f"csv-{pid}".ljust(20, " ").encode("us-ascii"))   ◁── We create an ID for our table.

client.put(table, plid)     ◁── We put the object in Plasma.
```

When we put an object in Plasma, we have to give it an ID (i.e. name it). We will use a name that is `csv-`, followed by the PID (process ID) of our process. This name is good enough for our intentions here, but you might need something with less clash potential with other name strings as a more general solution. Plasma requires a 20-byte ID, so we pad the name with spaces to get to a size of 20 and then encode our string using the US-ASCII codec, which will return a list of bytes. You can use any codec you'd like as long as it will convert one character to 1 byte, or you will end up with a byte array that is too long.

We use the object ID to denote and find our tables. There are other potentially more sophisticated techniques, such as using object metadata, but as long as we have a way to find our objects of interest, an object ID is enough for illustrative purposes.

> **WARNING**   If you do not have enough memory available, Plasma will evict older objects.

Before we implement the two other processes, let's create a support script to list all CSVs currently available in Plasma, which allows us to monitor what is in Plasma. We will also monitor for results, which we will name with the prefix `result-` (see `07-pandas/sec5-arrow-plasma/list_csvs.py`):

```python
import pyarrow as pa
import pyarrow.plasma as plasma

client = plasma.connect("/tmp/fast_python")

all_objects = client.list()     ◁─── We list all the objects.

for plid, keys in all_objects.items():
    try:
        plid_str = plid.binary().decode("us-ascii")
    except UnicodeDecodeError:      ◁─┐
        continue                       │ As decoding of IDs might not yield valid
    if plid_str.startswith("csv-"):    │ strings, we need to catch exceptions.
        print(plid_str, plid)
        print(keys)
    elif plid_str.startswith("result-"):
        print(plid_str, plid)
        print(keys)
```

After we get the list of all objects, which is returned as a dictionary, we look for IDs starting with either `csv-` or `result-`. Because not all IDs may actually convert to a string (i.e., other stuff may be being shared in the Plasma server), we are careful to catch all exceptions that cannot be decoded, and then we ignore them as they are not really errors.

For all relevant cases, we print the decoded ID, the original one and some metadata associated. Here is an example:

```
csv-579123           ObjectID(6373762d353739313233202020202020202020)
{'data_size': 822037944, 'metadata_size': 0, 'ref_count': 0,
 'create_time': 1616361341, 'construct_duration': 0,
 'state': 'sealed'}
```

Now let's implement our computation server. It will be in an eternal loop, looking for objects whose name starts with csv-. If one is found and a result doesn't exist yet, then perform the computation and put the result in Plasma according to the object ID naming conversion starting with result- (see 07-pandas/sec5-arrow-plasma/compute_stats.py):

```
import time

import pandas as pd
import pyarrow as pa
from pyarrow import csv
import pyarrow.compute as pc
import pyarrow.plasma as plasma

client = plasma.connect("/tmp/fast_python")
while True:
    client = plasma.connect("/tmp/fast_python")
    all_objects = client.list()

    for plid, keys in all_objects.items():
        plid_str = ""
        try:
            plid_str = plid.binary().decode("us-ascii")
        except UnicodeDecodeError:
            continue
        if plid_str.startswith("csv-"):
            original_pid = plid_str[4:]
            result_plid = plasma.ObjectID(
                f"result-{original_pid}".ljust(
                    20, " ")[:20].encode("us-ascii"))    ⟵  We check whether a
            if client.contains(result_plid):            ⟵  result already exists.
                continue
            print(f"Working on: {plid_str}")
            table = client.get(plid)                     ⟵ We get the table from Plasma.
            t0 = table.filter(
                pc.not_equal(table["total_amount"], 0.0))
            my_mean = pc.mean(
                pc.divide(t0["tip_amount"], t0["total_amount"])).as_py()
            result_plid = plasma.ObjectID(
                f"result-{original_pid}".ljust(20, " ")[:20]
                    .encode("us-ascii"))
            client.put(my_mean, result_plid)    ⟵  We put the result
    time.sleep(0.05)                                       on Plasma.
```

Most of our code has been presented in the current and previous sections. The only conceptual novelties are the use of the contains function to see whether a result already exists and the get function to get the table.

Finally, let's see the results (see `07-pandas/sec5-arrow-plasma/show_results.py`):

```python
import pyarrow as pa
import pyarrow.plasma as plasma

client = plasma.connect("/tmp/fast_python")

all_objects = client.list()

for plid, keys in all_objects.items():
    try:
        plid_str = plid.binary().decode("us-ascii")
    except UnicodeDecodeError:
        pass
    if plid_str.startswith("result-"):
        print(plid_str, client.get(plid, timeout_ms=0))
```

The is really nothing new in this code, but note that we get the object in the last line without blocking by specifying a timeout of 0. Plasma has blocking semantics by default, but you can specify a timeout if desired.

There is more to be said about Plasma (e.g., using a lower-level API to get and put objects or how to efficiently transfer pandas objects). However, because the development of the Arrow/Plasma architecture is still evolving, it is probably more important to get a grasp of the concepts for the IPC involved as we did here.

We will revisit Arrow in the next chapter when we discuss data persistence. Arrow has a lot to offer on the storage front.

Summary

- pandas is the most widely used data analysis library in the Python world, but it is not designed with efficiency, neither in terms of computational nor in-memory storage, as the first concern.
- Very simple techniques for loading data can dramatically decrease the memory footprint of pandas data frames by, for example, ignoring some columns that are not needed for computation or informing pandas about the type of each column in advance.
- Judicious use of indexing can decrease processing times, although the flexibility of pandas indexing is somewhat limited.
- Different row iteration strategies can have differences of more than two orders of magnitude in performance. Avoid explicit loops whenever possible and use vectorization operations.
- While pandas is built on top of NumPy, sometimes explicitly requiring that NumPy data structures are extracted from pandas can further increase performance speed.
- Cython can be used with pandas, albeit indirectly via NumPy data structures, and can substantially increase speed.

- For very large data frames *and* complex formulas, NumExpr may be an efficient strategy to perform data analysis.
- Apache Arrow can serve many tasks. In this chapter, we focus on how it can complement pandas, especially as a fast reader of data. But be sure to check other functionalities of the project.
- Arrow's architecture, through its Plasma server, can be used for efficient data transfer across processes on the same machine. This can be quite useful to process data with different languages and frameworks, as the format is shared by all languages where it is implemented.

Storing big data

This chapter covers

- Getting to know fsspec, an abstraction library over filesystems
- Storing heterogeneous columnar data efficiently with Parquet
- Processing data files with in-memory libraries like pandas or Parquet
- Processing homogeneous multi-dimensional array data with Zarr

When dealing with big data, persistence is of paramount importance. We want to be able to access—to read and write—data as fast as possible, preferably from many parallel processes. We also want persistent representations that are compact because storing large amounts of data can be expensive.

In this chapter, we will consider several approaches to make persistent storage of data more efficient. We will start with a short discussion of fsspec, a library that abstracts access to file systems, both local and remote. While fsspec isn't directly involved in performance problems, it is a modern library used by many applications to deal with storage systems, and its use is recurrent in efficient storage implementations.

We will then consider Parquet, a file format to persist heterogeneous columnar datasets. Parquet is supported in Python via the Apache Arrow project, which was introduced in the previous chapter.

Next, we will discuss chunked reading of very large datasets, sometimes called an *out-of-core approach*. Often, we have stored datasets that cannot be processed in-memory all at the same time. Chunked reading allows you to process data in parts with software libraries that you already know, which is a simple but very efficient strategy. Our example will take a large pandas data frame and convert it to a Parquet file. Finally, we will look at Zarr, a modern format and library to store multidimensional homogeneous arrays (i.e., NumPy arrays) in persistent memory.

For this chapter, you will need to install fsspec, Zarr, and Arrow, which provides the Parquet interface. To install conda, you can use `conda install fsspec zarr pyarrow`. The Docker image `tiagoantao/python-performance-dask` includes all the necessary libraries. Let's start with a small overview of the fsspec library, which allows us to deal with different types of filesystems, both local and remote, using the same API.

8.1 A unified interface for file access: fsspec

There are many systems for file storage, from the venerable local filesystem, to cloud storage like Amazon S3, to protocols like SFTP and SMB (Windows file shares). The list is large, especially if we consider that there are many other filesystem-like objects: for example, a zip file is a file and directory container, an HTTP server has a traversable tree, and so on.

Dealing with every type of filesystem means learning a different programming API for each one—a laborious, even painful, prospect. Enter fsspec, a library that abstracts away many filesystem types behind a unified API. With fsspec, you only need to learn a single API to interact with many filesystem types. There are a few quirks: for example, you cannot expect the behavior of a local filesystem to be the same as a remote one, but the library simplifies access to file systems substantially with minimal overhead.

8.1.1 Using fsspec to search for files in a GitHub repo

To illustrate how fsspec works, we will use it to traverse a GitHub repository in search of zip files and then determine whether or not those zip files contain CSV files. In this exercise, we are treating a GitHub repository as if it is a filesystem. This is not so far fetched as it may sound. When you think about it, a GitHub repo is essentially a directory tree with versioned content.

For a sample repository, we will use the one from this book. In `08-persistence/01-fspec`, you will find a zip file named `dummy.zip`, which contains two dummy CSV files. Our code will traverse the repository, find all zip files—in our case, only `dummy.zip` exists—open them, and use pandas' `describe` command to summarize all CSVs.

Let's start by accessing the repository with fsspec and listing the root directory:

```
from fsspec.implementations.github import GithubFileSystem

git_user = "tiagoantao"
git_repo = "python-performance"

fs = GithubFileSystem(git_user, git_repo)
print(fs.ls(""))
```

We import the class `GithubFileSystem`, pass the user and repository name, and list the top-level directory. Note that the root directory is represented by the empty string, not by the typical `/`. fsspec provides many other classes to access storage, like the local filesystem, compressed files, Amazon S3, Arrow, HTTP, SFTP, and so on.

The `fs` object has several methods common with Python's filesystem interfaces. For example, to traverse the filesystem, which we need to do to find all zip files, a `walk` method exists that is very similar to the `walk` method of the `os` module:

```
def get_zip_list(fs, root_path=""):
    for root, dirs, fnames in fs.walk(root_path):
        for fname in fnames:
            if fname.endswith(".zip"):
                yield f"{root}/{fname}"
```

`get_zip_list` is a generator that yields all complete paths to existing zip files. Note that the code is exactly what you would use with `os.walk` if the `root_path` was `/`.

> **fsspec interface limitations**
>
> While fsspec provides a unified and simple interface for filesystems, it cannot hide all semantic differences. Indeed, in some cases, we do not want it to hide all the differences. Using `GitHubFileSystem` as an example, here are two possible situations where differences can be seen:
>
> - *Extra functionality*—You can navigate the repository at *any* point in time, not just at the current time point of the master branch. You can specify a branch or a tag, and fsspec will allow you to inspect the repository at that precise point.
> - *Limitations*—Not only you will have the typical problems with remote filesystems (e.g., if you are not connected to the internet, the code won't work), but also if you query the server many times, it will rate-limit you.

Now that we have a list of zips in the repository, as a first, naïve solution, we will copy the zip files from the repository to the local filesystem. The idea here is that we will open them locally to see whether they have CSV files:

```
def get_zips(fs):
    for zip_name in get_zips(fs):
        fs.get_file(zip_name, "/tmp/dl.zip")
        yield zip_name
```

Now we can inspect the file inside. For this, we can, again naively, use Python's built-in `zipfile` module:

```
import zipfile
import pandas as pd

def describe_all_csvs_in_zips(fs):
    for zip_name in get_zips(fs):
        my_zip = zipfile.ZipFile("/tmp/dl.zip")
        for zip_info in my_zip.infolist():
            print(zip_name)
            if not zip_info.filename.endswith(".csv"):
                continue
            print(zip_info.filename)
            my_zip_open = zipfile.ZipFile("/tmp/dl.zip")
            df = pd.read_csv(zipfile.Path(my_zip_open,
            zip_info.filename).open())
            print(df.describe())
```

We open the file using the zipfile module here.

Note that the infolist method is specific to the zipfile module, something that needs to be learned.

Notice the new API that we need to learn for `zipfile`. We started with the constructor and then used the `infolist` method, but we may need to re-open the zip mid-listing due to `zipfile` semantics.

8.1.2 Using fsspec to inspect zip files

That previous code listing is just a simple illustration of the *mess* that fsspec is saving us from. fsspec provides an interface to zip files, and thus we can rewrite that code like this:

```
from fsspec.implementations.zip import ZipFileSystem

def describe_all_csvs_in_zips(fs):
        print(zip_name)
        for zip_name in get_zips(fs):
        my_zip = ZipFileSystem("/tmp/dl.zip")
        for fname in my_zip.find(""):
            if not fname.endswith(".csv"):
                continue
            print(fname)
            df = pd.read_csv(my_zip.open(fname))
            print(df.describe())
```

The find method, along with all others, exists for all kinds of filesystems, not just zip.

As with the find method, open is also available for all types of filesystems.

Other than creating the `ZipFileSystem` object, the interface is exactly the same as the one for GitHub and very close to common Python file interfaces. There is no need to learn the `zipfile` interface.

8.1.3 Accessing files using fsspec

You can also use fsspec to open files directly, although the semantics are a bit different from the standard `open`. For example, to open a zip file using fsspec `open`, we use the following code:

```
dlf = fsspec.open("/tmp/dl.zip")
with dlf as f:                        ◁─────┐ To open the file, we need to
    zipf = zipfile.ZipFile(f)                use the with statement.
    print(zipf.infolist())
dlf.close()
```

We are using Python's zipfile module again to parse the file.

The output is:

```
[
  <ZipInfo filename='dummy1.csv' filemode='-rw-rw-r--' file_size=22>,
  <ZipInfo filename='dummy2.csv' compress_type=deflate
    filemode='-rw-rw-r--' file_size=56 compress_size=54>
]
```

Notice the need to use the `with` dialect after `open` to get a proper file descriptor, which is different from the typical approach of just using the `open` function.

8.1.4   *Using URL chaining to traverse different filesystems transparently*

Let's go back to our zip file inside the GitHub repository. Note that because we can interpret the zip file as a container for files, this zip file is like having a filesystem inside another filesystem. fsspec has a declarative way of allowing us to get to our data quite easily: URL chaining. You can sometimes take a stream and reinterpret it as a filesystem. An example will make this clear; let's print the content of `dummy1.csv`:

```
dlf = fsspec.open("zip://dummy1.csv::/tmp/dl.zip", "rt")
with dlf as f:
    print(f.read())
```

Notice URL chaining in action: we take `dummy1.csv` from `/tmp/dl.zip`. You did not need to explicitly open the zip file; fsspec took care of that for you.

Remember that we referred to our implementation of `get_zips` as *naive*? It is naive because we do not need to explicitly download the file, courtesy of URL chaining:

```
dlf = fsspec.open(
  "zip://dummy1.csv::github://tiagoantao:python-performance@/08-"
  "persistence/sec1-fsspec/dummy.zip")
with dlf as f:
    print(pd.read_csv(f))
```

We are hardcoding the complete chained URL to make clear an explicit example of usage.

8.1.5   *Replacing filesystem backends*

Now, because fsspec abstracts away filesystem interfacing, it is very easy to replace a filesystem implementation. For example, let's replace GitHub with the local filesystem. It is as simple as:

```
import os
from fsspec.implementations.local import LocalFileSystem

fs = LocalFileSystem()
os.chdir("../..")
```

This assumes that you are running the script from the directory `08-persistence/sec1-fsspec`; as such, `../..` will be the root of the book repository.

We use `LocalFileSystem` instead of `GitHubFileSystem`, and that is *almost* it. Because we are running this code two levels deep from the top of the repository, we need to move up the tree—hence, the `chdir`. Now how the code works is on top of the local filesystem, not GitHub. For example, run `describe_all_csvs_in_zips(fs)`.

8.1.6 *Interfacing with PyArrow*

Finally, it is worth noting that PyArrow, which we discussed in the previous chapter, can interface directly with fsspec:

```
from pyarrow import csv
from pyarrow.fs import PyFileSystem, FSSpecHandler

zfs = ZipFileSystem("/tmp/dl.zip")
arrow_fs = PyFileSystem(FSSpecHandler(zfs))
my_csv = csv.read_csv(arrow_fs.open_input_stream("dummy1.csv"))
```

The important part here is that Arrow has the concept of the filesystem, which allows it to naturally integrate with fsspec. The Arrow filesystem can bridge with fsspec via `pyarrow.fs.FSSpecHandler`. After a fsspec filesystem is mapped this way, Arrow filesystem primitives can be used on top of it transparently.

> **TIP** fsspec supports the ability to partially download data from remote servers, which can be important in big data situations where we might only need a fraction of a big file. This can only be done if the server type that we are trying to use supports partial file downloading. For example, GitHub doesn't support it; conversely, S3 does. You can enable this feature by activating the cache when you call `open` by using the parameter `cache_type` with a value of `readahead`.

That was a bit of a sidetrack, as fsspec is not directly related to performance, although it is used in many performance-related libraries like Dask, Zarr, and Arrow. Now, let's go back to our normally scheduled programming, looking at approaches to efficiently store heterogenous columnar data, aka data frames.

8.2 *Parquet: An efficient format to store columnar data*

Storing data in CSVs is fraught with problems. First, because they can't accommodate typing of each column, it's not uncommon to have unexpected values in columns. In addition, the format itself is inefficient. For example, you can represent numbers much more compactly in binary form than in text. In addition, you cannot jump to a specific row or column in constant time, as it is not possible to compute the location of its position because each line in a CSV can vary in size.

Apache Parquet is becoming the most common format to efficiently store heterogeneous columnar data. This means you can access just the columns you need and also use data-compression and column-encoding formats to increase performance.

In this section, we will learn how to use Parquet to store data frames, drawing on the New York City taxi data from the previous chapter. As we walk through this task, I will also present a tour of many Parquet features.

> **WARNING**   Parquet is a file format that started in the Java world, specifically in the Hadoop ecosystem. While the available Python implementations are perfectly fit for production purposes, they do not implement the specification completely. For example, we cannot specify in full detail how we want to encode columns; neither we can inspect how a column is stored—something I will show here. But for the vast majority of use cases, the necessary functionality is present and will only increase over time.

Just as a reminder, the taxi dataset has information about all taxi runs in New York City for a period of time. Information includes, among other things, start and end time of the run, start and end location, cost, taxes, and tips. We will begin by using the same file as in the previous chapter, which includes taxi runs for January 2020. The first thing that we will do is convert the CSV file into Parquet. For this, we will use Apache Arrow, introduced in the previous chapter. The code can be found in `08-persistence/sec2-parquet/start.py`:

```
import pyarrow as pa
from pyarrow import csv
import pyarrow.parquet as pq

table = csv.read_csv(
    "../../07-pandas/sec1-intro/yellow_tripdata_2020-01.csv.gz")
pq.write_table(table, "202001.parquet")
```

We simply use `write_table` from the Parquet module of PyArrow. We end up with a 111 MB binary file. The compressed CSV is 105 MB, and the original uncompressed version, 567 MB. Because Parquet is a structured binary format, we should expect some differences in size for the same content. The point here is not to fixate on the details but to have an insight into the size relationships.

8.2.1   *Inspecting Parquet metadata*

Let's discover some of Parquet's features by inspecting the file:

```
parquet_file = pq.ParquetFile("202001.parquet")

metadata = parquet_file.metadata
print(metadata)
print(parquet_file.schema)
group = metadata.row_group(0)
print(group)
```

The abridged output is:

```
<pyarrow._parquet.FileMetaData object at 0x7f90858879f0>
  created_by: parquet-cpp-arrow version 4.0.0
  num_columns: 18
  num_rows: 6405008
  num_row_groups: 1
  format_version: 1.0
  serialized_size: 4099
<pyarrow._parquet.ParquetSchema object at 0x7f9193aeed00>
required group field_id=0 schema {
  optional int32 field_id=1 VendorID (Int(bitWidth=8, isSigned=false));
  optional int64 field_id=2 tpep_pickup_datetime (
    Timestamp(isAdjustedToUTC=false, timeUnit=milliseconds,
    is_from_converted_type=false, force_set_converted_type=false));
  ....
<pyarrow._parquet.RowGroupMetaData object at 0x7f90858ad0e0>
  num_columns: 18
  num_rows: 6405008
  total_byte_size: 170358087
```

We start by printing the metadata for the file. Here we simply get some summary information such as having 18 columns and 6,405,008 rows. Paquet also tells us that there is a single row group in the file. A row group is a partition of the total of rows: in larger files, there may be more than a single row group. A row group will have all the column data for the rows in the group. Remember, information in Parquet is organized by columns. This will become clear shortly.

We then print the schema of the file. An abridged version is:

```
required group field_id=0 schema {
  optional int32 field_id=1 VendorID (Int(bitWidth=8, isSigned=false));
  optional int64 field_id=2 tpep_pickup_datetime (
    Timestamp(isAdjustedToUTC=false, timeUnit=milliseconds,
    is_from_converted_type=false, force_set_converted_type=false));
  optional double field_id=5 trip_distance;
  optional binary field_id=7 store_and_fwd_flag (String);
}
```

**Here you have the definition of VendorID,
which has a bit width of 8 and is not signed.**

This code lists all the columns for our data. For example `VendorID` is an `int32`, but note that the bit width is 8 and that it is unsigned. `VendorID` had only two possible values plus a null, so it makes sense to reduce its implementation to just 8 unsigned bits. This could even be reduced to fewer bits as, in theory, Parquet supports such a reduction.

Then we have `tpep_pickup_datetime`, which is a time stamp. From a storage perspective, the time unit is the most important variable, as more precision will require more space. pandas defaults to nanosecond precision. Also, note `store_and_fwd_flag`: text is stored as general binary data.

8.2.2   *Column encoding with Parquet*

Let's now look at the existing metadata for several columns:

```
tip_col = group.column(13)   # tip_amount
print(tip_col)
```

The abridged output is:

```
physical_type: DOUBLE
   num_values: 6405008
   path_in_schema: tip_amount
   statistics:
       has_min_max: True
       min: -91.0
       max: 1100.0
       null_count: 0
       distinct_count: 0
       num_values: 6405008
       physical_type: DOUBLE
       logical_type: None
       converted_type (legacy): NONE
   compression: SNAPPY
   encodings: ('PLAIN_DICTIONARY', 'PLAIN', 'RLE')
   has_dictionary_page: True
```

**Statistical information about
the column starts here.**

**The compression algorithm
used in the column**

The metadata starts with the physical type, the number of values, and the column
name. The statistical information (there seems to be a negative tip—probably an entry
mistake) shows $-91 as the minimum and $1,000 as the maximum tip. Now things start
to get *really* interesting.

   With regards to the storage of data proper, Parquet can compress columns, which
saves disk space. Compressing columns can also provide potential computational
gains related to cache management problems discussed in the previous chapter. Different columns can have different compression types or no compression at all.

   In our example, the Snappy algorithm is used for compression. Snappy trades
more compression for speed, compared to, say, gzip, which is also an option. Make
sure to check what compression algorithms Arrow implements at the time of usage.
Facebook has some benchmarking information available at https://facebook.github
.io/zstd/#benchmarks to help you decide.

   For example, you can use ZSTD:

```
pq.write_table(table, "202001_std.parquet", compression="ZSTD")
```

We are using ZSTD on all columns in this example. In this case, you go down from 110
MB with Snappy to 82 MB.

   Parquet can encode columns not only with direct values but also by using dictionaries, where a long value is converted to an indirect reference, potentially saving a lot

of disk space. To understand how this can help, consider that tips are represented by a double requiring 64 bits, whereas there are only 3626 different values for tips:

```
print(len(table["tip_amount"].unique()))
```

A dictionary can reduce encoding from 64 bits to 12 bits per value, which is enough to encode up to 4096 values. We also need to store the dictionary, which is residual for 3626 values. However, because we have many distinct values, it might not make sense to use a dictionary. You can control whether a column is stored with a dictionary or not with `write_table`.

Last but not least, note that the encoding also has RLE, which stands for Run Length Encoding. Let's look at the advantage of RLE with a somewhat silly example. Let's create a data frame with a column with `VendorID` followed by another column *also* with `VendorID`, but ordered:

```
import pyarrow.compute as pc

silly_table = pa.Table.from_arrays([
    table["VendorID"],
    table["VendorID"].take(
        pc.sort_indices(table["VendorID"]))],
    ["unordered", "ordered"]
)
```

So it's the same data, with ordered and unordered versions. Let's now see how much space each column occupies on a Parquet file:

```
pq.write_table(silly_table, "silly.parquet")
silly = pq.ParquetFile("silly.parquet")
silly_group = silly.metadata.row_group(0)
print(silly_group.column(0))
print(silly_group.column(1))
```

The unordered file takes 953,295 bytes, and the ordered file takes 141 bytes! The way RLE works is by storing the value and the number of repetitions. With an ordered `VendorID` column, we have an extreme case: we have only three values (1, 2, and `null`), which are ordered. So in theory, RLE can store: 1 9094439 / 2 4945123 / null 65441.

RLE can compress data quite substantially. While our case is extreme in terms of efficiency, RLE typically works well for ordered fields or fields with few values. However, if you deviate from these assumptions, make sure you evaluate the compression benefit that you are getting.

Smaller files help with storage *and* processing time. Remember from chapter 6 that if you can have data in faster types of memory, you can sometimes have orders of magnitude gains in performance.

The format is extensible, so you can expect a new way to efficiently store data to be developed over time. The format also allows for data partitioning, which has several advantages from an efficiency perspective. Let's make it clear with an example.

8.2.3 *Partitioning with datasets*

To clarify what partitioning means and what the process entails, let's partition our dataset using `VendorID` and `passenger_count`. As partitions cannot be based on null values, we will remove those from our dataset. We only do this for this exercise; in general, you cannot remove null value rows just out of convenience:

```
from pyarrow import csv
import pyarrow.compute as pc
import pyarrow.parquet as pq

table = csv.read_csv(
    "../../07-pandas/sec1-intro/yellow_tripdata_2020-01.csv.gz")

table = table.filter(
  pc.invert(table["VendorID"].is_null()))
table = table.filter(pc.invert(table["passenger_count"].is_null()))

pq.write_to_dataset(
    table, root_path="all.parquet",
    partition_cols=["VendorID", "passenger_count"])
```

> **Note again that the syntax to do the computation with Arrow is very different from pandas.**

The equivalent to the first filter line in pandas would be `table = table[~table["VendorID"].isna()]`.

If you look at `all.parquet`, you will find a few surprises: The biggest surprise is that it is not a file anymore but a directory! The abridged contents will be something like this:

```
.
├── VendorID=1
│   ├── passenger_count=0
│   │   └── e59ac47b5193411e9772bfee9d423d61.parquet
│   ├── passenger_count=1
│   │   └── ee90fe5b818d4a37a32b5a415915610b.parquet
│   └── passenger_count=9
│       └── 002ff0bba1d340abb6174c5c64f779d7.parquet
└── VendorID=2
    ├── passenger_count=0
    │   └── 5809e29649524202a9b3cef5371c46d9.parquet
    └── passenger_count=9
        └── feaff7a23bbf4ae2b687b34dcaa10afb.parquet
```

The directory structure reflects our partitioning strategy. The first level of directories has an entry per `VendorID`, and the second level, one per `passenger_count`.

You now have two options. The easiest one—and arguably less interesting—is to load everything as a table:

```
all_data = pq.read_table("all.parquet/")
```

Here you will have all the data as a normal table. You can, alternatively, do the following to the same effect:

```
dataset = pq.ParquetDataset("all.parquet/")
ds_all_data = dataset.read()
```

But, as an alternative option, you can also load each parquet *file* separately. For example, let's load the file for the partition of vendor ID 1 with three passengers:

```
import os
data_dir = "all.parquet/VendorID=1/passenger_count=3"
parquet_fname = os.listdir(data_dir)[0]          ⊲
v1p3 = pq.read_table(f"{data_dir}/{parquet_fname}")
print(v1p3)
```

The name of the parquet file is not assured, so we get the first file in the directory.

If you look at the output, you will notice that the columns `VendorID` and `passenger_count` are missing, as they can be inferred from the directory.

> **WARNING**   What is inside each directory can vary. In our case, with PyArrow, it is a single Parquet file. For example, you can tell Parquet to further split each partition into a file by row group. So, make sure you investigate how the data is actually written to the disk and adapt the code accordingly.

What is the point of partitioning from a performance perspective? We can now load each Parquet file separately and process each one accordingly. For example, we can improve performance by using multiple processes on the same machine, each doing analysis on each file. We can even process different files on different machines. Implicitly, the filesystem can be more efficient as concurrent loads are done in different parts of the disk. There can also be a memory gain because we don't load the partition columns. Finally, partitioning opens the avenue for concurrent writes, which provides performance gains from parallelism. We will discuss concurrent writes in more detail in section 8.4.

The way data is partitioned matters from a performance perspective. For example, Vendor 1 has half the data of Vendor 2, which means that the cost of processing Vendor 2 will probably be double that of Vendor 1. This doubling may cause you to wait for the slowest of all the partitions because you want to be as uniform as possible. `VendorID` might be a good choice when compared with `passenger_count`. Parquet has many more features, but from a performance perspective, we now have a good overview of how we can benefit from the format.

8.3   *Dealing with larger-than-memory datasets the old-fashioned way*

In this section, we will work with Parquet and CSV files to go over two simple techniques to deal with data that is bigger than memory: memory mapping and chunking. There are more sophisticated ways of doing both tasks, and we will discuss them in section 8.4, as well as in the next chapter. But chunking and memory mapping are important concepts that underpin more sophisticated libraries. Therefore, understanding them is not only valid in itself but also fundamental to understanding more advanced techniques.

8.3.1 *Memory mapping files with NumPy*

Memory mapping occurs when a part of the memory is directly associated with a part of the filesystem. In the specific case of NumPy, an array that is persisted to storage can be assessed with the normal NumPy API, and NumPy will take care of bringing to RAM whatever parts we need from the array. In most cases, this is done transparently by the operating system kernel for NumPy. Conversely, it will change the persistent representation when we write. Because you are assessing memory, this can speed up your code by orders of magnitude. Figure 8.1 depicts memory mapping.

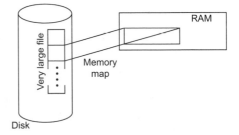

In this case, we will use a simple abstract example of creating a big array and accessing it. You can decide the size of the array. For this exercise, I recommend a size that is bigger than your memory but for which you have enough disk space. Allocation is quite simple:

Figure 8.1 Memory mapping mirrors a part of a file into memory.

```
import numpy as np

SIZE_IN_GB = 10        ◁———┐  Changes the size to a value appropriate for
                             your machine, as previously specified

array = np.memmap("data.np", mode="w+",
                  dtype=np.int8, shape=(SIZE_IN_GB * 1024, 1024, 1024))
print(array[-1, -1, :10])
```

The `np.memmap` call is quite straightforward: you pass it a file name, an open mode, and the type and shape of the array. If you list the files on your disk, you will find a file that is 10 GB in size.

The array will be initialized with all zeroes; hence, the print will show an array with 10 zeroes. Let's now add 2 to all elements in the array:

```
array += 2
```

The interface is exactly the same as for an in-memory NumPy array. But you will notice that this operation will take a few seconds. The time increases because the large file is being changed all across it; it's not a fast in-memory operation.

Let's now open the file and print the last value:

```
array = np.memmap("data.np", mode="r",
                  dtype=np.int8)
print(array.shape)
print(array[:-10])
```

The output is:

```
(10737418240,)
[2 2 2 ... 2 2 2]
```

The important point here is that the shape of the array is not saved with it, so if you map it without specifying the shape, you get a linear array. Therefore, you need to make sure that you recover the desired shape. We then print the last 10 elements of that array and we get ten 2s.

> ### NumPy copy-on-write
>
> NumPy memory mapping allows you to use a technique called *copy-on-write*. This permits you to have several copies of a disk array loaded into memory and pay a substantially lower price in terms of memory usage. This technique is prone to bugs in many circumstances, mostly because Python is not the best language to deal with shared data structures and because memory mapping semantics become unclear when you change the underlying file. I don't think the benefits justify the risks unless you are *sure* you will be performing only read operations. If you want to research this technique, I recommend the excellent article from Itamar Turner-Trauring, available at https://pythonspeed.com/articles/reduce-memory-array-copies/.
>
> I would generally steer away from explicit memory-mapping techniques that perform concurrency writes and sharing unless you are absolutely sure that every process is only reading. Also, if you are a developer of a low-level library, you might use memory mapping with writing, but you probably will not be using Python to implement the most efficient parts anyway, so the problem will be addressed in other languages.

Remember that even if you are not using memory mapping directly, many frameworks that you use will do that implicitly, so understanding it is useful. Let's now discuss another technique to deal with large files: chunking.

8.3.2   Chunk reading and writing of data frames

Chunking, as the name suggests, means processing a file in, well, *chunks*. You read (or write) the file in parts. You will definitely deal with chunking if you use Zarr (see section 8.4) or Dask (see chapter 10).

Here we will return to our trusty taxi example. We will convert the file from CSV to Parquet but in chunks. Although the file is small enough that we could do this in-memory in most computers, let's assume we are in a memory-constrained machine and that loading the full file in-memory is not possible.

We will use pandas to read the CSV file and Arrow to write the Parquet version. We could do everything with Arrow, which would be more efficient, but we want to demonstrate the pandas chunking interface:

```
import pandas as pd

table_chunks = pd.read_csv(
    "../../07-pandas/sec1-intro/yellow_tripdata_2020-01.csv.gz",
```

```
    chunksize=1000000
    )
print(type(table_chunks))
for chunk in table_chunks:
    print(chunk.shape)
```

> The type will be
> pandas.io.parsers.TextFileReader.

> Each chunk will be a data frame.

We only need to add the parameter `chunksize` to `read_csv`. You will not have a data frame from `read_csv`, but a generator of chunks. Each chunk will then be a data frame with a maximum size of 1 million rows.

We will now do the conversion proper. The first thing that we need to do is to reopen the file. We have iterated through all the chunks once, so we need to go back to the beginning:

```
table_chunks = pd.read_csv(
    "../../07-pandas/sec1-intro/yellow_tripdata_2020-01.csv.gz",
    chunksize=1000000,
    dtype={
        "VendorID": float,
        "passenger_count": float,
        "RatecodeID": float,
        "PULocationID": float,
        "DOLocationID": float,
        "payment_type": float,
    }
)
```

We also need to specify some column data types; the type of some columns will change from chunk to chunk. This is mostly the case with integer columns that have null values. When there are null values, the type will be promoted to `float` as there is no way to represent a null value in pandas with integers.

Now, we will traverse the chunks and create the Parquet file:

```
first = True
writer = None
for chunk in table_chunks:
    chunk_table = pa.Table.from_pandas(chunk)
    schema = chunk_table.schema
    if first:
        first = False
        writer = pq.ParquetWriter(
            "output.parquet", schema=schema)
    writer.write_table(chunk_table)
writer.close()
```

> We convert the pandas
> frame into an Arrow table.

> We create a writer object. We
> need to specify the schema at
> initialization.

The `ParquetWriter` interface allows us to write table after table in the same file. Each table will be written in a separate Parquet row group. It will be, in a sense, a chunk.

We can read the Parquet data in several ways:

```
pf = pq.ParquetFile("output.parquet")
print(pf.metadata)
for groupi in range(pf.num_row_groups):
```

> We can read each row
> group separately.

```
    group = pf.read_row_group(groupi)
    print(type(group), len(group))
    break
table = pf.read()
table = pq.read_table("output.parquet")
```

The metadata of the Parquet file will indicate that there are seven row groups. Parquet allows us to read row group by row group. If you have enough memory, there are two interfaces—in `ParquetFile` with `read` or in the `parquet` module with `read_table`—that take care of reading all read groups and creating a table in-memory.

Armed with the notion of chunking, which allows us to load and process the data in parts, we are now going to have a look at Zarr. Zarr is a library that allows us to manipulate very large homogeneous N-dimension arrays (i.e., NumPy objects).

8.4 *Zarr for large-array persistence*

Some of the biggest datasets in existence are not heterogeneous table data frames but multidimensional homogeneous arrays. Therefore, it is important to store these larger arrays efficiently.

Zarr allows us to efficiently store homogeneous multidimensional arrays with different backends and different encoding formats. Functionality like concurrent writing can be extremely useful to generate data efficiently.

There are a couple of very mature standards to represent array data (e.g., NetCDF and HDF5), but in our case, we will use the nascent format Zarr. Zarr is substantially more optimizable than any other format for efficient processing. For example, it allows for concurrent writes and different organization of the file structure, both of which can have massive implications on performance. Concurrent writes allow for many parallel processes to work simultaneously on the same structure. Different file structures allow us to take advantage of the performance properties of the filesystem.

While Zarr is a file format, it started in the Python space implemented in a library called Zarr. So you can be sure the Python version implements all the major features of the format. If you plan to use Zarr files from other programming languages, you should check first to see whether the libraries for those languages support such features. Zarr is, in a sense, the opposite of Parquet: Parquet came from the Java ecosystem to Python, so Python for Parquet still doesn't cover all the features. With Zarr, the Python implementation is the gold standard.

Zarr was started in the bioinformatics space, and we will be using a bioinformatics example. We will use data from an old genomics project called the HapMap (https://www.genome.gov/10001688/international-hapmap-project). This project has genomics variants (variation in DNA letters) for many individuals accross human populations. You don't need to know any of the scientific details for this exercise. We will introduce the minimal concepts needed as we go along.

For our example, we will start with a pre-prepared Zarr database that I generated from HapMap data in Plink format (https://www.cog-genomics.org/plink/2.0/). You don't need to worry about the original format, but if you are interested and for completion, you can find the code that generates the Zarr database that you should use in the repository in `08-persistence/sec4-zarr/hapmap` . The pre-prepared Zarr file can be found at https://tiago.org/db.zarr.tar.gz. It includes genetic information of 210 individuals across several human populations.

One of our objectives will be to generate another Zarr database that can be used to perform principal components analysis (PCA)—a unsupervised machine learning technique commom in genomics—which will require reformatting the data that we have from the original database. We will not run a PCA here but just prepare the file for that.

8.4.1 *Understanding Zarr's internal structure*

Let's start by sceing what is inside the database. While we traverse the database, we will remind ourselves of the necessary genomic concepts involved:

```
import zarr

genomes = zarr.open("db.zarr")      Prints the tree structure
genomes.tree()              ◁——————  of the file contents
```

Zarr is a tree container for arrays, so we have a directory structure where the leaf nodes are arrays. An abridged version of our file is:

```
├─ chromosome-1
│    ├─ alleles (318558,) <U2
│    ├─ calls (318558, 210) uint8
│    └─ positions (318558,) int64
├─ chromosome-10
│    ├─ alleles (216535,) <U2
│    ├─ calls (216535, 210) uint8
│    └─ positions (216535,) int64
```

Data is split in chromosomes, and there is a hierarchy per chromosome. Each chromosome has a list of positions genotyped (for which we get the DNA letters) in `positions`. The possible alleles (i.e., the DNA letters) per position are in the `alleles` array. The main matrix is in `calls`, where for the 210 individuals, we have the alleles for each marker. So, as there are 318,558 markers in chromosome 1, the `calls` matrix will be $318{,}558 \times 210$. For every individual and marker, there are two calls, which will be encoded in a single number.

Our objective is to create a concatenated matrix of all calls to submit to a PCA implementation. Do not worry about the genetics; what matters from our perspective is that we have a two-dimensional `calls` matrix with 0/1/2 values coded as unsigned integers with 8 bits, and two one-dimensional arrays, one with 64-bit integers (`positions`) and the other with strings of a size of up to two characters (`alleles`).

Before we delve into performance-related problems, let's briefly discuss how to traverse Zarr data. We can traverse the whole structure like this:

```
def traverse_hierarchy(group, location=""):          Gets all groups inside a group
    for name, array in group.arrays():      ◁
        print(f"{location}/{name} {array.shape} {array.dtype}")
    for name, group in group.groups():      ◁
        my_root = f"{location}/{name}"            Gets all arrays inside a group
        print(my_root + "/")
        traverse_hierarchy(group, my_root)

traverse_hierarchy(genomes)
```

When Zarr reads a file, it returns a `Group` object. The `groups` method will return a generator with all the subgroups inside, so we can rely on that to traverse a Zarr repository.

You can also use a simple directory-like nomenclature to access content, which depends on your subjective preference. For example:

```
in_chr_2 = genomes["chromosome-2"]
pos_chr_2 = genomes["chromosome-2/positions"]
calls_chr_2 = genomes["chromosome-2/calls"]
alleles_chr_2 = genomes["chromosome-2/alleles"]
```

`in_chr_2` will have a `Group` for the key `pos_chr_2`, `calls_chr_2` and `alleles_chr_2` will have respective the arrays `chromosome-2/positions`, `chromosome-2/calls` and `chromosome-2/alleles` ready for use.

Let's get some information from our data structures:

```
print(in_chr_2.info)
```

The output is:

```
Name         : /chromosome-2
Type         : zarr.hierarchy.Group
Read-only    : False
Store type   : zarr.storage.DirectoryStore
No. members  : 3
No. arrays   : 3
No. groups   : 0
Arrays       : alleles, calls, positions
```

What we have is a Group, containing three members, all of which happen to be arrays, there could also be subgroups inside the name.

Zarr supports many types of stores: in our case, we are using `zarr.storage` `.DirectoryStore`, but you can find classes for in-memory, zip files, DBM files, SQL, fsspec, Mongo, and so on.

As we will see shortly, `DirectoryStore` is very helpful in supporting advanced parallel features, but for now, let's look at the directory structure that it uses. In case you haven't noticed, `db.zarr` is not a file but a directory. The following code snippet is an abridged version of the directory structure:

```
.
├── chromosome-1
│    ├── alleles
│    └── calls
│    └── positions
├── chromosome-10
│    ├── alleles
│    └── calls
│    └── positions
...
```

The directory structure mimics the Zarr group structure, which makes it easy for development.

8.4.2 Storage of arrays in Zarr

Let's now discuss how arrays are stored, a substantially more complex and interesting subject:

```
print(pos_chr_2.info)
```

Now we will reorder the output and split it into several parts. Let's start with some basic information:

```
Type              : zarr.core.Array
Data type         : int64
Shape             : (333056,)
Order             : C
Read-only         : False
Store type        : zarr.storage.DirectoryStore
```

You should be able to interpret this information with what we studied in previous chapters: the object is a `zarr.core.Array`, the data type is a 64-bit integer with 333,056 numbers, and the array is C-ordered and can be written on.

Let's now look at chunk shape:

```
Chunk shape       : (41632,)
Chunks initialized : 8/8
```

Remember that chunking is a way to partition a big array into smaller equal parts (chunks) that can be more easily manipulated (figure 8.2).

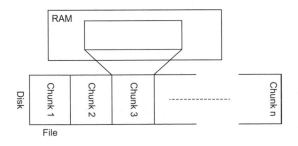

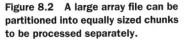

Figure 8.2 A large array file can be partitioned into equally sized chunks to be processed separately.

Zarr is telling us that each chunk is 41,632 elements in size; hence, we end up with eight chunks to accommodate 333,056 elements. When we created the array in the support script to create the pre-prepared version, we were a bit naive and did not specify the chunk size, and as such, Zarr tried to guess a reasonable value. Chunk size can—and should—be specified on creation. We will see why later in the section.

Note that all chunks are also initialized: however, under some circumstances, not all chunks need to be initialized (e.g., an empty array). Uninitialized chunks can potentially save a lot of disk space. Again, we will see that when we create arrays later.

If you go into the directory db.zarr/chromosome-2/positions, you will find eight files, named from 0 to 7; this is a file per chunk. This separation will make concurrent writes—a sophisticated feature not found in many array storage systems—easier with Zarr.

Finally, Zarr arrays can be compressed, thus saving a lot of disk space and potentially processing time, as discussed earlier in the chapter. Here is part of the output describing this:

```
Compressor         : Blosc(cname='lz4', clevel=5,
  shuffle=SHUFFLE, blocksize=0)
No. bytes          : 2664448 (2.5M)
No. bytes stored   : 687723 (671.6K)
Storage ratio      : 3.9
```

In our case, data was stored using Blosc with the LZ4 algorithm. The original size is 2,664,448 bytes—333,056 elements multiplied by 8 bytes for 64-bit integers, for a final storage of 687,723 bytes, thus a compression of 3.9 times. Given that the arrays are of homogeneous type, we should expect, on average, that compression will outperform the overall compression of heterogeneous data frames. Of course, this expectation is for an average case; for example, a random array is very difficult to compress.

For the calls array, we have a similar output but adapted to two dimensions. Here is an abridged version of print(calls_chr_2.info):

```
Shape              : (333056, 210)
Chunk shape        : (41632, 27)
Chunks initialized : 64/64
```

In this case, we have a matrix of dimension 333,056 × 210 and two-dimensional chunks.

> **TIP** You can chunk an N-dimensional array in fewer dimensions than N. For example, our two-dimensional array can be chunked only over one dimension. This choice may make sense if you need to process all information over one dimension at the same time. As with all chunking decisions, it depends on your use case.

Each dimension is split into eight intervals for a total of 64 chunks. If you list the contents of db.zarr/chromosome-2/calls, you will find 64 files conveniently named X.Y, where X and Y vary from 0 to 7, which refers to the chunk number on each dimension.

Finally, we have an array for all alleles, which is a string with two characters (e.g., AT, CG, TC, etc.). The abridged output from `print(alleles_chr_2.info)` is:

```
Data type          : <U2
```

This output is a Unicode string of fixed two-byte size. Remember from chapter 2 that Python string representation is sophisticated—or cumbersome, depending on the point of view—and assessing the size in bytes of a Python string is far from trivial.

For efficient access, it helps if we have strings of a fixed size and a representation that is predictable in size. Zarr provides two built-in representations for strings: if you only have ASCII characters, you can use a byte array, and if you have more than ASCII characters, Zarr provides a fixed-size Unicode representation, as opposed to the variable-size Python string implementation. If you need variable length strings and different encodings, Zarr provides encoders for those as well, but be careful about the performance implications of that much flexibility; if possible and reasonable in terms of storage, allocate a fixed long string.

Now that we have an overview of how Zarr data is organized, let's create an array that is the concatenation of all positions across all chromosomes. We need a single matrix from all chromosomes, as PCA requires a single matrix as input.

8.4.3   *Creating a new array*

We are now going to create a new array that can be used for unsupervised learning algorithms like PCA. This is simply a concatenation of all the call arrays (i.e., the calls for all chromosomes).

Before we can start, we must know the size of the array we need to allocate. To learn this, we traverse the existing Zarr file to extract the number of markers per chromosome, which will differ depending on your concrete problem:

```python
import zarr

genomes = zarr.open("db.zarr")

chrom_sizes = []
for chrom in range(1, 23):
    chrom_pos_array = genomes[f"chromosome-{chrom}/positions"]
    chrom_sizes.append(chrom_pos_array.shape[0])

total_size = sum(chrom_sizes)
```

This code simply checks the first dimension of all the one-dimensional arrays for positions. With this information, we can calculate the size of the all-encompassing Zarr array.

With the total size in hand, we can allocate the array:

```python
CHUNK_SIZE = 20000
all_calls = zarr.open(
    "all_calls.zarr", "w",
```

```
shape=(total_size, 210),
dtype=np.uint8,   # type change
chunks=(CHUNK_SIZE,))
```

⟵ **210 is the number of individuals in our dataset.**

The most important parameter in terms of performance is the chunk size. We chose a value that will put us above 1 MB per chunk, although you will have to calibrate chunk size for your specific case. The total of $20{,}000 \times 210$ is around 4 MB, but we are counting with some compression. We are assuming that all individuals will be read at once, so we chunk only on a single dimension. Feel free to vary the chunk size, you will see clear performance differences.

General ideas to decide on chunk size

It is very difficult to come up with general rules for the chunk size. You will need to have a look at your algorithms and use cases. That being said, here are some basic rules:

- You don't want chunks that are too small; they should typically be at least 1 MB or bigger.
- Your chunks should comfortably fit in memory.
- Try different values across different dimensions. These can have important effects on performance and on your ability to do all work in-memory.
- Chunk size and type of storage are not orthogonal. For example, `Directory-Store` will not scale well with thousand of chunks because of filesystem performance problems with too many files in the same directory. In this case, Zarr offers `NestedDirectoryStore` to spread chunks over subdirectories. But the important point is, it's better if you understand the limitations of different stores and parameterize chunking accordingly.

Let's get the info for `all_calls`. The abridged version is:

```
Type               : zarr.core.Array
Data type          : uint8
Shape              : (3976554, 210)
Chunk shape        : (20000, 210)
No. bytes          : 835076340 (796.4M)
No. bytes stored   : 345
Storage ratio      : 2420511.1
Chunks initialized : 0/199
```

The most important issue to note is the number of bytes stored and, relatedly, the number of chunks initialized. While the total expected size is 796.4 MB, only 345 bytes (!) are in use because no data has been saved (i.e., no chunk is initialized). By default, Zarr assumes all values in the array are 0 if not initialized. If, at this stage, you list the `all_calls.zarr` directory, you will find that it is empty and that it occupies no space at all.

Actually, a hidden file, called .zarray, has some metadata. If you open the file, you will find a file with a JSON version of the parameters that we passed to the Zarr array creation along with other defaults.

8.4.4   *Parallel reading and writing of Zarr arrays*

Now let's create the single concatenated array. We require a single array with all data for PCA analysis.

We will discuss two versions: the first is a sequential version and the second, a parallel one. Here is the first:

```
def do_serial():
    curr_pos = 0
    for chrom in range(1, 23):
        chrom_calls_array = genomes[f"chromosome-{chrom}/calls"]
        my_size = chrom_calls_array.shape[0]
        all_calls[curr_pos: curr_pos + my_size, :] = chrom_calls_array
        curr_pos += my_size


do_serial()
print(all_calls.info)
```

This code simply copies all chromosome calls in sequence to the all_calls array. Note that all the storage management is completely abstracted on top of a typical NumPy interface.

After you run the code, if you print the info for all_calls, few changes occur:

```
No. bytes          : 835076340 (796.4M)
No. bytes stored   : 297035153 (283.3M)
Storage ratio      : 2.8
Chunks initialized : 199/199
```

Now that all chunks are initialized, the store occupies 283.3 MB—a storage ratio of 2.8 compared to 796.4 MB for the total number of bytes. If you list the all_calls.zarr directory, you will find 199 files: one for each chunk.

The previous code takes a few seconds to run. While I won't ask you to run an example with many terabytes of data that will take hours, it is easy to see that, for more data, the time to do such a conversion could become prohibitively long.

So, as a second version, we will create a parallel version that will read from the chromosome arrays and write to the all_calls array. Both reads *and* writes will be parallel.

Not many libraries support parallel writing, but Zarr does. By putting each chunk in a separate file, the directory store makes it easy for Zarr to implement parallel writes. In this case, a simple design based on filesystem performance properties opens the possibility for a very important feature.

In theory, it is possible to write in whatever size you prefer, but doing this chunk by chunk will be the most efficient, as Zarr will not have to deal with concurrent writes on the same file. The fundamental point is that your chunk size should align with your use cases and you should try to process data on a chunk-by-chunk basis if possible.

In our case, we cannot go simply chromosome by chromosome; we have to write chunk by chunk. Here is the function to write a chunk in general:

```python
def process_chunk(genomes, all_calls, chrom_sizes, chunk_size, my_chunk):
    all_start = my_chunk * chunk_size        ◁──  The first write position is the chunk
    remaining = all_start                         number times the chunk size.
    chrom = 0
    chrom_start = 0
    for chrom_size in chrom_sizes:           ◁──  We traverse all chromosome sizes
        chrom += 1                                until we find where to start.
        remaining -= chrom_size
        if remaining <= 0:
            chrom_start = chrom_size + remaining
            remaining - -remaining                A chunk might require more
            break                                 than one chromosome.
    while remaining > 0:                      ◁──
        write_from_chrom = min(remaining, CHUNK_SIZE)
        remaining -= write_from_chrom
        chrom_calls = genomes[f"chromosome-{chrom}/calls"]
        all_calls[all_start:all_start + write_from_chrom, :] = chrom_calls[
          chrom_start: chrom_start + write_from_chrom, :]
        all_start = all_start + write_from_chrom
```

Do not stress if you do not understand the previous code in its entirety: the code is specific to the domain. What matters is the general approach. We are trying to work in a chunk-based way, which is appropriate for large files that do not fit memory.

We can now use a simple multiprocessing pool with a map call to process each chunk:

```python
from functools import partial
from multiprocessing import Pool

partial_process_chunk = partial(
    process_chunk, genomes,
    all_calls, chrom_sizes, CHUNK_SIZE)

def do_parallel():
    with Pool() as p:
        p.map(partial_process_chunk, range(all_calls.nchunks))

do_parallel()
```

We do a partial function application by defining `partial_process_chunk` so that the `Pool.map` call is easier. We then use a multiprocessing pool to process our map; for more details, see chapter 3.

Summary

- fsspec works as a unified interface for file storage, allowing for the same API to be used across many different backends.

- Because there is a unified API with fsspec, it is substantially easier to replace backends.

- While fsspec is not directly related to performance, several advanced libraries make use of it, including Arrow and Zarr.

- Parquet is a columnar data format that allows for more efficient storage of data: data is typed, potentially compressed, and organized by column.

- Parquet uses sophisticated strategies for data encoding, like dictionaries or run-length encoding, allowing for very compact representations, especially of data with clear patterns and repetitions. Furthermore, the format is extensible, and there may be even more performance enhancements in the future.

- Parquet allows for data partitioning, which gives programmers the ability to process data in parallel.

- The most common technique for dealing with larger-than-memory files is chunking. Chunking is supported in many libraries, including pandas, Parquet, and Zarr.

- Zarr is a modern library to process homogeneous multidimensional arrays. It originated in the Python world and provides NumPy-based interfaces.

- Zarr supports parallelism out of the box. Support for a concurrent writing process is of note as it is an uncommon feature in other libraries.

Part 4

Advanced Topics

Part 4 covers advanced topics. We start by discussing the advantages of using Graphical processing units (GPUs) to process big data. It turns out that the computing model of GPUs is very amenable to processing large datasets, especially N-dimensional arrays. We conclude this section by introducing Dask: a Python-based framework to do parallel processing across many computers, allowing us to scale out to many machines when we need to process very large amounts of data with complex algorithms.

Data analysis
using GPU computing

This chapter covers

- Using GPU architectures to improve many data analysis algorithms
- Using Numba to convert Python code to efficient GPU low-level code
- Writing highly parallel GPU code to work on matrices
- Using GPU-native data analysis libraries from Python

Graphics processing units (GPUs) were originally designed to make graphics applications more efficient: drawing and animation software, computer-aided design, and, of course, games!

At some point, it became clear that GPUs could not only do graphics processing but could also be used to do all kinds of computing, hence the appearance of general-purpose computing on graphics processing units (GPGPUs). GPUs are attractive because they have substantially more computing power than CPUs. They have been successfully used for many applications, such as scientific computing and artificial intelligence. They have massive applications in data science and in making computing more efficient in general.

GPGPUs use the architecture and programming paradigms imposed by the hardware of the GPUs and are built with two key considerations in mind. First, they need to do a lot of computation because graphics are very data-intensive. Second, they need to process many similar data points simultaneously, as every pixel in a graphics multiprocessor is computed at the same time. These requirements have a big effect on GPU design. For example, GPUs have many, many processing units, typically in the thousands, that are doing mostly similar tasks at the same time. In contrast, a typical CPU has a handful of processing units, each one doing different things at the same point in time. Processing speed in GPUs comes from the sheer number of processing units. In fact, each individual core is not very fast, at least compared to a CPU core. GPUs are thus massively parallel.

These crucial hardware differences mean that coding for GPUs is very different from coding for CPUs. It is not just a matter of recompiling existing code. Coding for GPUs, at least when we take care of it explicitly, implies a massive paradigm shift in how we think as programmers.

GPU computing can be advantageous for data analysis, but many people give up learning to code for GPUs due to the different mindset it requires. So this chapter focuses on the most important step in coding for high-performance GPU computing: the transition to that new way of thinking. Unlike the other chapters in this book, I will treat this as more of an introduction to an approach and a way of thinking. As such, I'll simplify the material to some degree and skip details. We will not discuss some important topics like thread synchronization, and we will assume trivially parallelizable problems so we can focus on understanding the programming paradigm instead. Many problems in data science are actually trivial to parallelize, so the material here is quite applicable to our field.

> **TIP** You can get more in-depth information on GPU computing from other sources. I recommend NVIDIA's CUDA C++ Programming Guide (http://mng.bz/61Bp). While geared for C and C++, the first four chapters will provide you with a mostly language-agnostic perspective on GPU architectures and programming concepts. Part 3 of *Parallel and High Performance Computing* by Bob Robey and Yuliana Zamora (Manning, 2021) is dedicated to GPUs; you can read chapter 9, "GPU Architectures and Concepts," for free by following this link: http://mng.bz/oJ6y.

We will start by looking at GPU architectures and their implications on algorithm and software development. I'll assume no prior knowledge and show you how GPUs work.

Because Python code cannot be run on GPUs directly, we will use Numba, which is a translator of Python to machine code that works with both GPUs and CPUs. Numba takes your Python code and compiles it at run time to a lower-level representation that is compatible with either your CPU or GPU. You can find an introduction to Numba in appendix B. Our examples will deploy Python code on the GPU explicitly.

After we are done with the hard part, which is fundamental to start understanding the programming model of GPUs, we will then make use of high-level data analysis libraries. While you can program GPUs directly, you can also use GPUs through libraries, which take care of most implementation details for you. Here, you will be using GPUs implicitly as external libraries will deploy computation on GPUs. For example, we will replace NumPy with CuPy. As we will see, even though libraries remove most of the burden of running code on GPUs, it is not simply a matter of replacing the library. Let's start by understanding GPU architectures from the perspective of the necessary changes in coding paradigms and performance.

> **NOTE** This chapter requires access to a GPU—namely, a recent NVIDIA GPU (i.e., Pascal architecture or newer). Thus, this chapter is vendor-dependent. While I would prefer to do vendor-agnostic content, the reality is that GPU computing happens mostly on top of NVIDIA GPUs using the CUDA architecture. This is especially important in the Python world with libraries like CuPy or cuDF. If you want to research vendor-agnostic ways to do GPGPU computing, check out OpenCL (https://www.khronos.org/opencl/) or Vulkan (https://www.vulkan.org/).

You will have to make sure that your installation has all the required NVIDIA drivers to do GPGPU computing. You will need to install the CUDA toolkit, along with CuPy, to run software on this chapter. This can be done in conda with `conda install -c rapidsai -c nvidia -c numba -c conda-forge cupy cudatoolkit`. There is a Docker image for GPU processing called `tiagoantao/python-performance-gpu`.

9.1 Making sense of GPU computing power

GPUs can, for some classes of algorithms, perform orders of magnitude better than CPUs. In this section, we will look at GPU architectures with the objective of understanding when and why GPUs can be more efficient for data analysis problems.

9.1.1 Understanding the advantages of GPUs

To understand why GPUs are so efficient, we will present a simplified conceptual model of CPU and GPU execution using a practical example. The objective of this simple example is to give you insight into why GPUs perform so well for many, but only certain classes of, parallel problems.

Consider the simple problem of getting an array of 100 elements and returning a doubled version of it:

```
import numpy as np
a = np.ones(100)
b = np.empty(100)
for i in range(100):
    b[i] = 2 * a[i]
```

If you have a naive single-threaded and single-core CPU, the low-level implementation, such as a pseudocode assembler, for the previous code could be:

```
TMPVAR = A[0]          ◁─────────────┐  Gets the first element of the array A and
TMPVAR = 2 * TMPVAR    ◁──────────┐  │  puts it into a register called TMPVAR
B[0] = TMPVAR          ◁───────┐  │  │
TMPVAR = A[1]                  │  │  │
TMPVAR = 2 * TMPVAR            │  │     Doubles the value in the register
B[1] = TMPVAR                  │
...
TMPVAR = A[99]                    Puts the value of the register in
TMPVAR = 2 * TMPVAR              the first position of array B
B[99] = TMPVAR
```

This pseudocode gets the first element of the array A into a register, doubles its value, and puts it on the first element of array B. This is repeated for all 100 elements of our array.

Now, remember from chapter 6 that retrieving values from main memory is an *extremely* expensive operation. Assume here that our naive CPU has no cache. Our read and write operations, TMPVAR = A[0] and B[0] = TMPVAR, take 90 units of time each, and our doubling operation, TMPVAR = 2 * TMPVAR, takes 2 units of time. We have 100 reads, 100 writes, and 100 doublings: 100*90 + 100*90 + 100*2. This adds up to 18,200 units of time. Remember, too, that our naive CPU is sequential, so one operation can only start after the previous operation is complete.

Now imagine a completely different execution model where you have 100 threads running in parallel, and *each* thread does a single memory read, followed by a single doubling and, finally, a single write. Let's assume that the cost of reading and writing is the same: 90 time units. But the cost of doubling is substantially more expensive; we have a lot of computing units, so they are slower by the unit—say, 40 time units.

So *all* threads emit a memory read request at the same time. One hundred time units later, *all* threads receive their data and then take 40 time units to perform the computation. Remember, all threads are operating in parallel at the same time and are independent of each other. Finally, they write to memory in parallel at 100 time units of cost. The total cost is 100 + 40 + 100 = 240 time units.

So, our "CPU" takes 18,200 time units whereas our "GPU" takes 240 time units: making the "GPU" roughly 75 times faster. However, if you only wanted to make the operation on a *single* value, then the "CPU" would take 202 time cycles, whereas the "GPU" would take 240 time cycles.

This example should provide you with some insight into the advantages and disadvantages of GPU computing. In essence, GPUs are great for dealing with memory latency and doing similar operations on lots of data, but they are not efficient at dealing with single operations. To use a metaphor, we can compare a CPU with a Ferrari and a GPU with a bus. If you only need to transport 5 people, the Ferrari will beat the bus. But if you need to transport 500 people, it's not even a fair competition.

One of the biggest obstacles that many developers face when learning or using GPUs is overcoming their intuitive feeling that most code should be sequential. While

it's true that a lot of code is sequential, many, if not most, of the *expensive* parts of the computation are very parallel. The quintessential example is pixels on a screen. There are 2 million pixels on an HD screen with a resolution of 1920 × 1080. Each pixel is processed independently, and thus we could, at least in theory, process all those pixels in parallel. Or consider N-dimensional arrays, which are exactly the type of data structures used in data science: each element of the array can be computed separately and thus all elements can potentially be computed in parallel. So GPUs are very applicable to many problems of interest.

To get a clearer understanding of why GPUs are appropriate for highly parallel problems, we need to look more closely at the architecture of these machines. We will do just that in the next section.

9.1.2 *The relationship between CPUs and GPUs*

The computation model of a GPU is very different from a CPU. To program a GPU efficiently—actually, to program a GPU at all—we need to understand the underlying architecture and how it is different from what we are used to.

The GPU is, for all intents and purposes, a co-processor. The CPU is the main processor, and code for it controls the top level of the computation. The nomenclature surrounding GPU computing makes this relationship quite clear: the *host* refers to the CPU, and the *device* is the GPU. The code in the host drives the overall computing process.

Most important from a performance perspective, for the overwhelming majority of CPU and GPU architectures, the CPU and GPU have different memory banks that are separated from each other. We thus have *host memory* (i.e., the memory available in the host) and *device memory* (i.e., the memory available in the GPU).

The cost of transferring data to and from the GPU memory can have a massive effect on performance, especially if the amount of computation that we do on the GPU is limited. Figure 9.1 depicts this relationship.

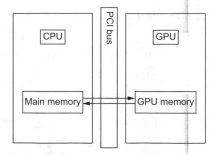

Figure 9.1   The CPU and GPU have separate memory spaces. We need to transfer our data to the memory associated with the GPU for computation and then get our results back into the CPU-associated memory, which can cost a substantial amount of time.

> ### GPU vendors and software portability
>
> Before we discuss the internal architecture of GPUs, I want to make a point about GPU vendors and software portability. There are two main vendors of GPUs for general-purpose computing: NVIDIA and AMD. In theory, there are vendor-agnostic interfaces that allow us to program in a non–vendor-dependent way. If you are interested in being vendor agnostic, you can check out software solutions for that, such as OpenCL or the Vulkan compute API.

(continued)

The practical reality is that NVIDIA almost completely dominates the general-purpose computing market. That can be seen at a lower-level programming for GPUs with the dominance of NVIDIA's Compute Unified Device Architecture (CUDA), as well as at the Python level, where many data analysis libraries supporting GPUs are CUDA based such as CuPy, CuDF, cuML, and BlazingSQL.

In this chapter we will be solely NVIDIA/CUDA based in terms of APIs. However, from a conceptual perspective, the information is transferable to the AMD space as well as vendor-agnostic libraries.

The problem with vendor dependence extends into the nomenclature: vendor-agnostic terminology can be different from NVIDIA terminology. I will try to present vendor-agnostic terms in as much as possible, but I will give NVIDIA equivalents when those have become common terms.

The trouble with naming is further complicated because, adding to vendor-specific terminology, there are some words that are based on the graphics origins of GPUs. For example, a CUDA core is also a streaming processor—not to be confused with streaming multiprocessor—and a shader.

9.1.3   *The internal architecture of GPUs*

GPUs have several streaming multiprocessors (SMs). The number can vary from 1 to 30 or even more. Each SM is composed of many streaming processors (SPs), which are sometimes called CUDA cores. Each SM has many SPs. See figure 9.2 for a simplified overview of the main GPU components.

For example, a NVIDIA RTX 2070 is based on the NVIDIA Turing 106 GPU, which has 36 SMs, each with 64 CUDA Cores for a total of 2304 CUDA cores; this GPU is like having the ability to run 2,304 threads simultaneously. As I said previously, we are opting here for simplification, as the architecture is substantially more complicated. Of particular importance for data science are the new tensor cores that can be used for AI computation; we will not cover these in this chapter, but you might want to research them for more advanced usage.

Memory organization is also important: each SM has a certain amount of L1 cache (check chapter 6 for cache concepts) that can be shared across all SPs in the same SM. We will not be making direct use of the L1 cache, which can be used to share states across threads running on the same SM. There is also L2 cache, which is shared by all SMs, and, finally, the GPU main memory. For example the TU 106 GPU has 64 KB of L1 cache per SM and 4 MB of L2 cache, and the RTX 2070 comes with 8 GB of main memory.

How will this affect our coding and performance design? You need to be explicitly aware of the architecture to run code on it, as we will see next.

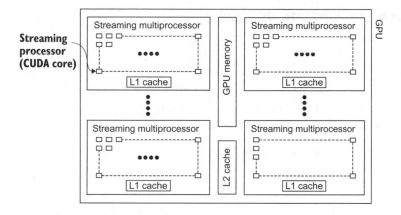

Figure 9.2   A simplified overview of the main GPU components: streaming multiprocessors that contain streaming processors (CUDA cores) and local cache. The GPU includes all the streaming multiprocessors along with some extra cache and the GPU main memory.

9.1.4   *Software architecture considerations*

Let's now see how the hardware architecture affects GPU code design. We will have a look at the steps necessary to run our previous simple example: multiplying a matrix by 2. Later in the chapter, we will actually code this, but for now let's revisit the high-level steps.

We have our matrix in the memory near the CPU, so the first thing we need to do is to transfer it to the GPU memory. This operation can be quite expensive, especially if we don't have much computation to do on the GPU.

Imagine a 1024×64 matrix (i.e., 65,536 elements). In a GPU, each element will be computed as a separate thread. So, we will have 65,536 threads. Each thread will run the *same code*. Threads need to be divided into thread blocks; all threads in a thread block are placed in the same SM and can share memory and synchronization primitives. In our case, nothing is needed to share across different threads as the algorithm is trivial, but we still need to divide our code in thread blocks.

If we assume, for example, the value of 32 threads per block, we will need 2048 blocks. Each block can be executed on different SMs.

So how do we call the code? Remember that the CPU drives everything, so the CPU will call an entry point on the GPU that will drive all the computations. The name for that entry point is the *kernel function*. We now have a very basic idea of the fundamentals of coding a GPU: the existence of an entry point—*kernel function*—and the running of the same code over many threads.

We will deploy low-level code to the GPU. Because there is no Cython equivalent to convert Python to OpenCL C (or CUDA C), we will use Numba. If you have never used Numba, see appendix B, which is an introduction to the technology.

9.2   *Using Numba to generate GPU code*

After some basic preparation, we are finally going to write our first GPU program using Numba. To understand the basic problems with GPU coding, we will start with the simplest of examples: doubling the value of an array. After that, we will implement a Mandelbrot generator, which you can then compare with a CPU version in appendix B. Again, if you've never used Numba, consider looking first at that appendix where Numba is introduced on the CPU.

9.2.1   *Installation of GPU software for Python*

Before we can start running our GPU code, we need to be sure that all the drivers and required software for the GPU are installed. Installing the software is not always trivial. It is not possible here to provide general instructions for different operating systems and architectures, but a few guidelines can be given.

You will probably need kernel drivers installed with the potential need to reboot your machine. You will need the CUDA toolkit, which comes in different flavors; if you are using Anaconda, doing `conda install cudatoolkit` is probably the easiest approach.

Numba has the ability to test the existing infrastructure and report on existing hardware and libraries. To check, run this in the following shell:

```
numba -s
```

You will have a very detailed view of your system. To determine whether the GPU is available, you need to see whether the hardware is detected and the libraries are available. For the hardware, search for something like this:

```
__CUDA Information__
CUDA Device Initialized                          : True
CUDA Driver Version                              : 11020
CUDA Detect Output:
Found 1 CUDA devices
id 0             b'Tesla T4'                              [SUPPORTED]
                    compute capability: 7.5
                        pci device id: 30
                          pci bus id: 0
Summary:
        1/1 devices are supported
```

This code will allow you to check whether the device is detected and supported. Some older GPUs might not be supported. You also need to make sure that all libraries are found. Another part of the report will include something like this:

```
CUDA Libraries Test Output:
Finding cublas from Conda environment
        named  libcublas.so.11.2.0.252
        trying to open library...         ok
Finding cusparse from Conda environment
        named  libcusparse.so.11.1.1.245
```

```
        trying to open library...        ok
Finding cufft from Conda environment
        named  libcufft.so.10.2.1.245
        trying to open library...        ok
Finding curand from Conda environment
        named  libcurand.so.10.2.1.245
        trying to open library...        ok
Finding nvvm from Conda environment
        named  libnvvm.so.3.3.0
        trying to open library...        ok
Finding libdevice from Conda environment
        searching for compute_20...      ok
        searching for compute_30...      ok
        searching for compute_35...      ok
        searching for compute_50...      ok
```

This code will allow you to discover all problematic libraries. Let's now write some GPU code.

9.2.2 *The basics of GPU programming with Numba*

Before we start with our code, let's get into the right mindset by looking at what we do *not* want to do. Remember, we are trying simply to double an array, so the following would be a potential solution with a CPU mindset:

```
def double_not_this(my_array):
    for position in range(my_array):   ◁─── for is a sequential operation.
        my_array[position] *= 2
```

This code is a sequential loop over the array. But our GPU code will use one thread per element, so our code should only handle a *single* element. Later, we will take care of telling the GPU to apply our code to all elements of the array. Here is the first version:

```
from numba import cuda
                              Compiles the
@cuda.jit            ◁─────   function to CUDA
def double(my_array):                           cuda.grid accesses the
    position = cuda.grid(1)   ◁─────────────     current position to be
    my_array[position] *= 2                      processed in the array.
```

There is no output to show here because this all happens on the GPU.

Yes, a function call handles a single element only! This approach is very different from what we are used to—outside vectorized approaches.

We annotate our function with the cuda.jit decorator so that Numba generates a CUDA version of our code. We then use the "magic" function cuda.grid to get the single and only position we will be changing; we will see later what is going on there. Finally, we change a single entry in the array based on position.

Our function cannot return values as it going to be implemented as a GPU kernel function, so we need to pass parameters to accommodate return values. If we try to execute the code

```
my_array = np.ones(1000)
double(my_array)
```

we will get an error:

```
Kernel launch configuration was not specified. Use the syntax:
```

```
kernel_function[blockspergrid, threadsperblock](arg0, arg1, ..., argn)
```

This error is because we must also tell Numba how to distribute the computation. As alluded to in the section on architecture, we have to divide the computation into thread blocks, and each block, into grids. This will work:

```
import numpy as np

blocks_per_grid = 50
threads_per_block = 20

my_array = np.ones(1000)
double[blocks_per_grid, threads_per_block](my_array)   ◁──  The call to the function
assert (my_array == 2).all()                                 uses a syntax that is not
                                                             very idiomatic.
```

We want to check that the function was applied to all elements of the array.

Notice that the syntax to call the function is not very idiomatic. At the end, we are checking that all elements are 2 using `assert`. We are trying to be careful because if we supply the wrong number of blocks, not all arrays may be computed.

We are issuing 20 threads per block, and as we have 1,000 elements, we will need 50 blocks. Generally, 32 threads are common. Give the memory hierarchy in GPUs, threads in the same block can share some states very fast. Here we will not be concerned with those types of algorithms, as they are for a more advanced stage. Thus, we can be quite flexible with our code distribution over the GPU.

That being said, sometimes it is not possible to have a `blocks * threads` that is equal to the number of elements in our array (e.g., in an array whose size is a prime number). In that case, we have to specify a `blocks * threads` that is slightly bigger than our array. Here is an example:

```
threads_per_block = 16
blocks_per_grid = 63

my_array = np.ones(1000)
double[blocks_per_grid, threads_per_block](my_array)
assert (my_array == 2).all()
```

In this case, we will have a total of 1,008 threads (16*63). If you are lucky, this code will work. It is also quite possible that it crashes!

You are calling the code for positions 0 to 1007, and the last eight positions, 1000 to 1007, were not allocated. Now, here you have to stop with the Python mindset and remember that your code was converted into a lower-level language. This conversion means that all the standard Python bounds checking will not be available and that you can get, as a "prize," a memory allocation error or, worse, a silent bug. We will see an example later of this type of bug.

Correcting this problem is quite easy:

```
@cuda.jit
def double_safe(my_array):
    position = cuda.grid(1)
    if position > my_array.shape[0]:
        return
    my_array[position] *= 2
```

We check whether the position is bigger than the array size and, if so, return. Now we can call the code confidently:

```
my_array = np.ones(1000)
double_safe[blocks_per_grid, threads_per_block](my_array)
assert (my_array == 2).all()
```

Finally, at this stage, we properly called code on the GPU!

Now, let's get back to the "magic" of cuda.grid to get the position to be computed. We will understand what is going on with that call by explicitly coding it ourselves. Having to code it ourselves is sometime necessary (e.g., with arrays that have more than three dimensions):

```
@cuda.jit
def double_safe_explicit(my_array):
    position = cuda.blockIdx.x * cuda.blockDim.x + cuda.threadIdx.x
    if position >= my_array.shape[0]:
        return
    my_array[position] *= 2
```

The thread call has access to which block and thread it is running. It also has access to the block dimension. cuda.blockIdx gives you the block index where the current thread is running. cuda.blockDim provides the block dimension, and cuda.threadIdx gives you the thread inside the group. With this information, you can make sure each thread addresses a different position in the array.

Location information for a thread can be one-, two-, and three-dimensional: You might have noticed the .x parameter on all the CUDA calls; .y and .z parameters can be used if you have two- and three-dimensional arrays.

Let's now look at the same function but for a two-dimensional array:

```
@cuda.jit
def double_matrix_unsafe(my_matrix):
    x, y = cuda.grid(2)
    my_matrix[y, x] *= 2
```

We now use `cuda.grid(2)` to get two indices. Notice that we returned to the unsafe code because we can now be quite sure that we will trigger an error. Let's run this code:

```
threads_per_block_2d = 16, 16
blocks_per_grid_2d = 63, 63

my_matrix = np.ones((1000, 1000))
double_matrix_unsafe[blocks_per_grid_2d, threads_per_block_2d](my_matrix)
print((my_matrix == 2).all())
```

This will print `True`, as all elements of the matrix are now 2. Notice that we have block and thread definitions that are two-dimensional like our data.

If you run this code and are lucky enough that it doesn't crash, it will most surely return erroneous results. This outcome occurs because we are not testing matrix boundaries, and when you go over in one row, you will land on the next row of the matrix, which was not possible with a one-dimensional array. So, there will probably be positions where the value is 4, not 2, as the code will be executed there twice.

Correcting this is quite simple, as we have previously seen. The following is our final version where we also are explicit with the matrix indexes:

```
@cuda.jit
def double_matrix(my_matrix):
    x = cuda.blockIdx.x * cuda.blockDim.x + cuda.threadIdx.x
    y = cuda.blockIdx.y * cuda.blockDim.y + cuda.threadIdx.y
    if x >= my_matrix.shape[0]:
        return
    if y >= my_matrix.shape[1]:
        return
    my_matrix[y, x] *= 2
```

Now that we have covered the basics, let's re-create our Mandelbrot example using a GPU.

9.2.3   *Revisiting the Mandelbrot example using GPUs*

We have gone over almost all the Numba concepts, so let's create a Mandelbrot renderer using a GPU. To put those concepts together and build the renderer, we will take a circuitous route, following what may seem like the logical approach, but ending up at a few dead ends that do not work. The goal here is to illustrate and explain exactly *why* these steps do not work, in the hopes that this understanding will save you from the pitfalls of just following your intuition.

Let's start by implementing the Mandelbrot function to compute the value for a single point:

```
from numba import cuda

@cuda.jit(device=True)
def compute_point(c):
    i = -1
    z = complex(0, 0)
    while abs(z) < 2:
        i += 1
        if i == 255:
            break
        z = z**2 + c
    return 255 - (255 * i)
```

Note the `device=True` addition to the `cuda.jit` decorator. We are telling Numba that this function needs to be invoked from *inside* the device. Device functions, unlike kernel functions, can return values.

Next, we will implement a first version that may seem sensible but does not work:

```
@cuda.jit
def compute_all_points_doesnt_work(start, end, size, img_array):
    x, y = cuda.grid(2)
    if x >= img_array.shape[0] or y >= img_array.shape[1]:
        return
    mandel_x = (end[0] - start[0])*(x/size) + start[0]
    mandel_y = (end[1] - start[1])*(y/size) + start[1]
    img_array[y, x] = compute_point(complex(mandel_x, mandel_y))
```

While this function compiles, if you try to call it, you will get the following:

```
NotImplementedError: (UniTuple(float64 x 2), (-1.5, -1.3))
```

The problem here is that Numba cannot handle tuples as input parameters (at least at the present time). But this points to a larger problem that we need to remember: *some Python functionality is not supported by Numba.* So, be sure to check Numba's documentation (http://numba.pydata.org/) to determine what functions are supported. It makes no sense for us to discuss here which specific features are unsupported, because Numba is changing all the time. It may very well be supporting new features between the time I am writing and the time you are reading this section.

So, to make this solution work, we have to create a version without tuples as input parameters:

```
@cuda.jit
def compute_all_points(startx, starty, endx, endy, size, img_array):
    x, y = cuda.grid(2)
    if x >= img_array.shape[0] or y >= img_array.shape[1]:
        return
```

```
mandel_x = (end[0] - startx)*(x/size) + startx
mandel_y = (end[1] - starty)*(y/size) + starty
img_array[y, x] = compute_point(complex(mandel_x, mandel_y))
```

There is a minor detail worth noticing in the last line: remember that with NumPy arrays the y coordinate goes first, so we write img_array[y, x].

Let's now make our call:

```
from math import ceil
import numpy as np
from PIL import Image

size = 2000
start = -1.5, -1.3
end = 0.5, 1.3

img_array = np.empty((size, size), dtype=np.uint8)
threads_per_block_2d = 16, 16
blocks_per_grid_2d = ceil(size / 16), ceil(size / 16)

compute_all_points[blocks_per_grid_2d,
    threads_per_block_2d](start[0], start[1], end[0], end[1],
    size, img_array)

img = Image.fromarray(img_array, mode="P")
img.save("mandelbrot.png")
```

The most important point that I'd like you to notice here is the specification of the number of blocks: given that we have 16 threads per block on each dimension, we need to have size / 16 blocks. As the number might not be an integer, we must round up to make sure all points are covered.

We can time this:

```
In [3]: %timeit compute_all_points[blocks_per_grid_2d, ...
72.6 ms ± 50.4 µs per loop (mean ± std. dev. of 7 runs, 10 loops each)
```

This compares with 539 ms for the best CPU version demonstrated in appendix B. Although, to be honest, this is not a fair comparison, as it pits a poor CPU against a good GPU. Furthermore, there are plenty of other factors, like algorithm type and CPU-to-GPU memory transfer, that have a massive effect on speed. Nonetheless, it should be clear that GPUs can deliver increased performance compared to CPUs for some algorithms.

Now that we have our first Mandelbrot generator based on GPUs with a substantial increase in performance, let's create another Mandelbrot generator. This time, we'll create it using NumPy vectorization, because it can be quite useful in accelerating data analysis, as we have seen before.

9.2.4 *A NumPy version of the Mandelbrot code*

Our final version is a NumPy universal function running on the GPU. We've gone over all the essential pieces, so it should be quite easy to put this together. Here is the computation point along with the vectorized version:

```
from cuda import vectorize

size = 2000
start = -1.5, -1.3
end = 0.5, 1.3


def compute_point_255_fn(c):
    i = -1
    z = complex(0, 0)
    while abs(z) < 2:
        i += 1
        if i == 255:
            break
        z = z**2 + c
    return 255 - (255 * i) // 255
```

We will be using a simpler version of the point calculation with the interaction limit hardcoded.

```
compute_point_vectorized = vectorize(
  ["uint8(complex128)"], target="cuda")(compute_point_255_fn)
```

The only small novelty of this code is the use of `target="cuda"` in the `vectorize` call on the last line.

Remember from the previous section that we need to prepare an array with positions for which we want computation:

```
def prepare_pos_array(start, end, pos_array):
    size = pos_array.shape[0]
    startx, starty = start
    endx, endy = end
    for xp in range(size):
        x = (endx - startx)*(xp/size) + startx
        for yp in range(size):
            y = (endy - starty)*(yp/size) + starty
            pos_array[yp, xp] = complex(x, y)


pos_array = np.empty((size, size), dtype=np.complex128)
img_array = np.empty((size, size), dtype=np.uint8)
```

We can now time the execution of this version:

```
In [6]: %timeit compute_point_vectorized(pos_array)
222 ms ± 3.05 ms per loop (mean ± std. dev. of 7 runs, 1 loop each)
```

The numbers are worse than the previous GPU version, but still better than the CPU version. The pattern here is different from the CPU version: in the CPU version, the fastest code was with an universal function.

NumPy functionality is limited with CUDA due to the computation model. Wouldn't it be nice if there was a native GPU implementation of NumPy? Enter CuPy. . . .

9.3   Performance analysis of GPU code: The case of a CuPy application

In this section, we will implement a solution using a native GPU version of NumPy: CuPy.

> **NOTE**   Many CPU-based data analysis libraries have GPU counterparts. So, you can use GPUs with little to no knowledge of how the GPU code works. As such, we will start by listing existing versions of GPU-based libraries for data analysis.

After we create our CuPy solution, we will use our code to discuss techniques to profile GPU code. Our CuPy example will serve as an excuse to introduce tools to analyze the performance of GPU solutions. But before we discuss code or profiling, let's get an overview of existing GPU-based libraries for data science.

9.3.1   GPU-based data analysis libraries

If you have access to GPUs, you don't have to code from scratch. There are a few GPU-based libraries that provide similar functionality—many times with very close interfaces—to existing known data libraries for CPUs. In many instances, you don't need to know anything about GPU programming. Table 9.1 provides a list of currently existing libraries along with their CPU counterparts.

Table 9.1   GPU-based libraries with CPU counterparts

GPU	CPU	Purpose
cuBLAS	BLAS	Basic linear algebra
CuPy	NumPy	N-dimensional array processing
CuDF	pandas	Columnar data analysis
CuGraph		Graph algorithms for data frames
CuML	scikit-learn	Machine learning
BlazingSQL		SQL interfaces on top of columnar data

Other libraries are able to accelerate existing analysis code. For example, cuDNN can increase the performance of machine learning libraries like PyTorch or TensorFlow.

You can consider these libraries for your data analysis projects based on GPUs. For example, we will develop a project based on CuPy.

9.3.2   *Using CuPy: A GPU-based version of NumPy*

We will develop a project using a high-level data science library, CuPy. CuPy is a GPU-based version of NumPy. Many high-level GPU libraries have similar interfaces with their CPU counterparts so not much new information needs to be introduced at that level. But, other than allowing us to see a real example of GPU-based data science code, we can use the code generated in this example to introduce profiling tools for GPU code. Our project will be, you guessed it, a Mandelbrot generator on top of CuPy arrays.

9.3.3   *A basic interaction with CuPy*

Before we implement our Mandelbrot generator, let's do some basic work with CuPy, which will allow us to discuss of the underlying mechanics going on with CuPy. We are simply going to create a matrix of 5000×5000 and double it:

```
import numpy as np
import cupy as cp

size = 5000

my_matrix = cp.ones((size, size), dtype=cp.uint8)
print(type(my_matrix))
np_matrix = my_matrix.get()
print(type(np_matrix))
2 * my_matrix

2 * np_matrix
```

While having similar interfaces, CuPy and NumPy are different libraries and expose different object types. It is not uncommon that you end up importing both for many analyses.

The type of `my_matrix` will be `cupy._core.core.ndarray`, whereas the type of `np_matrix` will be `numpy.ndarray`. The data for `my_matrix` resides on the GPU memory, so when you want do operations on it, there will be no memory transfer from the CPU to the GPU side. For example, the multiplication `2 * my_matrix` occurs completely in the GPU. A memory transfer from the GPU side will happen when you explicitly do `my_matrix.get()`, which will create an independent NumPy representation of the original matrix.

Basic profiling of GPU code should not be done with the typical Python tools like the `timeit` module or the `%timeit` magic of IPython. The GPU code executes independently from the CPU code, and a CPU perspective of execution time will not be representative of the GPU cost.

CuPy provides a simple mechanism to profile code. Let's run `2 * my_matrix` 200 times and see its cost:

```
from cupyx.time import repeat

print(repeat(lambda : 2 * my_matrix, n_repeat=200))
```

The output on my machine is:

```
<lambda>            :    CPU:    60.910 us    +/-14.344
                              (min:   19.158 / max:   101.755) us
                         GPU-0:  785.708 us    +/-12.013
                              (min:   749.760 / max:   822.656) us
```

So, on average, each execution takes 60 μs of CPU time and 785 μs of GPU time. I ran this code on a Tesla T4 GPU, which was hosted on an Intel Xeon at 2.50 GHz.

Now let's move on and finally implement our Mandelbrot generator using CuPy. Our larger objective here is not to show the interface because it is supposed to be similar, by design, with NumPy. We are also not going to talk about CuPy limitations compared to NumPy because these change over time, and when you read this text, they may have already changed.

Our objective with our next *two* Mandelbrot implementations is to explore how to extract the most performance out of the GPU. We will write processing functions that work on the GPU with CuPy. Our first will show the interaction of CuPy with Numba.

9.3.4 *Writing a Mandelbrot generator using Numba*

CuPy interacts seamlessly with Numba: you can write a Numba-decorated function and use it with CuPy.

> **TIP** CuPy has its own converter of Python code to GPU code that is somewhat competitive with Numba. At the current stage, its support for Python features is quite limited compared to Numba. I recommend trying Numba first, although, with time, maybe the native CuPy converter will become more feature-complete.

The following is our implementation of a Mandelbrot generator written in Numba that works with CuPy:

```
from math import ceil

import numpy as np
import cupy as cp
from numba import cuda
from PIL import Image

size = 2000
start = -1.5, -1.3
end = 0.5, 1.3

@cuda.jit
def compute_all_mandelbrot(startx, starty, endx, endy, size, img_array):
    x, y = cuda.grid(2)
    if x >= img_array.shape[0] or y >= img_array.shape[1]:
        return
    mandel_x = (end[0] - startx)*(x/size) + startx
    mandel_y = (end[1] - starty)*(y/size) + starty
```

```
c = complex(mandel_x, mandel_y)
i = -1
z = complex(0, 0)
while abs(z) < 2:
    i += 1
    if i == 255:
        break
    z = z**2 + c
img_array[y, x] = i
```

Nothing in this code is really new to you from a conceptual point of view when compared to what we discussed in the Numba for GPU section. The same is true for calling the code:

```
threads_per_block_2d = 16, 16
blocks_per_grid_2d = ceil(size / 16), ceil(size / 16)

cp_img_array = cp.empty((size, size), dtype=cp.uint8)

compute_all_mandelbrot[blocks_per_grid_2d, threads_per_block_2d](
    start[0], start[1],
    end[0], end[1],
    size, cp_img_array)
```

The only thing left to do is to save our image:

```
img = Image.fromarray(cp.asnumpy(cp_img_array), mode="P")
img.save("imandelbrot.png")
```

Here we need to convert our CuPy array into a NumPy version to be able to use the Pillow library to create an image representation. This means that data will be transferred from GPU to CPU memory.

Let's do some basic performance analysis:

```
from cupyx.time import repeat

print(repeat(
    lambda: compute_all_mandelbrot[blocks_per_grid_2d, threads_per_block_2d](
        start[0], start[1], end[0], end[1], size, cp_img_array),
    n_repeat=200))
```

The performance reported here is:

```
<lambda>            :    CPU:   684.475 us   +/-76.369
                               (min:   629.685 / max: 1387.853) us
                         GPU-0:70604.003 us   +/-89.377
                               (min:70519.264 / max:71290.688) us
```

It seems that `repeat` prefers to report 70,600 µs instead of the more visually pleasant 70 ms. Now that we have the first version of our Mandelbrot generator on top of CuPy, let's do a second version that embeds the CUDA C code into our Python code.

9.3.5   *Writing a Mandelbrot generator using CUDA C*

We will create a vectorized function to generate a Mandelbrot set. Our vectorized function will receive a matrix with all the positions and compute, for each one, the Mandelbrot value. We will be implementing our function using CUDA C.

As with the NumPy version, we start by preparing the position array. We will actually do that in NumPy and then transfer it to CuPy:

```
def prepare_pos_array(start, end, pos_array):
    size = pos_array.shape[0]
    startx, starty = start
    endx, endy = end
    for xp in range(size):
        x = (endx - startx)*(xp/size) + startx
        for yp in range(size):
            y = (endy - starty)*(yp/size) + starty
            pos_array[yp, xp] = complex(x, y)


pos_array = np.empty((size, size), dtype=np.complex64)
prepare_pos_array(pos_array)

cp_pos_array = cp.array(pos_array)
```

The code for input preparation is exactly as before. In the last line, we convert the NumPy array to a CuPy version on the GPU, which requires a memory transfer.

We must now prepare our `threads_per_block` and `blocks_per_grid` variables. To keep our C code as simple as possible, we will work in one, rather than two, dimensions:

```
threads_per_block = 16 ** 2
blocks_per_grid = ceil(size / 16) ** 2
```

We scale our one-dimensional blocks and threads per block as necessary. Here is our implementation:

```
c_compute_mandelbrot = cp.RawKernel(r'''
#include <cupy/complex.cuh>
extern "C" __global__
void raw_mandelbrot(const complex<float>* pos_array,
            char* img_array) {
    int x = blockDim.x * blockIdx.x + threadIdx.x;
    int i = -1;
    complex<float> z = complex<float>(0.0, 0.0);
    complex<float> c = pos_array[x];
```

```
    while (abs(z) < 2) {
        i++;
        if (i == 255) break;
        z = z*z + c;
    }
    img_array[x] = i;
}
''', 'raw_mandelbrot')
```

The point of this book is not to teach you C, so we are not going to delve into the details of this listing, but the code is designed with simplicity in mind and should be easy to understand. As before, we are not focusing on how we decide on the position to compute but, rather, on `blockDim.x * blockIdx.x threadIdx.x`. The C code is actually looking at the matrix as a one-dimensional array and that works.

Finally, let's use the previous function to compute the Mandelbrot set from the position array:

```
c_compute_mandelbrot((blocks_per_grid,),
    (threads_per_block,), (cp_pos_array, cp_img_array))
img = Image.fromarray(cp.asnumpy(cp_img_array), mode="P")
img.save("cmandelbrot.png")
```

Note the syntax to call the function while specifying the number of blocks and threads per block: it's different from the Numba approach. We finalize by transferring the CuPy array to a NumPy version to print it.

Let's do some basic performance analysis:

```
from cupyx.time import import repeat

print(repeat(
    lambda: c_compute_mandelbrot((blocks_per_grid,),
        (threads_per_block,), (cp_pos_array, cp_img_array)),
    n_repeat=200))
```

On my machine, I get:

```
<lambda>           :    CPU:    6.677 us   +/- 2.769
                               (min:   4.177 / max:   25.978) us
                       GPU-0: 3149.825 us   +/-801.397
                               (min: 2635.584 / max: 5881.088) us
```

This result of 3.1 ms is 20 times faster than the Numba version. If your Numba code is still not fast enough, there is one final step that you can take: an embedded CUDA C implementation.

Now that we have some code that makes use of the GPU, let's find out about some GPU performance analysis tools.

9.3.6   *Profiling tools for GPU code*

Here we will use some basic functions of NVIDIA profiling tools to analyze the performance of our Mandelbrot implementations. The profiling tools are general: they don't depend on CuPy and not even on Python—you can use them with any GPU code. To demonstrate this, we will be profiling the NumPy version of our Mandelbrot code using a vectorized GPU implementation.

We will use NVIDIA's Nsight Systems to do our performance analysis. We will assume offline usage, and we will capture performance analysis and separately analyze it using Nsight's GUI. This is the most flexible approach, as it assumes that the GPU machine is separate from the analysis machine—for example, when the GPU machine is on the cloud and you look at the performance data on your local machine.

After installing Nsight Systems, we can very easily profile the code by doing the following:

```
nsys profile -o numba python mandelbrot_numba.py
nsys profile -o c python mandelbrot_c.py
```

To profile the NumPy version with a vectorized GPU implementation, we can do:

```
nsys profile -o numpy python ../sec3-gpu/mandelbrot_numpy.py
```

We now have three profile traces: `numba.qdrep`, `c.qdrep`, and `numpy.qdrep`.

Remember that we have a `timeit` mean of 222 ms for the NumPy version and a GPU cost from `cupyx.time.repeat` of 70 ms for the Numba version and 3 ms for the CUDA C version.

We can collect some basic profile statistics from each. Let's start with the NumPy version:

```
nsys stats numpy.qdrep
```

This code will produce a lot of output. Let's concentrate on the main GPU calls:

Time%	Total ns	Calls	Avg ns	Min ns	Max ns	StdDev	Name
96.1	368748545	1	368748545	368748545	368748545	0	cuMemcpyDtoH
3.6	13654495	1	13654495	13654495	13654495	0	cuMemcpyHtoD
0.1	540957	2	270478	234726	306231	50561	cuMemAlloc
0.1	371672	1	371672	371672	371672	0	cuModLdDataEx
0.0	133176	1	133176	133176	133176	0	cuLinkComplete
0.0	66248	1	66248	66248	66248	0	cuLinkCreate
0.0	49602	1	49602	49602	49602	0	cuMemGetInf
0.0	37495	1	37495	37495	37495	0	cuLaunchKernel
0.0	2071	1	2071	2071	2071	0	cuLinkDestroy

Notice that our implementation spends a lot of time copying data in and out of the GPU: these are the `cuMemcpyDtoH` and `cuMemcpyHtoD` calls, which take more than 99% of the time.

We can also inspect the cost of just the computation (i.e., kernel) part. The following is the NumPy abridged version:

```
Time(%)  Total Time (ns)   Name
-------  ---------------   -----------------------------------------------
  100.0        365860777   cudapy::__main__::__vectorized_compute_point ...
```

The time cost is 365860777 ns, or 365 ms.

The time cost for the CuPy version using Numba is:

```
Time(%)  Total Time (ns)   Name
-------  ---------------   ------------------------------------------------
  100.0        189965876   cudapy::__main__::compute_all_mandelbrot ...
```

The result is 180 ms.

Finally, the time cost for CUDA C is:

```
Time(%)  Total Time (ns)   Name
-------  ---------------   --------------
  100.0          5876134   raw_mandelbrot
```

The result is 5.8 ms.

The NumPy version is twice as slow as Numba. The C version is 32 times faster than the Numba version for kernel execution.

Nsight Systems has a great GUI, invoked using `nsys-ui`, that allows you to explore traces and follow execution in real time. While it's difficult to catch such dynamism in a screenshot, figure 9.3 shows a zoomed-in portion of the trace for the C version of our Mandelbrot generator. The application can be followed by CPU and GPU events, but here we concentrate on the GPU ones. You can see two blocks of relevance. First, in the one on the left, a host-to-device transfer is copying the NumPy matrix for positions into a CuPy version on the GPU: `cp_pos_array = cp.array(pos_array)`. The second block is actually doing the Mandelbrot computation.

To sum up the two most crucial takeaways from this section.

- As with CPUs, if you have performance problems, it is better to quantify the problem with proper profiling than to guess.
- If GPU libraries exist that mimic the CPU APIs that you already know, the most efficient path is probably to use those libraries instead of writing your own code from scratch to implement the same functionality.

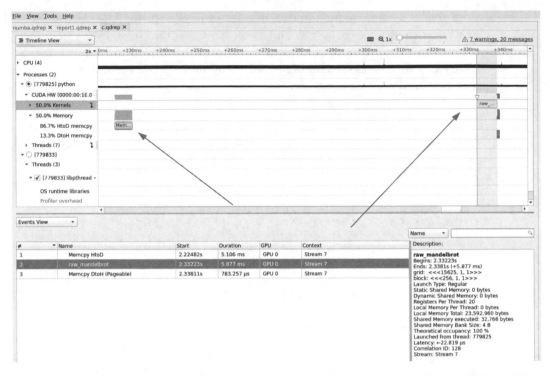

Figure 9.3   The GUI for Nsight Systems. Top left window: an outline of all processes allowing GPU and CPU usage. Main window: a temporal view of executions. Bottom left: temporal statistics of several GPU operations. Bottom right: details about one of the blocks from the main window.

Summary

- While CPUs provide a handful of computation units that are very fast and can work on different problems, GPUs typically provide thousands of computation units that are slow and expected to do similar workloads.

- GPUs provide computational power that is highly suited for efficient data processing, as many data science problems rely on data structures like matrices that lend themselves to parallelization via the use of the same algorithm over many data points.

- There are several GPU manufacturers, but in reality, the standard for GPU computing is based on NVIDIA hardware.

- When writing code for GPUs, we need to be aware that the compute model of GPUs is very different from CPUs and requires a different mindset from traditional sequential CPU computing.

- Standard Python code cannot be directly run on top of a GPU; we need to consider alternatives to be able to explore GPU power.

- There are already many Python libraries that allow the use of GPUs without needing to know how to program them directly.

- Many Python libraries are almost drop-in replacements for existing CPU versions. For example, CuPy exposes a similar interface to NumPy while working on GPUs, and cuDF has a similar interface to pandas.
- Numba can generate code for GPUs, but there is little value in just annotating existing Python code with Numba: code needs to be redesigned to explore the extreme parallelism that is possible with many algorithms working on large arrays.
- Numba code, even for GPUs, can interact seamlessly with NumPy, allowing it to offload highly parallel algorithms while still integrating with the traditional Python data analysis stack.

10
Analyzing big data with Dask

This chapter covers

- Scaling computation across many machines with extremely large datasets
- Introducing Dask's execution model
- Executing code using the `dask.distributed` scheduler

Processing large amounts of data sometimes requires more than a single computer because the data is too much to process or the algorithms require a lot of computing power. At this stage in the book, we know how to devise more efficient computational processes and how to store and structure our data more intelligently for processing. This final chapter will be about how to *scale out*—that is, use more than one computer to perform computations.

To scale out, we will be using Dask, which is a library to perform parallel computing for analytics. Dask integrates very well with other libraries in the Python ecosystem, like NumPy and pandas. Dask will serve our purpose to scale *out* (i.e., use more than one computer). However, it can also be used to scale *up* (i.e., use computational results in a single computer more efficiently). In that sense, it can be an alternative to the material presented in chapter 3 about parallelism.

There are other alternatives to Dask, Spark being the most common. Spark, coming from the Java space, is less well-integrated with other Python libraries compared to Dask. So I prefer to use a Python-native solution, which simplifies interaction with the Python ecosystem. Many of the concepts exercised here can still be used with other frameworks.

Dask has several different programming interfaces. At a higher level, some APIs are similar to NumPy, pandas, and other analysis libraries. However, Dask's interfaces, which are easy to use if you know the original libraries, allow for larger-than-memory objects like data frames and arrays, which pandas or NumPy don't. At a lower level, one interface is based on `concurrent.futures` (see chapter 3), and another allows you to use Dask to parallelize more general code (i.e., not only based on arrays and data frames).

The main objective in this chapter is to help you understand the underlying execution model of Dask, along with scheduling alternatives and larger-than-memory data usage. While we will discuss some performance problems, I believe that more is to be gained from understanding the underlying model of computation in Dask. Execution environments can vary a lot—from a single machine to very large clusters—and that can make concrete performance suggestions invalid or even deleterious. Thus, this chapter uses a different approach from most of the book: you are given the basic building blocks and will have to adapt them to your specific environment.

Dask has a different—namely, lazier—execution model compared to libraries like pandas or NumPy. So the first section will cover the substantial differences in semantics. Because we want to be on solid ground with regard to the model, we will not consider parallelism at all in the first section. We will also not consider larger-than-memory data structures. The first section will use an illustrative example based on the data frame interface of Dask, which is akin to pandas.

In the second section, I will discuss the partitioning of larger-than-memory data and present some performance implications of the Dask model. I will also introduce some best practices to accelerate computation.

In the third section, we will learn about Dask's distributed scheduler, which allows us to intelligently distribute computations across several computers and architectures: from HPC clusters to the cloud or GPU-enabled machines. Since it would be too much to ask readers to have a cluster or cloud to run this code, our example can be run on a single machine but will also be easy to scale out.

We will start with Dask's execution model. Given Dask's lazy nature, it has some important conceptual differences from existing libraries, like pandas or NumPy, that need to be understood before we actually implement parallel solutions. Dask is required to run the code in this chapter. You will also need the Graphviz library to draw task graphs. With conda, do `conda install dask`. Currently, it seems easier to install the Graphviz library bridge using pip (`pip install graphviz`), even with conda. You should also make sure that the Graphviz main application is installed. The Docker image is `tiagoantao/python-performance-dask`.

10.1 Understanding Dask's execution model

Parallel solutions are notoriously difficult, especially when executed over distributed architectures. Before we dive deep into parallelism with Dask, let's make sure we understand its execution model. We will write a pandas-like solution in Dask and ignore the underlying implementation: we don't care if it is serial or parallel. Limiting our discussion to model execution will allow us to understand the differences between Dask and, in this example, pandas. Then, in the next section, we will use a parallel and distributed solution.

In this example, we will take data from the US Census about taxes in the 50 US states. For each state, we will have information about all the taxes collected, including breakdowns of the amounts collected from each tax source. In other words, we will be able to see the total amount of tax collected, as well as the amounts collected as income tax, sales tax, property tax, and the like. We are trying to decide where to buy a house, and one of the factors we are considering is how much we would have to fork over in property taxes. So, we want to know which states earn a large portion of their tax income from property taxes and which states earn only a small amount of their total tax from property tax. Our sole concern is determining the percentage of the whole tax income that comes from property taxes.

The table we will work with is quite small, so it would be trivial to process with pandas, but data size is not the point here. It is the execution model we want to understand. The data can be found at http://mng.bz/41ND.

10.1.1 A pandas baseline for comparison

Let's start with the pandas version as our baseline. We will need to read the file and clean the data, and then we will compute the fraction of property tax for each state:

```
import numpy as np
import pandas as pd

taxes = pd.read_csv("FY2016-STC-Category-Table.csv", sep="\t")
taxes["Amount"] = taxes["Amount"].str.replace(",",
  "").replace("X", np.nan).astype(float)
pivot = taxes.pivot_table(index="Geo_Name",
  columns="Tax_Type", values="Amount")
has_property_info = pivot[pivot["Property Taxes"].notna()].index

pivot_clean = pivot.loc[has_property_info]
frac_property = pivot_clean["Property Taxes"] / pivot_clean["Total Taxes"]
frac_property.sort_values()
```

> **We clean up the Amount column so it can be converted to a float.**

> **We pivot the table along Tax_Type.**

We start by reading the file, which includes the US state (called `Geo_Name`), the type of tax, and the amount the state collected for that type of tax:

```
Geo_Name        Tax_Type        Amount
Alabama         Total Taxes     10,355,317
Alabama         Property Taxes  362,515
Alabama         Sales and Gross Receipts Taxes  5,214,390
Alabama         License Taxes   575,510
Alabama         Income Taxes    4,098,278
Alabama         Other Taxes     104,624
Connecticut     Total Taxes     15,659,420
Connecticut     Property Taxes  X
Connecticut     Sales and Gross Receipts Taxes  6,518,905
Connecticut     License Taxes   454,779
Connecticut     Income Taxes    8,322,645
Connecticut     Other Taxes     363,091
...
```

Then, for the `Amount` column, which includes nonnumbers, we convert Xs to NAs. We need to have only numbers, not strings, for our calculations.

Next, we pivot the representation: we create a new table with one column per tax type and only one row per US state. This representation makes computation simpler, as we only need one row to get all the information. The result is:

```
index       Income Taxes    Total Taxes ...  Property Taxes
Alabama     4098278         10355317         362515
Colorado    711711          12887859             NaN
```

We then remove all rows that lack property taxes and finally compute the percentage of taxes that come from properties:

```
Nebraska        0.000024
New Jersey      0.000147
Iowa            0.000147
Massachusetts   0.000213
....
Alaska          0.124577
New Hampshire   0.154625
Wyoming         0.177035
DC              0.326369
Vermont         0.338844
```

Let's now look at the Dask version.

10.1.2 Developing a Dask-based data frame solution

As you can see, in the equivalent Dask version, the code is *almost* the same:

```
import numpy as np                    We import the data frame
import dask.dataframe as dd    ◁───┘  interface of Dask.

taxes = dd.read_csv("FY2016-STC-Category-Table.csv", sep="\t")
taxes["Amount"] = taxes["Amount"].str.replace(",",
  "").replace("X", np.nan).astype(float)
taxes["Tax_Type"] = taxes["Tax_Type"].astype(
```

```
        "category").cat.as_known()
pivot = taxes.pivot_table(index="Geo_Name",
    columns="Tax_Type", values="Amount")
has_property_info = pivot[
    ~pivot["Property Taxes"].isna()].index

pivot_clean = pivot.loc[has_property_info]
frac_property = pivot_clean["Property Taxes"] / pivot_clean["Total Taxes"]
```

We need to specify that Tax_Type is categorical for pivot.

We use isna, not notna, because Dask does not support notna.

As you can see, the code is very similar. It *feels* the same, and you can almost copy it verbatim while importing dask.dataframe instead of pandas.

> **WARNING** While the Dask's data frame interface is indeed similar to pandas', some features are not implemented or are slightly different. We just saw the case of notna and the need to annotate a column as categorical, but plenty more cases exist. I have crafted this example to avoid a few extra differences in the implementation. The point is: the flavor is the same, and many operations are very similar, but there is still an implementation gap between pandas and Dask data frames.

The previous code doesn't do what you would expect if you were using pandas. What does it do? While the Dask code is very similar, it is doing something completely different.

print(frac_property) does *not* provide the result. Instead, Dask prepared an execution plan—a task graph—that will compute the result. The task graph has as nodes for the operations that need to be done, and it has edges for the dependencies across operations. Let's consider a concrete example next.

Dask can export a visualization of the task graph:

```
frac_property.visualize(filename="10-property.svg", rankdir="LR")
```

Figure 10.1 shows the part of the task graph corresponding to the first two lines of the code. pd.read_csv is represented by the first node. The left part of the assignment taxes["Amount"].str.replace(",", "").replace("X", np.nan).astype(float) is represented by the bottom line, and the assignment proper taxes["Amount"] = …, by the last node on the right.

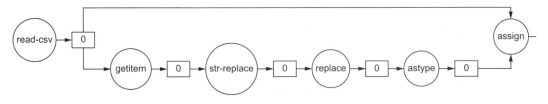

Figure 10.1   The start of the task graph for our property taxes calculation. The CSV reading and the recoding of Amount are included.

The computation is now ready to run. We can obtain the result by running:

```
frac_property_result = frac_property.compute()
```

This will compute the result and return a pandas data frame just like the one from the previous pandas example.

At this stage, we don't care how the computation was executed. It could have been serial, threaded, multiprocessed, on a cluster, on a GPU, or on the cloud. The fundamental point to understand for this section is that Dask is lazy in its execution: the code that you wrote creates a task graph to be executed later.

Now that you understand the difference between the lazy approach of Dask—where computation is done when it's needed—and the eager approach of pandas (or NumPy)—where computation is done when its specified—let's dig deep in terms of algorithm cost.

10.2   *The computational cost of Dask operations*

Let's discuss the algorithmic cost of several Dask operations. Our discussion will be irrespective of the execution environment. While the two subjects—algorithms and real execution platform—are, in practice, very intertwined, it is easier to grasp the consequences of algorithm complexity per se. There are consequences related to the way Dask splits data that doesn't fit in memory, and these are independent of whatever running infrastructure you have to execute the computation. The problems that we will consider here are quite general, and other parallel processing approaches, like Spark, have similar problems.

We will perform some very simple tasks. First, we will create a column called `year` that has just the last two digits from `Survey_Year`. So 2016 becomes 16. Then, we will create a column called `k_amount` that is the `Amount` but in thousands (i.e., divided by 1,000). Next, we will get the state with the maximum value. Finally, we will sort the states by total amount of taxes collected.

We will reuse the data from the last section. Although the dataset is tiny, we can force Dask to partition the computation in a similar way to a large dataset. In any case, what is "large" will depend on what hardware you have.

Before we partition, let's start by loading data and creating a year column with just the last two digits (e.g., 2016 is converted to 16):

```
import numpy as np
import dask.dataframe as dd

taxes = dd.read_csv("FY2016-STC-Category-Table.csv", sep="\t")
taxes["year"] = taxes["Survey_Year"] - 2000
taxes.visualize(filename="10-single.svg", rankdir="LR")
```

If you visualize the task graph, as shown in figure 10.2, you will see the file reading followed by the operations necessary to perform the subtraction.

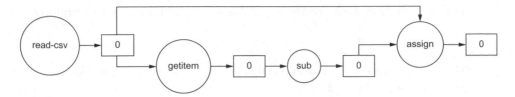

Figure 10.2   The tasks to read a CSV file and perform a subtraction on a column

Let's now see how the task graph would look if we had partitioned the data.

10.2.1 *Partitioning data for processing*

The CSV input is quite small, below 15 KB, but for the purpose of understanding what is going on, let's assume we can only process 5 KB at the same time. We can tell read_csv to process a maximum block, or chunk, of 5,000 bytes:

```
taxes = dd.read_csv("FY2016-STC-Category-Table.csv",
  sep="\t", blocksize=5000)
taxes["year"] = taxes["Survey_Year"] - 2000
taxes.visualize(filename="10-block.svg", rankdir="LR")
```

If we visualize the task graph, we now have three separate partitions, as in figure 10.3. The 15 KB is split into three so that a maximum of 5,000 bytes of input data can be processed.

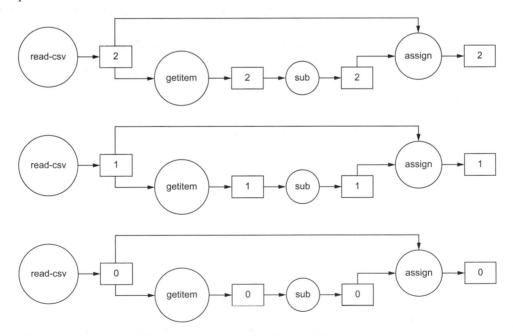

Figure 10.3   Reading a CSV and substracting using three partitions

Now that we have three partitions of a data frame, it's time to consider how a data frame is implemented in Dask. Remember that our objective is to force Dask to partition the data to understand how partitions affect the Dask task graph. Figure 10.4 provides a high-level overview of how the data is partitioned. In the implementation, the three partitions are rendered as three pandas data frames.

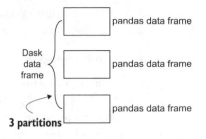

A similar implementation strategy is made for Dask arrays (the Dask equivalent of NumPy

Figure 10.4   A high-level view of how a data frame is implemented in Dask

arrays). A Dask array is implemented in each partition as a NumPy array. Dask, being a Python-based solution, makes use of existing libraries for its own inner workings. Let's return to implementing our solution.

Now that we have a basic view of the effect of partitioning on task graphs, let's look at a strategy to reduce repeated computations.

10.2.2 *Persisting intermediate computations*

As we discussed in the previous section, the column with amounts needs some parsing before we obtain a proper number. Because most of our computations will depend on having a correctly parsed number, we want to avoid continuously recomputing the string conversion every time we need that column. Instead, we can ask Dask to persist the intermediate state of a computation:

```
taxes["Amount"] = taxes["Amount"].str.replace(",",
  "").replace("X", np.nan).astype(float)
taxes = taxes.persist()
taxes.visualize(filename="10-persist.svg", rankdir="LR")
```

While the semantics of the `.persist` call will depend on the specific scheduler, let's assume that computation of all the nodes is started, so this will execute the task graph to clear the `Amount` column. After `.persist`, the computation for the amount will never be repeated. For this example, we are only dealing with a light computation, but a call to persist can also render very long graphs of computations.

The advantage of maintaining the data partitions is that we still have it all across the computing environment and can launch parallel queries over it. Contrast this with `compute`: you would get all your data back, and if you needed to compute more on top of it, you would need to repartition the data and send it to all processes executing the computation. Furthermore, if the full data frame is bigger than your memory, a `compute` would crash your local process.

> **TIP** Transferring data across processing units can be very expensive, especially over the network, as serialization of the data is required. On the other hand, we cannot persist everything, as that might require too much memory. Typically, nodes of the graph that are reused frequently and that produce small amounts of data are good candidates for the `persist` method.

Now that we optimized part of our computation, let's get back to computing the state with the maximum amount of taxes and order the states by total tax collected.

10.2.3 *Algorithm implementations over distributed data frames*

For some operations, the distributed implementations of algorithms may have completely different costs when compared to the sequential implementations that we are used to—in our case, comparing Dask data frames to pandas data frames.

Let's perform a simple operation. Remember that we want to convert the `Amount` column of the previous dataset to thousands of dollars:

```
taxes["k_amount"] = taxes["Amount"] / 1000
taxes.visualize(filename="10-k.svg", rankdir="LR")
```

The task graph for this operation is quite simple, as shown in figure 10.5. In this case, the computations occur in parallel over all partitions, which is quite efficient.

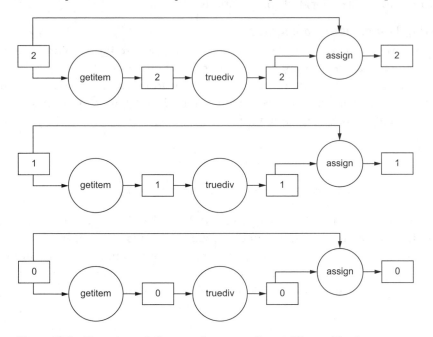

Figure 10.5   Many computations can happen on the partitions without any communication between them.

Let's now consider a more difficult operation to implement in a distributed system. Let's imagine we want to find the maximum value from the amount computed. Can you imagine what the task would look like? The code is:

```
max_k = taxes["k_amount"].max()
max_k.visualize(filename="10-max_k.svg", rankdir="LR")
```

Notice that one node per partition is responsible for computing the maximum for that partition. Unfortunately, all maximums per partition must be coalesced into a separate process to compute the maximum from all partitions. This process has some implications. When the maximum is computed, parallelism stops in the final node to get the maximum of all partitions. Thus, data must be transferred from the partitions that hold the amounts to the node computing the maximum. In the task graph for this operation (figure 10.6), you can see this data transfer in the transition from the three tasks called `series-max-chunk` to the tasks `series-max-agg`. In other words, we need to go from three parallel tasks to a single task to compute the maximum: this task bottlenecks ongoing parallelism.

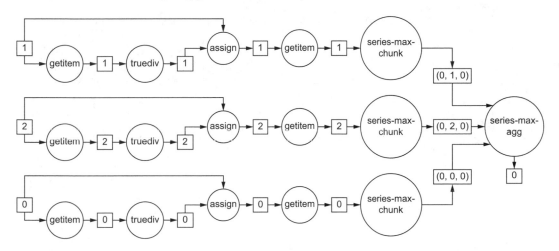

Figure 10.6 Some computations require reducing the parallelism—for example, the computation of a maximum.

The general principle is that the cost of operations using Dask when compared to pandas or NumPy can vary quite dramatically. If the operation requires communication between processes or a stop in parallel processing, you can expect an increase in cost. The precise implication can vary widely depending on your underlying architecture.

If you don't know the task graph topology of an operation, you can simply render the task graph of that operation to see the structure and find potential bottlenecks. For example, figure 10.7 shows the task graph for the (quite expensive) operation `sort_values`. In this specific case, `barrier` and `shuffle-collect` tasks impose a loss of parallelism on the whole graph:

```
sv = taxes.sort_values("k_amount")
sv.visualize(filename="10-sv.svg", rankdir="LR")
```

Sometimes you may need to check the task graph of two operations together because Dask may be smart enough to optimize them. For example, operations *following* `groupby` might be optimized in completely different ways. Optimization may even vary

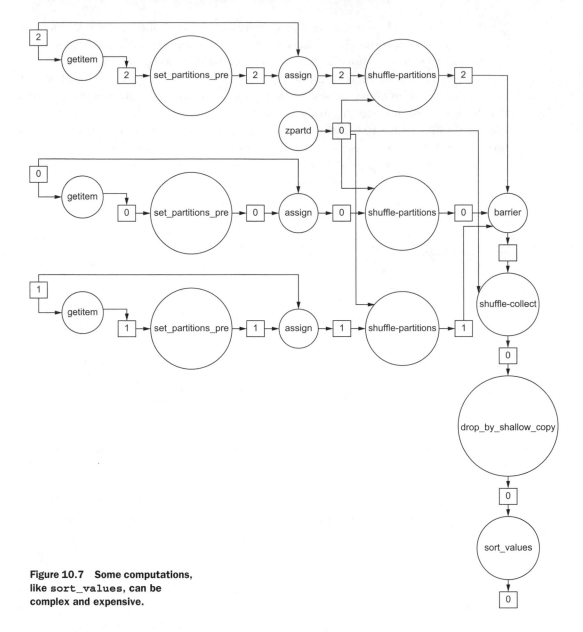

Figure 10.7   Some computations, like `sort_values`, can be complex and expensive.

across different Dask versions, so there is no general rule, other than to check how Dask renders the operations you are using.

I'm not listing cheap or expensive Dask operations here for two main reasons. First, whether or not operations are expensive depends on your execution environment. For example, a cloud will be different from a large multicore computer. Second, Dask is always evolving, and the implementation may change across versions. What is important is to understand the underlying principles.

10.2.4 *Repartitioning the data*

In some cases, depending on the task graph and execution environment, the granularity of the computation can benefit from repartitioning the data. For example, let's say we finalized a part of the computation that was very expensive, requiring more partitions and potentially more computing nodes. After this process, if we are entering a less-intensive part of the operation, we might reduce the number of partitions. In our case, let's reduce the partitions from three to two:

```
taxes2 = taxes.repartition(npartitions=2)
taxes2.visualize(filename="10-repart.svg", rankdir="LR")
```

As you can see in the task graph (figure 10.8), the problem with this repartitioning is that two of the three partitions are joined as one new partition. It would be more efficient if both new partitions had similar amounts of data.

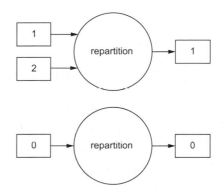

So let's see what it takes to balance the two partitions. The first problem we encounter is some semantic disparities between Dask and pandas. We should deal with these before we go any further.

The `repartition` method allows us to split the data not only based on the number of partitions but also by dividing the data frame index across partitions. We need to know the index, but we can do:

Figure 10.8 Repartitioning data using a different number of tasks

```
print(taxes.index)
```

The output is:

```
Dask Index Structure:
npartitions=3
    int64
      ...
      ...
      ...
dtype: int64
Dask Name: assign, 6 tasks
```

> **What we get here is a set of tasks to run, not the results.**

We will get a set of tasks to run, not the final index. So, we need to need to `compute` the index, with all the computational costs that entails, which, in most cases, defeats the purpose of the optimization that we are in the middle of doing.

Another potential alternative would be to get the boundaries of each partition. Dask allows us to get the boundaries of each partition by doing:

```
print(taxes.divisions)
```

Sadly, the output is:

```
(None, None, None, None)
```

Instead of getting the values of the index columns, we get `None`. Clearly, we cannot use `None` to compute better ways to repartition the data.

At this stage, we are in a frustrating situation: we would like to get the index to repartition the data, but the index is nowhere to be found. When you do `read_csv` with Dask, you will not get the index with values—*even* if you have persisted the data frame (at least with the current version of Dask).

We can set the index to get to a starting point to repartition by index. Let's use `Geo_Name` and `Tax_Type` as the index columns:

```
taxes = taxes.set_index(["Geo_Name", "Tax_Type"])
```

Unfortunately, with the current version of Dask, this operation doesn't work, as Dask doesn't support multi-indexes. An important lesson here is that Dask, while trying to mimic pandas' interface and semantics as much as possible, has several limitations and differences imposed by the complexity of dealing with distributed data structures. Dask does its best, but expect some differences like we just discussed.

> **TIP** Be sure to check that you have the most recent version of Dask. Maybe some of the limitations documented here have been solved.

OK, let's try to use an index with a single column:

```
taxes = taxes.set_index(["Geo_Name"])
print(taxes.npartitions)
print(taxes.divisions)
```

The output is:

```
3
('Alabama', 'Iowa', 'North Carolina', 'Wyoming')
```

This result is great as we have three clear partitions: one starting with Alabama, another starting with Iowa, and the final going from North Carolina to Wyoming.

How does Dask know the partitions if it is lazy? We did not ask it explicitly to compute the new data frame. Nonetheless, in some cases, `set_index` is eager: all computations required to render the data frame that is going to be indexed are triggered, which can potentially use a lot of compute resources.

Importantly, Dask is not always lazy, so for some operations, you will need to be mindful of the potential computational costs. You should check the documentation of the operations that you use, especially if their performance makes you suspect that some of them are eager.

Now that we finally have the index, let's repartition our data from three to two partitions:

```
taxes2 = taxes.repartition(divisions=[
  "Alabama", "New Hampshire", "Wyoming"])
print(taxes2.npartitions)
print(taxes2.divisions)
```

The output is:

```
2
('Alabama', 'New Hampshire', 'Wyoming')
```

Remember that, as a general rule, repartitioning is an expensive operation and should only be done either when you get small or intermediate results or if you believe (i.e., profiled) that repartitioning is advantageous.

The general arguments that we made for the relationship between Dask's data frame interface and pandas' can be extended to the relationship between Dask arrays and NumPy arrays. Dask arrays are mostly implemented with lazy operations and only implement a subset of NumPy's interface, and they sometimes have slightly different semantics.

Next, we will store to disk our distributed data frame.

10.2.5 *Persisting distributed data frames*

To store our `taxes2` data frame to disk, we can simply do:

```
taxes2.compute().to_csv("taxes2_pandas.csv")
```

In this case, we are computing the `taxes2` distributed data frame into a pandas data frame. We let pandas take care of writing the data. Bringing all data from the computing nodes to our master might be too expensive, or the data might not even fit in memory, so this option may not be viable.

> **WARNING** Be careful with the meaning of *persist*. Here we are using *persist* to mean transferring data to persistent storage like a hard disk. However, Dask also has the `.persist` method, which computes and stores the object on each partition.

We can ask for Dask to make the nodes write their data by doing:

```
taxes2.to_csv("partial-*.csv")
```

Remember that we have two partitions, so you will end up with not one, but two CSV files: `partial-0.csv` and `partial-1.csv`, both with headers. If you want a single CSV file, you will have to concatenate the files accordingly.

The Parquet format (see chapter 8) can actually render a single persistent version with each partition dumping its data independently:

```
taxes2.to_parquet("taxes2.parquet")
```

If you look at the file system, you will find a directory with the following content:

```
taxes2.parquet/
  _common_metadata
  _metadata
  part.0.parquet
  part.1.parquet
```

This can be read as a single Parquet "file." The following is a simple example using Apache Arrow (see chapter 7):

```
from pyarrow import parquet
taxes2_pq = parquet.read_table("taxes2.parquet")
taxes_pd = taxes2_pq.to_pandas()
```

So, Parquet as a format is amenable to distributed writing while still providing a consistent view of all the data.

At this stage, we understand how Dask task generation works, but we have talked little about execution. It's now time to proceed to the final step: using Dask for efficient parallel computing on top of heterogeneous architectures—namely, scheduling.

10.3   *Using Dask's distributed scheduler*

We have already seen that Dask tends to be lazy and only creates a computational graph, which must eventually be evaluated. To distribute the evaluation of the nodes of the computation graph across computational resources, Dask uses a scheduler. When you compute a task graph without explicitly configuring a scheduler, Dask automatically uses a default that depends on your collection. Let's take data frames as an example:

```
import dask
from dask.base import get_scheduler
import dask.dataframe as dd


df = dd.read_csv("FY2016-STC-Category-Table.csv")
print(get_scheduler(collections=[df]).__module__)
```

The function `get_scheduler` will return a function to execute the task graph. In our case, it is defined in the module printed in the output:

```
'dask.threaded'
```

As the name implies, the default scheduler for data frames is multithreaded. Dask offers two other simple schedulers: a multiprocessing one and a single-threaded one. The single-threaded scheduler is particularly good for debugging and profiling as it reduces the complexity by being strictly sequential. The single-threaded scheduler is a great choice for debugging. But for production, we will be using a more complex scheduler: the new Dask distributed scheduler supersedes all other Dask schedulers while allowing for much more flexibility

The distributed scheduler allows you to schedule tasks on more than one machine. This scheduler has implementations for HPC clusters, SSH connections, and cloud providers, among others. It also has an implementation to run on the local machine, which can be single- or multithreaded or based on multiple processes; thus, it includes all computing methods of built-in schedulers.

Next, we will use a local machine configuration so you don't need access to a cluster or the cloud, but all the fundamental building blocks will be available to scale out from a single machine.

> **NOTE** As a reminder, there is a certain overlap of this content with chapter 3: you can use Dask to parallelize code on a *single* computer as we did with Python's native libraries. But Dask adds the most value when you scale out (i.e., use more than one machine).

We will use the Mandelbrot generation scenario from the previous chapter to practice the array interface from Dask. Remember that there are other alternatives to make the Mandelbrot implementation more efficient (e.g., Cython or Numba). Given that we are doing a pure Python implementation over arrays, a Cython or Numba implementation would be much more efficient. Actually, the most efficient implementation, especially for very large images, would be Dask *with* Cython or Numba. Let's start by looking at dask.distributed's architecture.

10.3.1 The dask.distributed architecture

The architecture depicted in figure 10.9 has the following components:

- *A single centralized scheduler*—This scheduler is responsible for scheduling tasks for all workers. The scheduler has a web dashboard that users can use to check how computations are performing.
- *Workers*—Workers are responsible for executing the workload. Each machine may have many workers. You can configure a worker to have as many threads as you want. Hence, in practice, you have parallelism either via threading—say, with a single worker with as many threads as CPU cores—or via processes with one worker per CPU core. Each worker also has a dashboard and a tiny attached process, called a *nanny*, to continuously monitor the state of the worker.
- *Clients*—These clients can connect to Dask, use the scheduler to deploy tasks on it, and inspect the scheduler and worker dashboards.

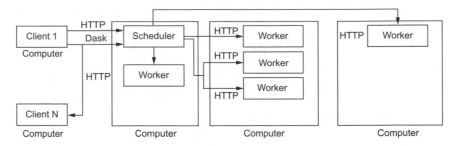

Figure 10.9   Dask's execution architecture

Typically, the components will also include some kind of shared storage, like a shared file system, but that will depend on your particular circumstances.

In our case, we will only use one machine. So, we will start all the processes on a single machine. There are simpler ways to deploy the architecture, but this way makes all components quite explicit.

Let's start with the scheduler:

```
dask-scheduler --port 8786 --dashboard-address 8787
```

We can start workers on the same machine as the scheduler like this:

```
dask-worker    --nprocs auto 127.0.0.1:8786
```

--nprocs auto lets the script decide how many workers it will start on our machine and how many threads.

On my machine, which has four cores and two threads per core, I end up with four workers, each having two threads. We can get this information from the scheduler dashboard: point your browser to http://127.0.0.1:8787 and choose the Workers tab in the menu. I get the result in figure 10.10.

| Status | Workers | Tasks | System | Profile | Graph | Info |

CPU Use (%)

Memory Use (%)

name	address	nthreads	cpu	memory	memory_limit	memory %	num_fds	read_bytes	write_bytes
Total (4)		8	1.0 %	383 MiB	8 GiB	4.9 %	92	50 KiB	48 KiB
tcp://127.0.0.1:	tcp://127.0.0.1:	2	2.0 %	94 MiB	2 GiB	4.8 %	23	12 KiB	12 KiB
tcp://127.0.0.1:	tcp://127.0.0.1:	2	2.0 %	97 MiB	2 GiB	5.0 %	23	14 KiB	13 KiB
tcp://127.0.0.1:	tcp://127.0.0.1:	2	0.0 %	96 MiB	2 GiB	4.9 %	23	10 KiB	10 KiB
tcp://127.0.0.1:	tcp://127.0.0.1:	2	0.0 %	96 MiB	2 GiB	4.9 %	23	14 KiB	13 KiB

Figure 10.10   Listing of all workers on Dask's dashboard

Deciding how many workers per machine and threads per worker is quite complicated and depends on the workload. For many problems based in NumPy, which, when correctly configured, is multithreaded, we can start with a single worker with a single Python per machine. NumPy will use as many threads as necessary, and we will leave it to the library to make the decision. A similar argument for allowing the script to determine the number of workers and threads could be made for code optimized with Numba or Cython as both can release the GIL. That being said, your workload may be different. In our case, it is indeed different: most of the burden is in pure Python, so we will use one process per core.

We will then replace the worker as previously defined with this one:

```
dask-worker --nprocs 4 --nthreads 1 --memory-limit 1GB 127.0.0.1:8786
```

We have four processes using a single thread. We also specify 1 GB of memory, which is half the total that I have available on my machine: I do this because I am running more stuff on my local machine, but you could probably go higher on dedicated machines. Be sure to adapt the values to your configuration.

For pedagogical reasons, we will reduce the workers to two so that we can discuss interworker communication, using only 250 MB per worker. On my machine, the code is:

```
dask-worker --nprocs 2 --nthreads 1 --memory-limit 250MB 127.0.0.1:8786
```

Next, we will connect to our scheduler using Python code. But, before we solve a concrete problem, let's inspect the infrastructure:

```
from pprint import pprint
import dask.dataframe as dd
from dask.distributed import Client

client = Client('127.0.0.1:8786')
print(client)
for what, instances in client.get_versions().items():
    print(what)
    if what == 'workers':
        for name, instance in instances.items():
            print(name)
            pprint(instance)
    else:
        pprint(instances)
```

We connect to the scheduler on the port specified on the startup of dask-scheduler.

get_versions returns information about the various components in the Dask system.

We connect to the scheduler by creating a Client object pointing to the entry point. The first print returns:

```
<Client: 'tcp://192.168.2.20:8786' processes=2 threads=2, memory=500.00 MB>
```

This output reflects the infrastructure that we created: two workers, with one thread and 250 MB per worker.

After that, we print all software versions of all the components involved. The scheduler is as follows:

```
scheduler
{'host': {'LANG': 'en_US.UTF-8',
          'LC_ALL': 'None',
          'OS': 'Linux',
          'OS-release': '5.13.0-19-generic',
          'byteorder': 'little',
          'machine': 'x86_64',
          'processor': 'x86_64',
          'python': '3.9.7.final.0',
          'python-bits': 64},
 'packages': {'blosc': '1.9.2',
              'cloudpickle': '1.6.0',
              'dask': '2021.01.0+dfsg',
              'distributed': '2021.01.0+ds.1',
              'lz4': None,
              'msgpack': '1.0.0',
              'numpy': '1.19.5',
              'python': '3.9.7.final.0',
              'toolz': '0.9.0',
              'tornado': '6.1'}}
```

You can find information about the host, including the operating system, type of processor, and Python version, as well as the libraries installed.

Here is an abridged version for our two workers and our client:

```
workers
tcp://127.0.0.1:32931
{'host': {'LANG': 'en_US.UTF-8',
...
          'python-bits': 64},
 'packages': {'blosc': '1.9.2',
....
                'tornado': '6.1'}}
tcp://127.0.0.1:34719
{'host': {'LANG': 'en_US.UTF-8',
...
                'tornado': '6.1'}}

client
{'host': {'LANG': 'en_US.UTF-8',
...
                'tornado': '6.1'}}
```

Making sure that the library versions are compatible is important in a heterogeneous cluster with many machines. In our case, as our machine is simultaneously client, scheduler, and both workers, so we can be sure that all versions are in sync. However, when more than one machine is involved, you might have to debug the library versions. Now let's deploy our code.

10.3.2 *Running code using dask.distributed*

We start by connecting to the scheduler:

```
from dask.distributed import Client

client = Client('127.0.0.1:8786')
```

The client will be used implicitly in all our calls unless we override it. Remember from the previous section that Dask data structures have default schedulers, but the default will be automatically replaced by the distributed scheduler.

> **TIP** The client object exposes an explicit interface that is very similar to the concurrent.futures API. If you want to use such an interface, see chapter 3. Here we will use the distributed framework via data science type interfaces— in this case, dask.array, which mimics NumPy.

We will use a NumPy universal function approach. Indeed, the code to compute a single point in the Mandelbrot set is exactly the same as the previous chapter:

```
def compute_point(c):
    i = -1
    z = complex(0, 0)
    max_iter = 200
    while abs(z) < 2:
        i += 1
        if i == max_iter:
            break
        z = z**2 + c
    return 255 - (255 * i) // max_iter
```

To compute the Mandelbrot set, we must prepare a matrix in which each cell has a two-dimensional position encoded in a complex number. In the previous chapter, we used this code:

```
def prepare_pos_array(size, start, end, pos_array):
    size = pos_array.shape[0]
    startx, starty = start
    endx, endy = end
    for xp in range(size):
        x = (endx - startx)*(xp/size) + startx
        for yp in range(size):
            y = (endy - starty)*(yp/size) + starty
            pos_array[yp, xp] = complex(x, y)    ⟵── Can you guess what
                                                     this line does?
```

In theory, the previous code works, but in practice, it would be a disaster. Note that the last line is not storing the position in the array's cells: it is actually creating a task in the task graph to compute the result. To make this clear, let's create a tiny image of size 3×3 (i.e., with a block size of 3):

```
size = 3
pos_array = da.empty((size, size), dtype=np.complex128)
prepare_pos_array(3, start, end, pos_array)
pos_array.visualize("10-size3.png", rankdir="LR")
```

Figure 10.11 depicts the task graph. Nine tasks are created, each to update an individual pixel/cell. This solution will work for a minuscule image but not for larger images. For a 1000×1000 image, we would be dealing with 1 million tasks.

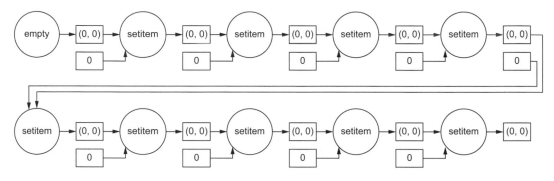

Figure 10.11   Task graph to run the initialization code for just nine pixels

A theoretical alternative would be to create a local NumPy array, initialize it locally, and then scatter it. That approach would work as long as the NumPy array would fit in memory, but that would defeat part of the purpose of Dask: to work with larger-than-memory data structures.

As a more realistic alternative, Dask allows us to do computations on each independent partition of the whole data structure, substantially reducing the number of tasks:

```
size = 1000
range_array = da.arange(0, size*size).reshape(size, size)
range__array = pos_array.rechunk(size // 2, size // 2)    ◁——
range__array.visualize("10-rechunk.png", rankdir="TB")
range_array = range_array.persist()
```
We chunk the array in four blocks of size (500, 500).

We are now using an image size of 1000×1000. We will initialize the array with a range number that will allow us to compute the two-dimensional coordinates (see the following code snippet for details). We start with a one-dimensional array sized 1000×1000 and then reshape it as `(1000, 1000)`.

We then rechunk the array in chunks of `(500, 500)`, ending up with four blocks. Finally, we persist the array across the four blocks to prepare to compute the two-dimensional positions.

Let's now prepare the position array. That is, we will create an array that has a two-dimensional position encoded as a complex number:

```
def block_prepare_pos_array(size, pos_array):
    nrows, ncols - pos_array.shape
    ret = np.empty(shape=(nrows,ncols), dtype=np.complex128)
    startx, starty = start
    endx, endy = end
    for row in range(nrows):
        x = (endx - startx) * ((pos_array[row, 0] // size ) / size) + startx
        for col in range(ncols):
            y = (endy -
    starty) * ((pos_array[row, col] % size) / size) + starty
            ret[row, col] = complex(x, y)
    return ret
```

This function converts the range array into an array of positions based on the value in the original cell. Do not worry much about the algorithm: it converts a one-dimensional coordinate to a two-dimensional one. The fundamental point is another; let's look at this code to discover it:

```
pos_array = da.blockwise(
    lambda x: block_prepare_pos_array(size, x),
    'ij', range_array, 'ij', dtype=np.complex128)
pos_array.visualize("10-blockwise.png", rankdir="TB")
```

This code tells Dask to apply the initialization code of block_prepare_pos_array to each of the four blocks. We specify range_array as the input parameter. Notice that there are two parameters: ij (i.e., i and j) that tells Dask the relationship between the shape of the input parameter and the output parameter (i.e., they have the same shape).

This code creates only four tasks, as shown in figure 10.12. If we used the original code, we would have 1 million tasks.

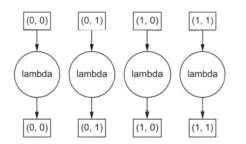

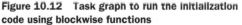

Figure 10.12 Task graph to run the initialization code using blockwise functions

Now, it's time to call our Mandelbrot code on our matrix:

```
from PIL import Image

u_compute_point = da.frompyfunc(compute_point, 1, 1)

image_arr = u_compute_point(pos_array)
image = Image.fromarray(image_np, mode="P")
image.save("mandelbrot.png")
```

We use `frompyfunc`, which converts a native Python function into a NumPy ufunc. Then we call it over our `pos_array` matrix.

Next, we will do some very basic profiling on our code. Mostly, we want to see the effect on the performance of using larger images. The code to perform some simple profiling is as follows:

```
from time import time

def time_scenario(size, persist_range, persist_pos, chunk_div=10):
    start_time = time()
    size = size
    range_array = da.arange(0, size*size).reshape(size, size).persist()
    range_array = range_array.rechunk(size // chunk_div, size // chunk_div)
    range_array = range_array.persist() if persist_range else range_array
    pos_array = da.blockwise(
        lambda x: block_prepare_pos_array(size, x),
        'ij', range_array, 'ij', dtype=np.complex128)

    pos_array = pos_array.persist() if persist_pos else pos_array
    image_arr = u_compute_point(pos_array)
    image_arr.visualize("task_graph.png", rankdir="TB")
    image_arr.compute()
    return time() - start_time
```

Our function runs the Mandelbrot code, as previously explained, which allows us to parameterize the size of the image. We also allow the parameterization of the chunking along with persisting the two intermediate arrays. The function returns the number of seconds it took to execute, which serves as a rough profiling of our code.

Let's run the code for a size of 500 (i.e., an image size of 500 × 500) with a chunk divisor of 2 (i.e., four blocks):

```
size = 500
time_scenario(size, False, False, 2)
```

Figure 10.13, which depicts the task graph, shows that we have four blocks, and the number of computations—the `lambda` and `frompyfunc` nodes—is also four.

Now, let's run the previous code with a size of 5,000 (i.e., an image of 5,000 × 5,000) with a chunk divisor of 10 (i.e., 100 blocks). But before we do that, open the web browser pointing to http://127.0.0.1:8787 (i.e., Dask's dashboard):

```
size = 5000
client = client.restart()        ◁─────   After running this line, reload the
time_scenario(size, True, True, 10)        web browser on the dashboard
                                           to get a clean version.
```

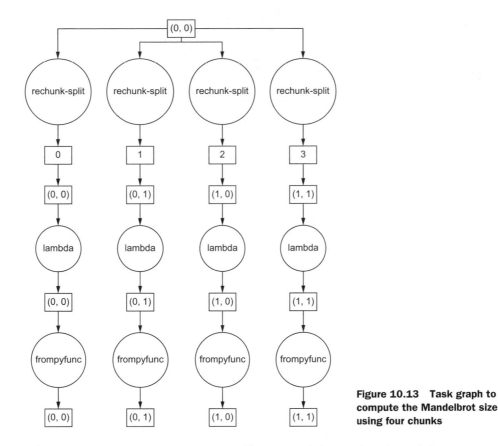

Figure 10.13   Task graph to compute the Mandelbrot size using four chunks

When you run `time_scenario`, you will see a real-time animation of the computation ongoing. While I cannot show you a video here, figure 10.14 displays the dashboard while the computation is ongoing. There are five charts on the main dashboard. Remember that we have four workers, and we will have a task graph with a similar topology as in figure 10.13 but with 100 columns, not just four:

- The small top-left chart reports the bytes stored all across the workers.
- The second chart on the left reflects the memory used per workers, so it's a more detailed version of top-left chart.
- The bottom-left chart enumerates the number of tasks processing on each worker.
- The main chart (top-right) has time on the X axis and workers on the Y axis. Each block represents a task from the task graph. Different colors (shown in grayscale here) are assigned to different task types.
- Finally, the bottom-right chart gives you the status of all tasks

I encourage you to explore all pages in the Dask dashboard. For example, the Profile page will give you a SnakeViz type visualization of the code profile, and the Graph page will show you the real-time status of all tasks in the task graph.

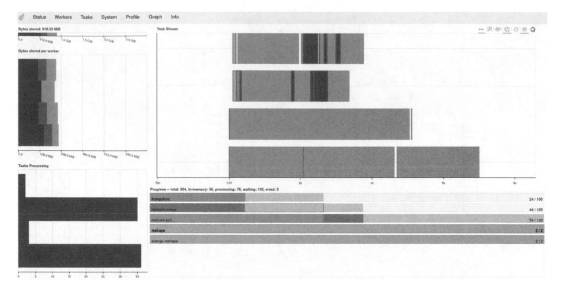

Figure 10.14   The main screen of Dask's dashboard

Finally, let's explore how Dask deals with datasets that are larger than memory.

10.3.3   *Dealing with datasets larger than memory*

Remember that Dask allows you to deal with datasets larger than memory. When you are using multiple computers and, hence, more memory, Dask distributes the data structures through those computers.

But the last-resort solution to dealing with larger-than-memory datasets is to spill them to disk: that is, store them temporarily on disk. However, as you can expect, performance pays a price.

We will run our Mandelbrot code for a very large size of 10000×10000. In one case, we will `.persist` intermediate arrays but not in the other case:

```
size = 10000
print(size, False, False, time_scenario(size, False, False))
print(size, True, True, time_scenario(size, True, True))
```

The output for this code on my computer is:

```
10000 False False 696
10000 True True 752
```

The second version is slower because the memory needed to persist the intermediate matrices and ongoing computations is larger than the memory available for the workers. This memory problem can be easily seen on the dashboard. For example, figure 10.15 displays the two top-left charts. The title of the first one clearly states that spillage is occurring. Also, the different colors (depicted here in grayscale) on both charts indicate that the data is stored in different places.

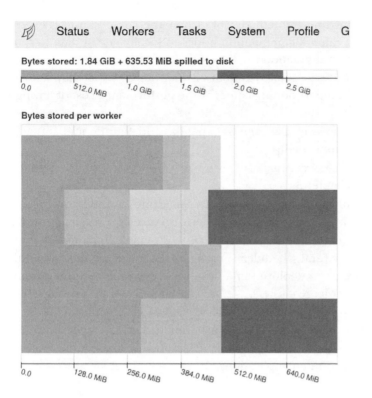

Figure 10.15 The top-left part of Dask's dashboard depicts spilling.

Spilling can cause delays that are orders of magnitude slower than a fully in-memory version. Several alternatives are available that you could consider, the most obvious being adding more memory or more machines. In any case, if you have spilling, either try to avoid it or make sure performance doesn't take a large hit.

This chapter provided an introduction to the basic concepts around Dask. With this information in hand, you can understand the fundamental blocks involved in performance problems while using Dask and apply those to completely different underlying architectures, each with their specific performance bottlenecks.

Summary

- Dask allows you to distribute computation among many machines.
- Dask also allows you to work with larger-than-memory objects like data frames and arrays.
- Dask implements subsets of widely known APIs like pandas and NumPy, but Dask APIs have different semantics as Dask's are mostly lazy, not eager.
- In Dask, you can inspect task graphs before execution, which allows you to understand the computation that will be executed and, in some cases, consider alternatives to optimize it.

- Dask allows for fine-grained control of how the computation is executed. For example, you can ask computation nodes to locally persist data to reuse it efficiently in later computations.

- You can repartition data across nodes if that helps to speed up later computation. However, repartitioning comes at the performance cost of having to transmit data across nodes.

- At the lower task level, Dask relies on pandas and NumPy, and at that level, you can use those libraries directly.

- Dask provides a `concurrent.futures` type of interface, similar to the interface discussed in chapter 3.

- Basic algorithms for data analysis must take into consideration Dask's use of partitioned data. Partitioning makes performance of several algorithms considerably different than the sequential versions available in pandas or NumPy.

- Dask provides several schedulers; among those, the distributed scheduler allows computations to be deployed in a wide variety of architectures—from a single machine to very large clusters.

- Dask provides a scheduler, `dask.distributed`, that can allocate tasks over many architectures, varying from a single machine to a scientific cluster or the cloud.

- `dask.distributed` provides a powerful dashboard that can be used to analyze and profile distributed applications.

appendix A
Setting up the environment

This appendix covers

- Setting up Anaconda
- Setting up your Python distribution
- Setting up Docker
- Hardware considerations

This appendix provides some recommendations on how to set up your environment. We will be using Python 3.10 as the base for our code.

You can use any operating system that you like. Nowadays, most production code is commonly deployed on Linux, but you can also use Windows or Mac OS X. There is little difference between using Mac and Linux. Using Windows is more difficult. If you choose to do so, I recommend that you install some Unix tools, like a Bash shell, or you can use the Windows subsystem for Linux; Cygwin is also an option.

An alternative route, available on all operating systems, is to use the provided—and totally optional—Docker image, which includes the required software. If you follow this route, be sure to install Docker for your operating system. I provide a default Docker image, although some chapters require specialized software, in which case I provide specialized Docker images. If so, you will find specific instructions in those chapters.

A complete list—too long to list here—of the software used in this book can be found on the code repository inside the various `Dockerfiles`. This list can be useful even if you don't use Docker. The repository for the book can be found at https://github.com/tiagoantao/python-performance.

A.1   Setting up Anaconda Python

Anaconda Python is probably the most common distribution for data science and engineering. I recommend using it to run the code in this book. After installing Anaconda, create an environment for the book:

```
conda create -n python-performance python=3.10 ipython=8.3

conda install pandas numpy requests snakeviz line_profiler blosc
```

Some chapters will require extra software. In these cases, I suggest you clone the original environment and create a new one for each chapter. This can be done with:

```
conda create --clone python-performance -n NEW_NAME
```

After cloning, you can install any required software in the new environment without compromising the original one.

I also suggest you create a separate environment for each chapter to avoid clashes between distinct packages and libraries. Package management is still problematic even when using a good package manager, like conda, so it's easier to have separate environments.

Updating conda environments

If you are a long-time Anaconda user, it's probably better if you create a new environment with:

```
conda create -n python-performance python=3.10
conda activate python-performance
```

Updating old environments can take a lot of time or even fail. If you are a new Anaconda user, you should consider creating a separate environment for the book material or, preferably, each chapter.

A.2   Installing your own Python distribution

You can choose whichever Python distribution you prefer, but I strongly recommend Anaconda Python, the de facto standard in data science and high-performance computing. If you install Anaconda (not the smaller version, Miniconda), you will have most of the software that we will use out of the box. *I assume throughout the book that you are on Anaconda. If you use another distribution, you might need to adapt the installation instructions provided in the chapters (for the chapters that have specific needs).* I would recommend checking a tool like Poetry (https://python-poetry.org/) that can partially help you with package management

You will need some very standard libraries, like NumPy and SciPy. To produce charts, we will use matplotlib. Different chapters require a specific library, like Cython, Numba, Apache Arrow, or Apache Parquet. If you are using neither conda nor Poetry, you will probably be dependent on `pip` to install software.

A.3 *Using Docker*

If package installation is something you want to avoid or you are using Windows and want a more typical environment, I provide Docker images with everything you need to run the code. These Docker images will provide a Linux environment for you, irrespective of your host operating system.

The base image can be run as follows:

```
docker run -v PATH_TO_THE_REPOSITORY:/code  ti tiagoantao/python-performance
```

The first time you run this code, it will download the image, which can take some time and bandwidth. You will have a shell, and you will be able to find the code in the directory `/code`. For chapters with specific software requirements, I provide tailored Docker images.

A.4 *Hardware considerations*

The software that we use in this book is fairly standard, but we are at the level that the setup can be tricky and actually derail some of the optimizations, for example:

- The way you compile and link the library can have a massive effect on performance (see chapter 4 on NumPy). If you install the recommended distribution, you are *probably* safe that you have a highly performant version. If you don't (and especially if you compile it yourself), be sure to read the last section of chapter 4.
- If you use the provided Docker image and given that you are inside a virtual environment, it's quite difficult to know whether you have full control of what is going on in the machine, which will make profiling and especially CPU caching less reliable.
- Similar arguments can be made if you are on a desktop where you are doing a lot of other tasks in parallel.
- Cloud instances also will suffer from the same problem unless you have access to the whole physical machine, which is possible (although expensive) and less common than being on a shared physical computer.

- Different hardware configurations can have completely different performance profiles. For example, an SSD disk typically has a much better read performance than a disk with physical spinning plates. This variability in performance applies to CPUs, CPU caches, internal buses, memories, disks, and networks—especially for profiling and caching issues (CPU, disk, or network).
- Addressing the previous point from a different perspective, a well-configured bare-metal production machine may be the best place to see a few of the techniques presented here in full force.
- Chapter 9 on GPUs requires access to a recent NVIDIA GPU—at least with a Pascal architecture.

We will discuss all these issues in depth throughout the book. But the larger point is that the practical examples you will see, while interesting per se, should be viewed as a conduit to develop essential insights about performance issues, which you might have to adapt to your specific cases. At a more advanced level, deep understanding is the real objective. Practical examples are the means but surely not the end.

appendix B
Using Numba to generate efficient low-level code

Numba is a framework to auto-magically convert Python code to native code—CPU or GPU. It is, on the CPU side, an alternative to Cython. The reason we have an entire chapter on Cython and not Numba is because in this book we are interested in understanding how things work and not only in making them work. Numba, which is great otherwise, is not great from a pedagogical approach—due to being "magical."

To solve real-world problems, Numba is as good as, if not better than, Cython as it requires less work on your part and produces similar results. From a usability perspective, I recommend you consider Numba as an alternative to Cython. Actually, it's probably more pragmatic to consider Numba first.

Numba takes a Python function and dynamically converts it into optimized machine code when you try to run that function. In other words, it is a just-in-time (JIT) compiler.

In this appendix, we will develop an example for the CPU. You can use this content as an introduction to Numba that you need for the GPU chapter, or you can just take it as self-standing to learn Numba for the CPU.

To run this code, you will need to install Numba. If you use conda, you can do `conda install numba`. If you use Docker, the image is `tiagoantao/python-performance-numba`.

Our example will be computing the Mandelbrot set, and we will be running both a native Python version and a Numba version to compare speeds. You have probably seen the iconic image—a variation is shown in figure B.1. The Mandelbrot set is computed on the complex space—we will be using complex numbers—and studies what happens to the behavior of iterating the equation $z = z^2 + c$,

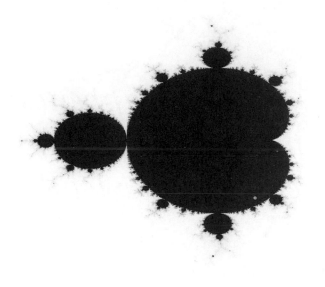

Figure B.1   A grayscale rendering of the Mandelbrot set

where c is a point in space and z starts at (0, 0). This computation is simpler than it seems. Let's look at the code to understand the details:

```
def compute_point(c, max_iter=200):
    num_iter = -1
    z = complex(0, 0)
    while abs(z) < 2:
        num_iter += 1
        if i == max_iter:
            break
        z = z**2 + c
    return 255 - (255 * num_iter) // max_iter
```

⟵ **We need to specify the maximum number of iterations, as this can be infinite.**

⟵ **Python has native support for complex numbers.**

⟵ **The Mandelbrot equation z = z² + c**

Our input is a point in space, c. We are interested in the number of iterations until the absolute value of the equation $z = z^2 + c$ with z starting at (0, 0) is above 2. The number of iterations determines the color of the pixel for position c. We impose a maximum number of iterations as points close to 0 but may never get above 2, and the number of iterations would thus be infinite.

So, we stop the iteration when the distance to the origin of z is larger than 2. Points very far away from the origin stop at the first iteration, and points close to the origin iterate forever. To avoid an infinite number of computations, we define a maximum number of iterations with max_iter. Around the border, the number of iterations changes in a chaotic way (the gray tones in figure B.1). The image shows the conversion of the number of iterations to a gray tone with a maximum number of iterations of 255 in the complex space between 1.5 − 1.3i and 0.5 + 1.3i.

The main function to compute the Mandelbrot set is thus quite simple. The version here is actually slightly more complex than the standard version, as we rescale the output to between 0 and 255, irrespective of the number of iterations. Rescaling will make drawing a grayscale 8-bit image simpler. (I use a grayscale image due to the limitations of using color in the printed book.)

B.1   Generating optimized code with Numba

We are now going to create a Numba version of the function by using the @jit decorator:

```
from numba import jit

compute_point_numba = jit()(compute_point)
```

Don't be fazed by the decorator: decorators are nothing more than syntactic sugar. Because in our case we want both versions—native and Numba—to compare performance, using a decorator is more convenient, as the @ syntax would only expose the Numba version.

As Numba is a JIT, the first call of the function will compile it to an LLVM representation; this is a one-time operation. We will do a dummy call so that later the performance analysis isn't biased by this one-time step:

```
compute_point_numba(complex(4,4))
```

You have to be careful with functions that might have side effects: make sure the dummy call doesn't have undesired consequences. In most production scenarios where you aren't performing benchmarking, you can simply ignore this step.

Now we have two versions: the native (compute_point) and the Numba-optimized (compute_point_numba). We will need to call these functions for every point we want to draw. We will have a start and end corner and our resolution: we will have the same resolution on the X and Y coordinates:

```
def do_all(size, start, end, img_array, compute_fun):
    startx, starty = start
    endx, endy = end
    for xp in range(size):
        x = (endx - startx)*(xp/size) + startx  # precision issues
        for yp in range(size):
            y = (endy - starty)*(yp/size) + starty  # precision issues
            img_array[yp, xp] = compute_fun(complex(x,y))
```

This simple function goes through all the points. If you are thinking that it is amenable to a vectorization approach, you are correct; we will get to that later. size is the number of pixels in each dimension, start and end are the positions on the complex space, img_array is the output array, and compute_fun is the function that we will use to compute the value at each position.

There is just a small nuance regarding how we compute the x and y coordinates. We could, in theory, add a delta to the current position like this:

```
x = startx
deltax = (endx - startx) / size
for xp in range(size):
    ....
    x += deltax
```

The problem with this approach, which would be slightly faster, is that precision errors would accumulate from iteration to iteration, to the point that we may get erroneous results. So, we will stick with the more expensive x = (endx - startx)*(xp/ size) + startx.

To generate the image, the parameters are:

```
size = 2000
start = -1.5, -1.3
end = 0.5, 1.3

img_array = np.empty((size, size), dtype=np.uint8)
```

We also need to initialize the array that will serve as the output.

Let's now compare the time to run the native and Numba versions. With IPython, we could do:

```
In [2]: %timeit do_all(size, start, end, img_array, compute_point_numba)
4.71 s ± 105 ms per loop (mean ± std. dev. of 7 runs, 1 loop each)

In [3]: %timeit do_all(size, start, end, img_array, compute_point)
50.4 s ± 2.94 s per loop (mean ± std. dev. of 7 runs, 1 loop each)
```

On my computer, I get a ten-fold increase in performance.

As we can see from this example, Numba is quite good at optimizing Python code automatically, but it can also experience a problem that we saw earlier in Cython: if it cannot get rid of the CPython object machinery, performance suffers. Let's create a somewhat artificial example to demonstrate this problem. While in our earlier example Numba performed an admirable job at automatic conversion, we can force Numba to generate CPython-bound code to see how it affects performance:

```
compute_point_numba_forceobj = jit(forceobj=True)(compute_point)
```

The run time is:

```
In [2]: %timeit do_all(size, start, end,
  img_array, compute_point_numba_forceobj)
1min 46s ± 2.46 s per loop (mean ± std. dev. of 7 runs, 1 loop each)
```

Now, we have 1 min, 46 s. Note that this example is a worst-case scenario. Sometimes Numba can optimize parts of the code, even if it fails to optimize all of it.

To force Python compilation, add `nopython=True` to the decorator. If Numba fails to compile the function, be sure to check Numba's documentation at https://numba.readthedocs.io/en/stable/user/5minguide.html to see which Python functionalities are supported: we will not go through those here as they change over time.

B.2   *Writing explicitly parallel functions in Numba*

Numba also allows you to write parallel threaded code, as sometimes you can release the GIL:

```
from numba import prange                                      We specify parallel=True,
                                                              and we release the GIL with
@jit(nopython=True,parallel=True,nogil=True)   ◀─────┘        nogil=True.
def pdo_all(size, start, end, img_array, compute_fun):
    startx, starty = start
    endx, endy = end
    for xp in prange(size):        ◀──────  We use the prange function.
        x = (endx - startx)*(xp/size) + startx
        for yp in range(size):
            y = (endy - starty)*(yp/size) + starty
            b = compute_fun(complex(x, y))
            img_array[yp, xp] = b
```

When we use `prange`, we are asking Numba to parallelize that loop. Because the code is GIL-free (i.e., no interactions with CPython are required), parallelization is possible. As such, the result is:

```
In [3]: %timeit pdo_all(size, start, end, img_array, compute_point_numba)
1.41 s ± 35.6 ms per loop (mean ± std. dev. of 7 runs, 1 loop each)
```

The performance is a bit over three times the serial version on my machine. This result is obviously better, but not linear with the eight cores that I have available. Numba functions can, in some cases (i.e., when Numba can sidestep the Python interpreter completely), generate code that is truly parallel.

B.3   *Writing NumPy-aware code in Numba*

Now that we converted pure Python code with Numba, let's consider a version using a NumPy universal function, as integrating in NumPy is fundamental for data science applications. Numba functions can be turned into NumPy universal functions, which is a common use case in data science. The process is quite simple:

```
from numba import vectorize

compute_point_ufunc = vectorize(
    ["uint8(complex128,uint64)"],
    target="parallel")(compute_point)
```

We use the `vectorize` function to wrap `compute_point`. We specify that the function can be run and is parallel. We also have to supply a list of types of function signatures. Optional arguments, like `max_iter`, become mandatory in practice.

The way we use this code is different: we need to pass a matrix of positions for which we want the result:

```
size = 2000
start = -1.5, -1.3
end = 0.5, 1.3

def prepare_pos_array(start, end, pos_array):
    size = pos_array.shape[0]
    startx, starty = start
    endx, endy = end
    for xp in range(size):
        x = (endx - startx)*(xp/size) + startx
        for yp in range(size):
            y = (endy - starty)*(yp/size) + starty
            pos_array[yp, xp] = complex(x, y)


pos_array = np.empty((size, size), dtype=np.complex128)
prepare_pos_array(start, end, pos_array)
```

`prepare_pos_array` simply prepares the input array with all the coordinate positions to be computed. The downside to this approach is that we need memory to store both the position and results array.

Let's time the run:

```
%timeit img_array = compute_point_ufunc(pos_array, 200)
```

The output on my machine is:

```
In [2]: %timeit img_array = compute_point_ufunc(pos_array, 200)
539 ms ± 7.17 ms per loop (mean ± std. dev. of 7 runs, 1 loop each)
```

This result is almost three times faster than the non-NumPy parallel version, all without a lot of work.

This appendix should allow you to get started with Numba. If you are interested in generating GPU code using Numba, check out chapter 9.

index

Symbols

@ (np.matmul) operator 91
@jit decorator 271
/tmp/fast_python UNIX socket 181
cython: linetrace=True directive 117
%timeit benchmarks 145

A

add4.c source code 113
algorithms
    algorithm implementations over distributed
        data frames 246–248
    CPU caching and algorithm efficiency 138–139
    effect of different compression algorithms on
        storage performance 143–144
all_calls array 208
alleles array 202
annotations, Cython
    importance of 111–113
    using to increase performance 110–111
Apache Arrow
    delegating work to more efficient languages
        and systems 179–184
        implications of language interop
            architecture 179–180
        zero-copy operations on data with Plasma
            server 180–184
    reading data into pandas with 174–179
        data analysis 178–179
        reading CSV files 176–178
    relationship between pandas and 175–176
array library 88
array programming 88

arrays
    array access in Cython
        advanced 124–132
        basic performance analysis 130–131
        bypassing GIL's limitation on running
            multiple threads at a time 127–130
        cleaning up all internal interactions 121–122
        optimizing with memoryviews 119–122
        spacewar example using Quadlife 131–132
    as representation alternative to lists 37
    large-array persistence with Zarr 201–209
        creating new arrays 206–208
        internal structure 202–204
        parallel reading and writing of arrays
            208–209
        storage of arrays 204–206
    NumPy 88–97
        applying 92–94
        broadcasting in NumPy 90–92
        copies vs. views of existing arrays 76–81
        developing vectorized mentality 94–97
as_strided function 88
async def coroutine 50
async for 52
async keyword 49–50
async with 52
asynchronous functions 49
asynchronous processing
    architecting a complete high-performance
        solution 68–71
    building asynchronous server scaffold 46–52
        alternative approaches 52
        communicating with clients 48–49
        programming with coroutines 49–50
        sending complex data from synchronous
            client 50–52

asynchronous processing *(continued)*
  concurrent version of framework 55–60
    asynchronous execution with futures 57–59
    GIL and multithreading 59–60
    using concurrent.futures to implement
      threaded server 55–57
  creating robust version of server 72–73
  implementing framework 54–55
  multiprocessing for implementation of
    framework 60–68
    monitoring progress of solution 63–65
    solution based on concurrent.futures 60–62
    solution based on the multiprocessing
      module 62–63
    transferring data in chunks 65–68
  overview of 53–54
  test scenario 54
asyncio module 49
await call 49–50

B

barrier tasks 247
Basic Library Algebra System (BLAS) 97
big-data analysis
  computational cost of operations 243–252
    algorithm implementations over distributed
      data frames 246–248
    partitioning data for processing 244–245
    persisting distributed data frames 251–252
    persisting intermediate computations 245–246
    repartitioning data 249–251
  distributed scheduler 252–263
    architecture of 253–256
    larger-than-memory datasets 262–263
    running code using 257–262
  execution model 240–243
    developing Dask-based data frame
      solutions 241–243
    pandas baseline vs. 240–241
big-data pipelining, laziness and generators
  for 39–41
big-data storage
  fsspec library 187–191
    accessing files 189–190
    inspecting zip files 189
    interfacing with PyArrow 191
    replacing filesystem backends 190–191
    searching for files in GitHub
      repositories 187–189
    URL chaining 190
  old-fashioned techniques 197–201
    chunk reading and writing of data
      frames 199–201
    memory mapping with NumPy 198–199

  Parquet 191–197
    column encoding 194–195
    inspecting metadata 192–193
    partitioning with datasets 196–197
  Zarr 201–209
    creating new arrays 206–208
    internal structure 202–204
    parallel reading and writing of arrays
      208–209
    storage of arrays 204–206
BLAS (Basic Library Algebra System) 97
blocks_per_grid variable 232
Blosc 140–144
  data compression 140–142
    effect on storage performance 143–144
    using data representation insights to
      increase 144
  read speeds and memory buffers 142–143
book-mkl environment 100
brighter3_arr variable 93
broadcasting, in NumPy 90–92
bytes type 37

C

C-level definitions 110
c.qdrep profile trace 234
cache management warning 23
cache_type parameter 191
caching
  CPU caching and algorithm efficiency 138–139
  reducing network usage using local caches
    22–23
callback function 63
calls array 205
calls matrix 202
cdef function 114
cdivision annotation 174
chunk generator 66
chunk_runner 66
chunk_size 66
chunking
  chunk reading and writing of data frames
    199–201
  transferring data in chunks 65–68
chunksize parameter 67, 200
Client object 255
close process 64
cloud-based infrastructure, high-performance
  computing and 11
clusters 136
code re-implementation
  array access
    advanced 124–132
    basic performance analysis 130–131

code re-implementation *(continued)*
    bypassing GIL's limitation on running
        multiple threads at a time 127–130
    cleaning up all internal interactions 121 122
    optimizing with memoryviews 119–122
    spacewar example using Quadlife 131–132
   overview of Cython 107–114
    annotations 110–113
    naive implementation in 108–110
    typing function returns 113
   overview of techniques for 106–107
   parallelism with cython 132–133
   profiling Cython code 114–119
    using line_profiler module 116–119
    using Python's built-in infrastructure 115–116
   writing NumPy generalized universal functions
    in Cython 122–124
columnar-data storage 191–197
   column encoding 194–195
   inspecting metadata 192–193
   partitioning with datasets 196–197
Compute Unified Device Architecture
   (CUDA) 232–233
compute_fun function 271
concurrency 13
   concurrent version of MapReduce
    framework 55–60
    asynchronous execution with futures 57–59
    GIL and multithreading 59–60
    using concurrent.futures to implement
        threaded server 55–57
   multiprocessing solution based on
    concurrent.futures 60–62
concurrent.futures API 257
concurrent.futures executor 56
concurrent.futures module 55, 62
   multithreading solution based on 60–62
   using to implement threaded server 55–57
connection pooling 152
contains function 183
ConvertOptions class 177
cooperative scheduling 49
coroutines 49–50
counter function 61
cpdef function 114, 121
cProfile module 21–22, 27
CPUs
   algorithm efficiency and CPU caching 138 139
   relationship between GPUs and 217–218
CSV files, reading into pandas with Arrow
   176–178
ctypes module 107
CUDA (Compute Unified Device
   Architecture) 218
cuda.grid function 221

cuda.jit decorator 221, 225
cuMemcpyDtoH call 235
cuMemcpyHtoD call 235
CuPy library 228–235
   basic interaction with 229–230
   GPU-based data analysis libraries 228
   GPU-based version of NumPy 229
   profiling tools for GPU code 234–235
   writing Mandelbrot generator using CUDA
    C 232–233
   writing Mandelbrot generator using
    Numba 230–232
Cython 107, 114
   annotations
    importance of 111–113
    using to increase performance 110–111
   array access
    advanced 124–132
    basic performance analysis 130–131
    bypassing GIL's limitation on running
        multiple threads at a time 127–130
    cleaning up all internal interactions 121–122
    optimizing with memoryviews 119–122
    spacewar example using Quadlife 131–132
   naïve implementation in 108–110
   pandas and 173–174
   parallelism 132–133
   profiling code 114–119
    using line_profiler module 116–119
    using Python's built-in infrastructure 115–116
   typing function returns 113–114
   writing NumPy generalized universal
    functions 122–124
CYTHON_TRACE macro 117

D

darken_pixel function 124
Dask
   computational cost of operations 243–252
    algorithm implementations over distributed
       data frames 246 248
    partitioning data for processing 244–245
    persisting distributed data frames 251–252
    persisting intermediate computations
       245–246
    repartitioning data 249–251
   distributed scheduler 252–263
    dask.distributed architecture 253–256
    larger-than-memory datasets 262–263
    running code using dask.distributed 257–262
   execution model 240–243
    developing Dask-based data frame
       solutions 241–243
    pandas baseline vs. 240–241

dask.distributed architecture 253
dask.distributed clients 253
dask.distributed scheduler
    architecture of 253–256
    running code using 257–262
dask.distributed workers 253
data analysis
    big-data analysis with Dask
        computational cost of operations 243–252
        distributed scheduler 252–263
        execution model 240–243
    GPU computing 215–219
        advantages of GPUs 215–217
        CuPy library 228–235
        generating GPU code with Numba 220–228
        internal architecture of GPUs 218
        relationship between CPUs and GPUs 217–218
        software architecture considerations 219
    increasing speed 166–170
        indexing 166–167
        row iteration strategies 167–170
    reading data into pandas with Arrow 178–179
data compression 140–142
    compressed vs. uncompressed data 158–159
    effect on storage performance 143–144
    using data representation insights to
        increase 144
data processing efficiency
    data deluge 4–7
    modern computing architectures and 7–11
        cloud-based infrastructure 11
        hardware changes 8–10
        network changes 10–11
    Python
        Global Interpreter Lock 13
        limitations of 12–13
    summary of solutions 14–16
Data Structures and Algorithms in Python
        (Goodrich, Tamassia, and Goldwasser) 31
data types
    data type precision 162–163
    type inference of columns 160–162
    typing function returns 113–114
datetime format 161
def emiter(word) form 54
def function 61, 114
dependencies, NumPy 97–99
device memory 217
df_10 data frame 168
df_100 data frame 168
dictionaries, complexity of 30–31
distributed scheduler, Dask 252–263
    architecture of 253–256
    larger-than-memory datasets 262–263
    running code using 257–262

distributor default dictionary 56
Docker, setting up 267
download_all_data call 21

E

extended_world variable 127

F

FIFO (first-in, first-out) queues 70
for loops 92, 95, 111, 132, 168
for-based approaches 168–169
Fowler, Matthew 45
frompyfunc node 260
fs object 188
fsspec library 187–191
    accessing files 189–190
    inspecting zip files 189
    interfacing with PyArrow 191
    replacing filesystem backends 190–191
    searching for files in GitHub repositories
        187–189
    URL chaining 190
fsspec.open 189
futures, asynchronous execution with 57–59

G

general-purpose computing on graphics
        processing units (GPGPUs) 8, 213
generators
    as alternative to standard functions 40–41
    big-data pipelining 39–41
    Mandelbrot generators
        NumPy version of code 227–228
        using GPUs 224–226
        writing using CUDA C 232–233
        writing using Numba 230–232
get function 183
get_all_files function 37
get_distance function 25
get_extended_world function 133
get_file_temperatures generator 40
get_scheduler function 252
get_zip_list generator 188
getsizeof function 32–33, 77
getsizeof module 32–35
GIL (Global Interpreter Lock) 4, 13
    bypassing limitation on running multiple
        threads at a time 127–130
    multithreading and 59–60
GitHub repositories, searching for files in 187–189
GithubFileSystem class 188

Global Interpreter Lock (GIL) 4
Goldwasser, Michael H. 31
Goodrich, Michael T. 31
goto call 113
GPGPUs (general-purpose computing on
    graphics processing units) 8, 213
GPU computing 215–219
  advantages of GPUs 215–217
  CuPy library 228–235
    basic interaction with 229–230
    GPU-based data analysis libraries 228
    GPU-based version of NumPy 229
    profiling tools for GPU code 234–235
    writing Mandelbrot generator using CUDA
        C 232–233
    writing Mandelbrot generator using
        Numba 230–232
  generating GPU code with Numba 220–228
    installation of GPU software for Python
        220–221
    Mandelbrot example using GPUs 224–226
    NumPy version of Mandelbrot code 227–228
    programming with Numba 221–224
  internal architecture of GPUs 218
  relationship between CPUs and GPUs 217–218
  software architecture considerations 219
Group object 203
groups method 203

H

handle_interrupt_signal handler 73
HDDs (hard disk drives) 139
host 217
host memory 217

I

if statements 127
ij parameters 259
image_pixel parameter 123
imap function 63
img_array output array 271
implementation-dependent 34
in method 31
index method 31
indexing 166–167
infolist method 189
init_worker initializer function 72
int object 51
int type 33, 111, 114
Integrated Surface Database, NOAA (US National
    Oceanic and Atmospheric
    Administration) 18

IP (internet protocol) 11
IPC (Interprocess Communication) 175
iterrows method 168

J

join call 64

K

kernel function 219
kernprof convenience script 25

L

lambda node 260
language interop architecture 179–180
LAPACK (Linear Algebra PACKage) 97
laziness, big-data pipelining 39–41
line profiling
    detecting performance bottlenecks 25–27
    profiling Cython code 116–119
line_profiler module 116
line_profiler package 25–26
linear variable 83
LineProfiler object 117
lists
    arrays as representation alternative to 37
    complexity of 30–31
    searching in 28–29
live function 126–127
live_core internal variables 127
local caches, reducing network usage 22–23
local networks, performance implications of
        using 147–152
    basic recovery on the client side 151–152
    naive client based on UDP and msgpack
        148–150
    sources of inefficiency with REST calls 148
    suggestions for optimizing network
        computing 152
    UDP-based servers 150–151

M

main entry point 70
main function 72
Mandelbrot generators
    NumPy version of code 227–228
    using GPUs 224–226
    writing using CUDA C 232–233
    writing using Numba 230–232
map function 40
map_async function 63

map_reduce framework 53
map_reduce function 64
mapper function 56
MapReduce frameworks
    architecting a complete high-performance
        solution 68–71
    building asynchronous server scaffold 46–52
        alternative approaches 52
        communicating with clients 48–49
        programming with coroutines 49–50
        sending complex data from synchronous
            client 50–52
    concurrent version of 55–60
        asynchronous execution with futures 57–59
        GIL and multithreading 59–60
        using concurrent.futures to implement
            threaded server 55–57
    creating robust version of server 72–73
    implementing 54–55
    multiprocessing for implementation of 60–68
        monitoring progress of solution 63–65
        solution based on concurrent.futures 60–62
        solution based on the multiprocessing
            module 62–63
        transferring data in chunks 65–68
    overview of 53–54
    test scenario 54
marshal module 51
may_share_memory function 79
memory
    accelerating NumPy with NumExpr 144–147
        effect of hardware architecture on results 146
        fast expression processing 145–146
        when not to use 147
    Blosc 140–144
        data compression 140–142
        effect of different compression algorithms on
            storage performance 143–144
        read speeds and memory buffers 142–143
        using data representation insights to increase
            compression 144
    data loading 158–166
        compressed vs. uncompressed data 158–159
        data type precision 162–163
        recoding and reducing data 164–166
        type inference of columns 160–162
    local networks 147–152
        basic recovery on the client side 151–152
        naive client based on UDP and msgpack
            148–150
        sources of inefficiency with REST calls 148
        suggestions for optimizing network
            computing 152
        UDP-based servers 150–151
    memory buffers 142–143

memory mapping with NumPy 198–199
memory usage estimation 32–39
    alternative representations 35–36
    arrays as representation alternative to lists 37
    creating utility function for 38–39
    difficulties with getsizeof module 32–35
    modern hardware architectures 137–140
        counterintuitive effect on performance
            137–138
        CPU caching and algorithm efficiency
            138–139
        persistent storage 139–140
Memory hierarchy chart 9, 138
memoryview built-in type 79
memoryview class 79
memoryview object 87, 121
memoryviews, optimizing array access in
    Cython 119–122
modern computing architectures
    data processing efficiency and 7–11
        cloud-based infrastructure 11
        hardware changes 8–10
        network changes 10–11
    memory and 137–140
        counterintuitive effect on performance
            137–138
        CPU caching and algorithm efficiency
            138–139
        persistent storage 139–140
msgpack library, naive client based on 148–150
multiprocessing 13, 60, 71
multiprocessing module 55–56, 62–63, 70
multithreading
    GIL and 59–60
    multithreading solution based on concur-
        rent.futures module 60–62
    multithreading solution based on
        multiprocessing module 62–63
my_funs function 52
my_number type 112

N

naive implementation 190
nanny Dask worker process 253
NOAA (US National Oceanic and Atmospheric
    Administration) Integrated Surface
    Database 18
nogil annotation 122–123
None object 121
not_equal operation 178
np.array function 77
np.memmap call 198
np.vectorize 94–95

Numba
generating efficient low-level code
generating optimized code 271–273
writing explicitly parallel functions 273
writing NumPy-aware code 273–274
generating GPU code with 220–228
installation of GPU software for Python
220–221
Mandelbrot example using GPUs 224–226
NumPy version of Mandelbrot code 227–228
programming with Numba 221–224
writing Mandelbrot generator using 230–232
numba.qdrep profile trace 234
NumExpr 144–147
effect of hardware architecture on results 146
fast expression processing 145–146
pandas on top of 171–173
when not to use 147
NumPy
accelerating with NumExpr 144–147
effect of hardware architecture on results 146
fast expression processing 145–146
when not to use 147
array programming 88–97
applying 92–94
broadcasting in NumPy 90–92
developing vectorized mentality 94–97
explicit use of with pandas 170–171
GPU-based version of 229
Mandelbrot code 227–228
memory mapping with 198–199
performance and 76–88
tuning internal architecture 97–101
dependencies 97–99
threads 100–101
tuning in Python distribution 99–100
views
copies vs. views of existing arrays 76–81
inner workings of 81–86
making use of for efficiency 86–88
writing generalized universal functions in
Cython 122–124
writing NumPy-aware code with Numba
273–274
numpy.lib.stride_tricks module 88
numpy.qdrep profile trace 234

O

open function 190
os module 188
out-of-core approach 187

P

pandas
Cython and 173–174
Dask execution model vs. 240–241
delegating work to more efficient languages
and systems with Arrow 179–184
language interop architecture 179–180
zero-copy operations on data with Plasma
server 180–184
explicit use of NumPy 170–171
increasing data analysis speed 166–170
indexing 166–167
row iteration strategies 167–170
memory and time optimization when loading
data 158–166
compressed vs. uncompressed data 158–159
data type precision 162–163
recoding and reducing data 164–166
type inference of columns 160–162
on top of NumExpr 171–173
reading data into pandas with Arrow 174–179
data analysis 178–179
reading CSV files 176–178
relationship between pandas and Arrow
175–176
Parallel and High Performance Computing
(Robey and Zamora) 214
parallelism 13
GIL and multithreading 59–60
in Cython 132–133
multiprocessing for implementation of
MapReduce framework 60–68
monitoring progress of solution 63–65
solution based on concurrent.futures 60–62
solution based on the multiprocessing
module 62–63
transferring data in chunks 65–68
parallel reading and writing of arrays 208–209
writing explicitly parallel functions with
Numba 273
Parquet 191–197
column encoding 194–195
inspecting metadata 192–193
partitioning with datasets 196–197
parquet module 201
ParquetFile 201
ParquetWriter interface 200
partitioning
big-data analysis with Dask
partitioning data for processing 244–245
repartitioning data 249–251
with datasets 196–197
PCA (principal components analysis) 202
PEP 393–Flexible String Representation 36

percall columns 21
.persist method 245, 251
persist method 245, 251
persistence
    Dask
        persisting distributed data frames 251–252
        persisting intermediate computations
            245–246
    large-array persistence with Zarr 201–209
        creating new arrays 206–208
        internal structure 202–204
        parallel reading and writing of arrays
            208–209
        storage of arrays 204–206
    peformance and persistent storage 139–140
persistent storage, peformance and 139–140
pickle module 51, 61
PID (process ID) 182
Pipe primitive 71
Plasma server, zero-copy operations on data
    with 180–184
Pool object 67
Pool.map call 209
Pool.map function 63
Pool.map_async function 63
pos_array matrix 260
prange function 273
preemptive scheduling 49
principal components analysis (PCA) 202
process ID (PID) 182
profiling
    of applications with IO and computing
        workloads 18–23
        computing minimum temperatures 19–20
        cProfile module 21–22
        downloading data 19–20
        reducing network usage using local
            caches 22–23
    of code to detect performance bottlenecks
        23–28
        line profiling 25–27
        visualizing profiling information 24–25
    of Cython code 114–119
        using line_profiler module 116–119
        using Python's built-in infrastructure 115–116
programming model 76
pstat module 24, 115
put_nowait 70
PyArrow, interfacing with fsspec library 191
PyPI (package repository) 60
PyPy (Python implementation) 60
Python
    Global Interpreter Lock 13
    hardware considerations 267–268
    installing Python distribution 266–267

laziness and generators 39–41
limitations of 12–13
lists, sets, and dictionaries 28–31
    complexity of 30–31
    searching in lists 28–29
    searching using sets 29–30
memory usage estimation 32–39
    alternative representations 35–36
    arrays as representation alternative to lists 37
    creating utility function for 38–39
    difficulties with getsizeof module 32–35
profiling applications 18–23
    computing minimum temperatures 19–20
    cProfile module 21–22
    downloading data 19–20
    reducing network usage using local
        caches 22–23
profiling code 23–28
    line profiling 25–27
    visualizing profiling information 24–25
setting up Docker 267
setting up Python 266
Python Concurrency with Asyncio (Fowler) 45
PyTuple_New performance flag 119
__Pyx_PyInt_AddObjC function 113
__Pyx_PyInt_From_int performance flag 119
__Pyx_PyObject_GetItem perfomance flag 119
__Pyx_SafeReleaseBuffer performance flag 119

Q

Quadlife 131–132
Queue class 70
queue module 69–70

R

random array 142–143
range function 40
read function 37
read interface, ParquetFile 201
read speeds 142–143
read_table, parquet module 201
reducer function 56
rep_tile array 142–143
repartition method 249
report_progress function 61, 65
request_text function 150
REST calls, sources of inefficiency with 148
Robey, Bob 214
rot90 operation 87
row iteration 167–170
RPC (remote procedure calls) 175

S

scale out 238
scale up 238
schedulers 45
scipy.linalg SciPy linear algebra module 99
SDDs (solid-state drives) 139
self_destruct parameter 165
send_text function 150
series-max-agg tasks 247
series-max-chunk tasks 247
sets
   complexity of 30–31
   searching using 29–30
shape array 77
shuffle-collect tasks 247
signal library 73
single element 221
singular value decomposition (SVD) 98
sleep call 57
slice operation 87
SMs (streaming multiprocessors) 218
socketserver built-in module 150
solid-state drives (SDDs) 139
SPs (streaming processors) 218
store_and_fwd_flag Boolean flag 162
stride 83
stride_tricks module 88
submit function 57
submit_job function 70
SVD (singular value decomposition) 98
swapaxes operation 87
SWIG 107
synchronous clients, sending complex
    data from 50–52
sys module, Python 32

T

Tamassia, Roberto 31
target="cuda" 227
taxes2 distributed data frame 251
TCP (Transmission Control Protocol) 148
terminate process 64
threading module 55–56, 71
threads_per_block variable 232
threads, NumPy 100–101
time_scenario 261
timeit module 27–28, 111, 229

tip_amount series 170
tkinter module 130
TLS (Transport Layer Security) 148
to_bytes function 51
to_numpy method 171
to_numpy(copy=True) 171
total_amount series 170
Transmission Control Protocol (TCP) 148
transpose operation 87
"Tsunami of Data" (The Guardian) 7

U

UDP (User Datagram protocol)
   naive client based on 148–150
   UDP-based servers 150–151
URL chaining 190
user code 54

V

vectorize function 227, 274
views, NumPy
   copies vs. views of existing arrays 76–81
   making use of for efficiency 86–88
   view machinery 81–86
visualizations, of profiling information 24–25

W

walk method 188
with dialect 190
worker function 70

Z

Zamora, Yuliana 214
Zarr 201–209
   creating new arrays 206–208
   internal structure 202–204
   parallel reading and writing of arrays 208–209
   storage of arrays 204–206
zero array 142–143
zero-copy operations, on data with Plasma
    server 180–184
zip files, inspecting with fsspec library 189
zip function 40
zipfile module 189

RELATED MANNING TITLES

Python Concurrency with asyncio
Matthew Fowler

ISBN 9781617298660
376 pages, $59.99
February 2022

The Quick Python Book, Third Edition
by Naomi Ceder
Foreword by Nicholas Tollervey

ISBN 9781617294037
472 pages, $39.99
May 2018

Grokking Concurrency
by Kirill Bobrov

ISBN 9781633439771
225 pages *(estimated)*, $49.99
Summer 2023 *(estimated)*

Parallel and High Performance Computing
by Robert Robey and Yuliana Zamora

ISBN 9781617296468
704 pages, $69.99
May 2021

For ordering information, go to www.manning.com